Exploring the Power of Solo, Silence, and Solitude

EDITED BY

Clifford E. Knapp & Thomas E. Smith

ASSOCIATION FOR EXPERIENTIAL EDUCATION

Design: Carol Burkey
Cover Photo: Richard Szwaja

Association for Experiential Education
3775 Iris Avenue, Suite 4
Boulder, CO 80301-2043
303.440.8844 • 866.522.8337
www.aee.org

ISBN: 0-929361-23-7

This publication is sold with the understanding that the publisher is not
engaged in providing psychological, medical, training, or other professional
services. Its contents is not intended as a definitive guide, but as a resource.

Published and printed in the United States.

Table of Contents

Foreword

By Rita Yerkes

This work, edited by Cliff Knapp and Tom Smith, is a fascinating collection of author perspectives on the meaning of solo, silence, and solitude to the learner's experiences and inner spirit. The diversity of author backgrounds and experience with the subject matter is impressive, and their writings are enlightening.

Beginning with Smith's chapter on "Going Outside to Go Inside," the editors weave a tapestry of theoretical perspectives about the power that wilderness, solitude, reflection, and vision quests have on the human experience and our search for meaning. The authors demonstrate how opportunities for silence and reflection are necessary to maximize experiential learning. Many of them indicate that experience is not complete unless the learner has the opportunity for personal reflection. To this end, various authors share their research, and program and personal experiences utilizing silence and solitude as tools in the journey of human development.

This body of work will be a welcome addition to your personal and professional library collections. It comes at a time in our culture when its suggestions and tools are needed more than ever before. Bob Henderson, one of the authors, captures this need in his choice of a quote by Erazim Kohak (1984):

> *We obliterate solitude with electronics and blind ourselves with the very lights we devised to help us see. There is nothing wrong with our artifacts; there is something wrong with us.*
>
> (Kohak, 1984, p. xii)

The strongest attributes of this text are the chapters that share the authors' experiences — both personal and with groups they've guided — using solos and reflection. Their insights and recommended practices will be helpful to novices as well as experienced trip leaders and educators. Their suggestions are practical, realistic, and timely.

While the research included in this book provides interesting assumptions and findings, it only scratches the surface of the topic. It leads this writer to ask, if solo and reflection are important tools in achieving experiential learning outcomes, why has research lagged behind in this area? Perhaps the message the authors wanted to convey to us in the field is "come join us and enable us to do more."

Lastly, this publication ends with an interesting discussion between the editors that reflects on the experience of working on this text. In it they raise questions that can serve as the foundation for further research and group discussions. The appendix of noted quotations rounds out the work and is an asset to individuals, as well as solo facilitators. The editors, authors, and publisher of this book have achieved their goal: to have the reader experience the power of solo, silence, and solitude.

Reference

Kohak, Erazim. (1984). *The embers and stars: A philosophical inquiry into the moral sense of nature.* Chicago: The University of Chicago Press.

Acknowledgements

We want to thank all the students and colleagues who have helped us learn about solo, silence, and solitude. Their willing involvement and perceptive feedback throughout the years has contributed to our teaching methodology and philosophy of outdoor leadership. There are too many to mention by name.

Because we believe, as many Native Americans do, that the wind is symbolic for the breath of life and for the telling of stories and blows from the four main directions, we want to spread our thanks into the winds.

First, we turn to the South, the place of trust, cooperation, and friendship. We give thanks to each other for the joyous adventure of creating this project. We have known each other professionally for more than 30 years, and now we know each other more personally from having worked together all these months. "Thanks, Cliff." "Thanks, Tom."

Second, we turn to the West, the place of quiet, reflection, and the demands of working alone with notepaper and computer. We thank our life partners, Jan and Charlotte, and our families, who gave us the space and time needed to complete this task. It was not always easy to have us "disconnect" with them and "hook up" to the computer, but they rose to the challenge. "Thanks, Jan, Dawn, Eve, and Jenny." "Thanks, Charlotte, Judd, Brian, Mike, Kathy, and Jenny."

Third, we turn to the North, where wisdom and insight abound. We give our thanks to those authors who took the time to write about solo, silence, and solitude for this collection of readings. They have responded willingly to our urging and pushing them to meet timelines and to write more clearly. We have learned much from them. When you, reader, finish this book, we think you will thank them too. "Thanks to all of you."

Finally, we turn to the East, where illumination and the big picture can be viewed. We want to give our heartfelt thanks to Natalie Kurylko, AEE's publications manager and our editor for this project. What a job she did! Because of her competence and caring, this book turned out better than either of us expected. We want to acknowledge you, Natalie, for a job well done.

Cliff Knapp & Tom Smith, November 2005

Preface

By Clifford E. Knapp & Thomas E. Smith

Why would a person of sound mind and body choose to leave worldly comforts and the security of friends and loved ones to spend time outside alone? What benefits could normally socially conditioned humans gain by isolating themselves from their communities for any period of time? What kind of person would willingly retreat into silence and solitude to be alone and possibly feel lonely? Who would carefully prepare themselves over many years to lead others in spending solo time in silence and solitude? If you have ever wondered about these questions and others related to solo and solitude experiences, this book may hold some answers for you.

We have thought long and hard about what makes solo important and essential to some people. Many have journeyed into the wilderness beyond themselves and then into the wilderness within themselves to discover the value and benefits of time spent on solo. They also have prepared themselves as leaders of solos and have facilitated a variety of solitude experiences for others. More than that, they have pondered what was happening to them and others while on solo and have recorded some of these thoughts and feelings on paper. These insights are made available to you in this book because of our dedication to, belief in, and passion for this important topic. The goal of this collection of writings is to stimulate others to explore the power and potential of solos, silence, and solitude.

The papers fall roughly into four categories. The papers in Part I, Theoretical Frameworks, discuss the theory and practice of solo taking and facilitating. The papers in Part II, Research Results, present study findings to ground the theory and practice that follow in the next two categories. The papers in Part III, Leadership in Action, address how and why these authors lead solo and solitude experiences for others. Readers who want to know what can happen as a result of experiencing solo under the guidance of competent and caring leaders can turn to this section for some answers. The last section, Personal Perspectives, contains six papers by authors who tuned into themselves as they participated in their own solo, silence, and solitude experiences. They share how their solos impacted them and their families. These are intimately personal reflections about solo that hopefully hold messages for others too.

In Appendix I, we discuss some important questions and issues related to solo. We use this opportunity to raise new questions not covered in the book's papers and to elaborate on questions that have been raised by others. Appendix II is a collection of quotations about solo, silence, and solitude. Readers may enjoy them on their own, share them with others who appreciate the solo experience, or provide them to those they lead to solo experiences. Appendix III offers brief descriptions of a number of activities that can be used in pre-solo preparation or during the solo experience.

As many of the authors note, the solo journey to the wilderness beyond and within has a long tradition in history and has been recognized as a powerful experience for personal growth. Many experiential educators spend considerable amounts of time, money, and energy preparing to lead others in the solo. They may enter professions such as teaching, counseling/therapy, coaching, leadership development, and therapeutic recreation in order to share the power of the solo with others.

We define the term *solo* in the broadest sense possible. We consider the solo experience to include multi-day wilderness quests involving considerable preparation and fasting (like those many Plains Indians completed as part of coming-of-age rituals), or an experience as short and simple as a 20-minute retreat to a quiet spot to meditate, reflect, or journal to relieve stress, enhance awareness of self and nature, or reflect on life experiences. The solo can be completed with or without a teacher or facilitator and can include walking a labyrinth, hiking in the wilderness, sitting alone in a park, or finding inner peace in a crowd by going inside your mind.

Solo time can provide awareness, understanding, and clarification of one's place, purpose, and direction in life. It can help one analyze relationships with others, the Earth, and divine and sacred powers. On the other hand, solo time can create fear, anxiety, physical discomfort, self-doubt, and insecurity if the person is not physically and/or mentally prepared for being alone or if the conditions of the environment become harsh and unyielding. There is clearly a connection between going out to nature's various ecosystems and going into our mysterious mind. Sometimes in order to go inside ourselves, we need to go outside; and sometimes in order to go outside ourselves, we need to go inside to gather the strength and courage needed for the challenge.

We hope that this collection of stimulating papers will prompt deeper thinking, feeling and discussion about the solo experience and perhaps answer some of the questions readers may have about the process of preparing, implementing, and reaching closure. More important than answering old questions may be the raising of new ones to encourage further inquiry into this fascinating topic. Both of us have found that exploring solo, silence, and solitude has enriched our lives and contributed to changing our attitudes and behaviors related to solos. We hope that this book will do the same for you. Reflect on the thoughts of the authors or discuss them with colleagues. Better still, take some solo time and discover (or re-discover) the connection between the wilderness beyond and the wilderness within.

PART I

Theoretical Frameworks

CHAPTER 1

Going Outside To Go Inside: Frameworks for the Solo Experience

By Thomas E. Smith

I only went for a walk and finally concluded to stay out,
til sundown, for going out, I found, was really going in.

(Muir, 1938, p. 419)

The solo is one of the most powerful experiences facilitated by adventure educators. It can be a growth and learning experience and a time for introspection and reflection. Kurt Hahn, founder of the Outward Bound Schools, knew the value of the solo. He insisted that "true learning required periods of silence and solitude as well as directed activity, and each day his students took a silent walk to commune with nature and revitalize their power of reflection" (James, 2000, p. 3).

I often think of solo experiences when I contemplate the question first raised by Thomas James: "Can the mountains speak for themselves?" (James, 1980). Solitude puts people in touch with both the wilderness beyond and the wilderness within. During solo those mountains can speak for themselves — silently sending words of wisdom from the beyond to the within, and into the conscious mind of the participant. This paper will argue for the importance of a structured framework within which individuals approach experiences of solitude. I will outline different formats for the solo and provide references for further reading.

The success of the solo experience, whether it involves gentle walking or rigorous hiking, camping at a sacred spot in the wilderness, or taking an hour alone in a special place, is affected by an individual's pre-solo mindset. Participants' past experiences with solitude, as well pre-solo input from the program materials and the facilitator — publicity brochures, assigned readings, orientation discussions, and solo-preparation activities — all contribute to a participant's pre-solo mindset. Without understanding the purpose of solo, knowing what to expect and how to use the time in solitude, the whole experience can fail (MacIntosh, 1989).

Structuring frameworks for the solo abound. Before students solo, program leaders should provide an underlying rationale (philosophy) for the experience, guide them in setting personal goals, and teach them appropriate activities for their time in solo. Some leaders rely totally on letting "the mountains speak for themselves," and just send their students off to solitude to let the experience unfold. My argument against this approach is that the solo experience can be more meaningful for participants if they understand and accept the format and goals of the experience. The soloist must be prepared to listen to the mountains.

I am defining the term solo in the broadest sense. There are many ways one can go on solo journey to *the wilderness beyond* and *the wilderness within*. If one understands the complex circles of life and the connectedness of all things, then going outside and going inside is really the same journey (Smith, 1980, p. 7).

Wilderness Quests

Most outdoor adventure education professionals think of solo as a solitary experience in the wilderness. A two- or three-day solo campout is integral to most Outward Bound (OB) and National Outdoor Leadership School (NOLS) courses, and many other wilderness adventure programs. Twenty-five years ago, solo was facilitated primarily as a survival experience, but this is no longer the case. OB instructors now have a keen appreciation for the contribution of solo to the process of reflection, and they frame solo as an opportunity for self-discovery (Bevington, 2003, p. 2).

> Solo is not a survival exercise, but rather an opportunity to reflect on experiences, relax, and recharge. During solo, which may last up to three days, each student is assigned an isolated campsite, provided with adequate food and water, given enough gear to have comfortable shelter, and regularly checked on by an instructor.
>
> (North Carolina Outward Bound School, 2004, p. 2)

> A solo provides an important break from traveling and a unique opportunity to rest, reflect, and practice self-discovery. With adequate food and equipment, you will spend time alone at an assigned campsite. You will be within hearing distance of other group members, and your instructor will check in with you at least once a day.
>
> (Voyageur Outward Bound School, 2004, p. 2)

Purists may criticize some of the contemporary safety practices now used by OB, but safety and health considerations clearly support these procedures. OB has recognized that solo can be more meaningful for students if there is less emphasis on the issue of survival in the wilderness and more on the pre-solo focus of participants' thoughts, expectancies, and goals.

> *I try to do a better job of framing the experience — and what they want and should get out of it. I'm less concerned about what they can't take, or can't do, because I now believe that maybe if they are a bit more comfortable while they are out there, they will get more out of it.*
>
> (Goodwin, 2003, p. 2)

While the experience of wilderness solo is only one element of programs offered by OB, NOLS, and other wilderness adventure programs, it is a core offering for others. These wilderness programs are designed to enhance self-discovery and creative energies, cultivate environmental awareness, and promote personal growth and spiritual development through solo experiences. The offerings may be called Wilderness Quests, Fasting Quests, Vision Quests, Spirit Quests, or Perceiving Quests. Typically these programs involve some days of pre-solo preparation, and then the individual spends days alone in the wilderness, sometimes fasting.

> *Since ancient times, people have sought healing, rejuvenation, self-knowledge and greater empowerment in their lives through journeys and retreats into the wilderness. What can be found in the purity of the wilderness can be found nowhere else as readily. It is in such settings, with beauty, harmony, and grandeur, that human beings can best come to know themselves by connecting through the living earth to a higher presence and purpose.*
>
> (Spirit Quest, 2003, p. 1)

Most of these programs spend considerable time frontloading the actual solo journey, and their promotional brochures outline a context for the proposed experience.

> *There is a way to begin to heal our fragmentation in the modern world. It requires going into nature to look deep within ourselves, to discover and measure our own growth through the seasons of our lives, taking time out from our doing to enter just being. Spending time alone, seeking purpose and direction, listening to the voice of Spirit, creating ceremony to mark one's changes, and returning to one's people with a story that gives life new meaning.*
>
> (Rites of Passage, 2004, p. 1)

Wilderness solo experiences are now being facilitated by counselors, psychotherapists, executive coaches, corporate trainers, and spiritual growth teachers, as well as educators and outdoor adventure leaders. These programs are usually quite structured, sometimes providing pre-solo reading assignments and a list of readings and activities for use during time in solitude. Such solos often involve daily visits from the leader to counsel participants and guide their introspection.

Although many programs label their solos a *vision quest*, after traditional practices of the Native American Plains tribes, only a few of them authentically adhere to traditional practices. The Lakota call this quest a *Hanbleceya*, which, translated into English, means crying for a vision. The vision quest is a sacred rite of passage for many traditional Native American youth, involving preparation by purifying body, mind, and spirit in the sweat lodge, fasting, and sometimes using natural psychotropics, such as peyote or toxic mushrooms (Ellie Crystal, 2004).

Nineteenth century anthropologists and cultural historians first used the term vision quest, seeing the parallel between the Indians' ritual and ancient shamanic practices of seeking a vision state and a path to the spirit world. The vision quest can be a search for purpose, meaning, and direction for one's life, and a search for connection with the spirit world. The term vision quest has become so closely associated with the sacred Native ritual that some contemporary leaders who facilitate similar experiences have chosen to use other terms out of respect for the indigenous Americans. "I choose the name Wilderness Solo instead of Vision Quest to honor the distinction of the authentic Native vision quest" (Jane Perry, 2004, p. 2).

Steven Foster and Meredith Little's books, *The Vision Quest: Passing from Childhood to Adulthood* (1983), and *Vision Quest: Personal Transformation in the Wilderness* (1992), popularized the procedure with outdoor leaders, experiential educators, and the general public. They founded The School of Lost Borders in 1984, which has facilitated thousands of people through vision quest experiences. Like some Native Americans, they speak of the three phases of the quest as (a) dying, (b) passing through, and (c) being reborn, and they follow traditional procedures closely, including the use of the sweat lodge for holistic purification before and after the journey into the wilderness. Still, they are careful to point out that their offering is an adaptation of indigenous tradition developed for contemporary times.

Students of Foster and Little have started other outdoor programs that offer the vision quest experience. Rites of Passage, Inc., describes the quest as follows:

> *We have taken the universal elements of a rite of passage in constructing a*
> *program designed for people living in our modern society. Our staff are guides,*

serving to mirror and support the participants by helping them first to prepare for their solo and then to understand and integrate their experience.... The group begins at a campground near the wilderness, where we can get acquainted and begin preparations for the quest. We'll review flora, fauna, first aid and safety procedures, and begin to present tools such as the medicine wheel teachings.... For the next three days and nights you will enact the Vision Quest, living by yourself in the wildness of nature. In the weakness of fasting [or eating slightly], you become more open and transparent. You live between the inner world of dreams, feelings, fantasies and the outer world of cold night air, the warming sun, the sound of a coyote howling, the sight of a lizard doing pushups, the vast view of a desert plateau. You may be visited by dragons, whose names are loneliness, boredom, fear, and regret — among others. You engage them with your heart and spirit, recognizing them as worthwhile opponents. They push you into your depths.

(Rites of Passage, 2004, pp. 3–4)

Like Outward Bound leaders, facilitators of these quests attend to safety and health issues. One common procedure is to send people into the wilderness in pairs. Although the two people set up personal campsites some distance from one another, they also establish a stone pile *post office* or cairn where they check in daily at different times. They can leave messages there for each other or for supervising leaders if they experience distress.

Solo Journey Across Cultures

Walking, hiking, biking, or paddling in solitude is another historic pattern of the solo. Solo treks to the wilderness have long been recognized as valuable. Confucius, Christ, Immanuel Kant, and the great American naturalists, Emerson, Thoreau, and Muir, have advocated the solo journey. Colin Mortlock's books, *The Alternative Adventure* (1987) and *Beyond Adventure* (2001), tell of his journeys of self-discovery through long solo walks in wild places.

Walking tends to help the body follow basic rhythms — balancing muscles, breathing, and thinking. It can provide escape from the fast-paced and cacophonic noise of the everyday world. A walk in the forest or through a meadow, along a creek, beach, or mountain, turns attention to the lessons of the wild.

Walking is the great adventure, the first meditation, a practice of heartiness and soul primary to humankind. Walking is the exact balance between spirit and humility

(Snyder, 1990, p. 14).

Courses that incorporate solo experiences often assign Thoreau's *Walden* (1970), or have students read his lecture *Walking* (http://ecotopia.org/ehof/thoreau/walking.html).

There are many wonderful essays and quotations that speak to the joys and lessons of solo walking. A collection of poems, quips, and wisdom titled *Walking, Strolling, Sauntering, Meandering, Hiking, Walk-Abouts,* can be found at http://www.gardendigest.com/walking.htm (Garofalo, 2004).

The Australian Aborigines practice a rites of passage ritual called *walkabout* that involves solo walking. The walkabout is somewhat like the Native American vision quest, although it involves hiking in the outback alone instead of waiting at a sacred place for a vision. The walkabout has been suggested as an educational curriculum design by Maurice Gibbons (1974, 1984). Gibbons' thinking was stirred by the book and movie of that name, in which an Aboriginal boy goes on a dreaming journey to discover himself and establish contact with the spirit world. In the movie, the boy explains his adventure to people he meets. "You leave everything and start walking until you find yourself" (*Walkabout*, 1971, re-release, 1996). Walkabouts may last for many months. The paths followed and places visited usually have historic and spiritual significance, as well as pragmatic value, because many of them are sources of water.

Like the term vision quest, walkabout is now used generically in outdoor adventure programs. Most of these programs do not adhere to Aboriginal tradition, though some of them provide students a pre-solo format grounded in the essentials of the tradition. Some walkabout programs involve groups traveling into the wilderness, during which there may or may not be solo time. If one did model a solo experience after Aboriginal traditions, it would need to last many days (or weeks) and might involve visiting a number of sacred places in the wilderness.

There are a number of parallels between the Native American vision quest, the Aboriginal walkabout and the historic *hero's journey*. Myths and legends throughout the world refer to the heroic journey. Joseph Campbell, building on C.G. Jung's studies of world mythology, noted that heroic journeys typically involve leaving the world of everyday life to travel where challenges are met and fears are overcome, as the hero searches for special knowledge, healing powers, personal visions, and connections to spirits (Campbell, 1969). Campbell wrote that all those who take a heroic journey follow a path from the known to the unknown and return forever changed by the experience, having acquired knowledge and a vision they did not possess before.

The hero's journey has often been interpreted as a metaphor for the process of personal growth, self-discovery, and spiritual enlightenment. The solo experience, as facilitated by experiential education professionals, could be described as a hero's journey. In literature and drama, many heroic figures go on a quest to find meaning and purpose. Facing the unknown and frightening realities, and dealing with the complexity of their emotions forces them to discover and uncover previously untapped personal strengths.

> *At critical choice points along the way, the hero may experience invaluable assistance and find unexpected personal resources. Having dealt with the perils of the quest, the hero returns home, forever changed and usually more related to both the inner and the outer worlds.*
>
> (Halliday, 2002, p. 1)

In this sense, participants in challenge/adventure programs are on a hero's journey. Experiential educators can find wonderful stories and quotations to use in orienting participants to all aspects of the adventure program, especially the solo. Many of the references cited by Joseph Campbell in *The Hero With a Thousand Faces* can help facilitators ready participants for solitude.

Hermitage and Solitude

There may be pre-solo value in considering what could be called the ultimate solo — that of the hermit or the monk who spends many years in solitude or silence. Several books discuss hermitage living and the solitary life (e.g., Allchin, [Ed.], 1977; Colegate, 2002). Such works provide stories and quotations about the problems and the joys of solitude, and about its contribution to one's connection to nature, discovery of self, and communion with spiritual worlds. These types of readings can guide participants to a mindset that makes their solo experience more meaningful.

Pre-solo preparation is especially necessary in the modern Western world, where solitude is quite undervalued — perhaps not even understood. Most participants have little experience with solitude, and many have considerable anxiety and fear about being alone. A former Outward Bound instructor noted that for many participants the wilderness solo is their "first time to truly experience being alone" (Frank, 2002, p. 3). The wisdom gained by hermits and monks might not only help students overcome negative anticipations about the solo experience but even guide them to positive expectancies about being alone.

Although experiences of solitude may be uncommon today, there is a still a certain fascination with those who turn to a life of solitude.

> *The idea of the hermit's life — simplicity, devotion, closeness to nature — lurks somewhere on the periphery of most people's consciousness, a way glimpsed, oddly familiar, not taken.*
>
> (Colegate, 2002, p. 97)

Thomas Merton, who lived part of his life in solitude as a Trappist monk, wrote of his love of the solitary life, and suggested that in peeling back the layers of interactional sociology, one discovers the ultimate solitude of existence.

> *The solitary life, being silent, clears away the smoke-screen of words that*
> *man has laid down between his mind and things.... To love solitude and to seek*
> *it does not mean constantly traveling from one geographical possibility to*
> *another. A man becomes solitary at the moment when, no matter what may be*
> *his external surroundings, he is suddenly aware of his own inalienable solitude*
> *and sees that he will never be anything but solitary.*

(Merton, 1956)

Experiences of solitude can be more meaningful for our participants when we help them ponder the thoughts of those who found special meaning in solo time.

Sacred Places

The word *sacred*, derived from French and Latin, means consecrated or set apart by and for the gods or God. Thousands of places on this earth have been identified as sacred. Sometimes these places are related to the religious and spiritual traditions of the indigenous people of the geographic region. Whether in the high peaks of the Himalayas, on the path to Mt. Fuji, at the base of the majestic California redwoods, by the holy springs of Ireland, or on Bear Butte in the South Dakota Black Hills, these sacred places hold special powers for many. They are places where one can feel the pulse of the earth, become keenly aware of the connectedness of all things, and find answers to longstanding personal questions.

Yi-Fu Tuan, a geographical philosopher, called the connection between people and a special place *geopiety* (Tuan, 1976). He suggested the term be used to describe a variety of emotional and spiritual connections between person and place. There seems to be a parallel between Tuan's ideas about a person being in special relationship with a place and Martin Buber's thoughts about the *I-Thou* relationship in contrast to the *I-It* relationship. While we approach most things as just that — separate things (I-It), we reach a different level of awareness when we sense that we are in an interactive relationship with those things (I-Thou). When we talk to and listen to particular aspects of our environment on an intimate basis, we are in an I-Thou relationship (Buber, 1996).

Tuan's concept of geopiety was reviewed for experiential educators over a decade ago (Knowles, 1992), but few have explored these ideas in relation to the solo experience. We do know that many who spend time on a wilderness solo find or create a special place where they sense a special relationship with the land. If that solo spot was not acknowledged as a sacred place before the solo, the experience tends to make it sacred for that individual.

Thoreau found his sacred place on Walden Pond. John Muir's sacred place was in the High Sierras, especially Yosemite Valley. One of my sacred places is the Boundary Waters on the Minnesota-Canada border. I have traveled there alone many times, to connect with Mother Earth, to sort out confusions, choices, and directions, and to heal from the pains of personal loss.

Special Places

Working with Joseph Chilton Pearce's notions about children growing from family connections to earth connections, David Sobel developed a theory of children's place-making in their environment (Sobel, 1992). His work on special places has spawned creative ideas about having children locate and develop a special spot in the world to call their own. He first observed children building tree houses, bush shelters and forts, and recognized that part of their motivation was to connect to the earth and create places for escape to solitude. Some educators have explored the concept of special places and incorporated the idea into their programs or curricula.

Sobel's idea is that children often find literal places in the world in preparation for making figurative places in the world as adults. If we accept his hypothesis, we could apply it to how the solo experience is to be facilitated. Perhaps many of our participants, young and old, have never discovered the joys of having their own *special places*. The solo experience might be organized to help them find that personal place to seek an emotional grounding for further holistic development. For those who have had experiences with special places, the solo can provide a rekindling of the warm and secure feelings found there.

Consider the following essay from a 10-year-old boy in Adjungbilly, Australia, whose teacher had organized a program for students to discover their special place.

> *Walking quickly, I take the road that leads me to my special place. Across the creek and up the creek and up the hill, climbing ever higher. Reaching the top, I pause to survey my kingdom, the special place I call my own. Kangaroos that chew the grass, bees that hum looking for pollen and nectar, and velvety brown rabbits that hop around chasing each other through the tall, wavy grass. My throne is a smooth flat rock, shaped and carved by the weather. A black and white rag flutters from time to time, reminding me that it's getting cold. I take one final look and stand against the setting sun. As I reluctantly leave my kingdom, I trudge slowly homeward.*
>
> (Tim, Age 10, 2004)

Outdoor educators and other teachers have discovered the value of having children find special places, secret spots, magic spots, quiet spots, and cozy nests in the park, the woods, or even the classroom. These are places for children to find solitude. "Quiet times can be planned each morning and around significant activities of the day — for meditation, prayer, journaling, or reading" (Anderson-Hanley, 1997, p. 33). In the outdoor setting, these special places typically involve solo time for introspection and reflection. Time alone in a special place or secret spot may be the first solo experience for many individuals and may be the solo format of choice for many experiential education groups.

Connecting With Nature

Many of the activities facilitated by traditional outdoor/environmental educators, challenge/adventure leaders, and the emerging professionals in the new field of ecopsychology (Roszak, Gomes, & Kanner, 1995) involve solitude. Steve Van Matre incorporates exercises such as having students spend time with a square foot of earth, or a bucket of pond water (Van Matre, 1976). Others are the oft-used exercises of *hug a tree* or spending time alone beside a special tree (Rockwell & Williams, 1983). Joseph Cornell (1978, 1987), Michael Cohen (1989), and James Swan (1992) suggest many wonderful activities, some of which can be facilitated as solo experiences.

Ruth Baetz, in her book *Wild Communion: Experiencing Peace With Nature* (1997), offers suggestions for solo experiences that lead to special connections with nature. Like Van Matre and other nature-awareness educators, she emphasizes relaxation, breathing, listening, and opening the senses to discovery:

> *I sit in a nook of untended bushes and grasses. I shift my eyes ever so slightly to make the dewdrops on the grass shine with rainbow colors. I count my breaths to one hundred with my eyes closed, just stilling my mind and being aware of the sounds and the feel of the sun and breeze. This little place can nourish me with its beauty.*

(Baetz, 1997, p. 71)

Ecopsychologists have suggested that connecting with nature is not only a healing process for the individual, but may even be a prerequisite for psychological, social, spiritual, and cultural health (Roszak, 1979; Duncan, 2003). The solo experience, if taken for only a few days, hours, or even a few minutes, can provide the individual an opportunity for discovering the healing powers and psychological benefits of wild places. Discovering one's relationship with nature may be one of the goals of some solo experiences, but it is often the major goal of others.

Connecting With God

Throughout history and in some contemporary programs that offer solo experiences, the purpose of going to the wilderness is to find special relationship with the Supreme Being or Divine Power. It was on solo journey that Moses received communication from God. Mohammed returned from a solo retreat and began to write. Traditional Native Americans took their vision quest in order to contact and understand the *Great Mystery*.

From the religious perspective, there are three frameworks for the solo. First there is the view of *nature theology*, which defines nature as God and God as nature. The soloist can find God in nature. The term *natural theology* dates back to the 17th or 18th century and holds that knowledge of God can be drawn from nature. This position differs from the traditional nature theology viewpoint in that it suggests that God is contained in and discovered through revelation. In this scenario, the soloist discovers God *through* nature. A third approach involves one strengthening an already discovered relationship with God through the solo experience. In this case, the solo might be considered as "walking and talking with God."

Some might be tempted to say that wilderness experiences, stationary or moving, taken under this format are not really solos, because one is never alone. Many years ago, my son went on a wilderness adventure with a church group. Everything else in the program, including a ropes and teams course, group initiatives, rock climbing and mountain hiking, was in preparation for the final 48-hour *duo*. The leaders purposely called it duo, because it was to be an occasion for the individual and God to spend special time together.

The Wilderness Within

Wilderness Beyond, Wilderness Within (1980) was the title of my first book. I have often used that metaphor for the whole process of challenge/adventure education as a methodology for facilitating people's personal growth. It can also serve as a format for the solo experience. Joan Halifax wrote, "Nature's wilderness is the locus for the elicitation of the individual's inner wilderness, the great plain of the spirit" (Galland, 1980, p. 115). Sacred spaces or places can be found in *the wilderness beyond*, but they can also be found at our center, in that *personal wilderness within*. "We go to the outside to get to the inside, and the outside becomes the inside, and the inside becomes the outside" (Smith, 1980, p. 7).

> *So you want to learn? To grow?*
> *To understand? To know?*
> *Then do not run wildly through the trails of life.*
> *Slow down. Come to Center. Breathe deeply.*

Sense the colors of the world about you.
Listen to the sounds of the environment.
Reach down and touch the Earth.
Reach up and draw forth the energy of the Sun.
Look. Better even, stare,
At all the little things of the world,
At all the big things of the world,
At all the living things of the world,
And at all the dying things of the world.
As your eyes fill, rest them in closure,
But keep on looking, inward, deep at your Center.
That is where the wisdom is to be found.

(Smith, Journal Notes, 1977)

Shifting focus from the outside to the inside, learning to enhance awareness of the inside, or seeking to empty out and open oneself to a higher order consciousness, is a longstanding human tradition. Monaghan and Viersek have listed more than 35 practices that can teach a person "to know where you are in life … to allow your emotions to flow" (1999, p. 11). Activities such as chanting, drumming, sufi dancing, tai chi, labyrinth walking, visualization, and active imagination can all be part of pre-solo or solo experiences. Leaders might teach students the basic procedures for relaxing, breathing, stretching, listening, focusing, and centering as part of the solo experience.

After all, to educate, according to the original Latin, means to bring out or draw forth that which is within the student. As I first wrote more than 20 years ago, "We don't need teachers, we need releasers" (Smith, 1980, p. 137). Most introspective exercises that send the individual to the inside occur during solo experiences. Whether used as a tool for the solo adventure in the wilderness beyond or as a separate experience to explore the mysteries of the wilderness within, reflection and discovery of one's personal resources is a solo experience. As Linda Winkelried-Dobson observed several years ago, "A student must first experience himself as the knower of knowledge" (1988, p. 24).

Summary

The philosophical framework for solo experiences is very important, and participants need to understand that framework as they move toward solitude. As leaders, the words written in our publicity and program brochures, the readings we suggest, the quotations we read, and the pre-solo orientation and campfire discussions all contribute to the participant's mindset. We can describe the solo experience as one of survival, simple rest and relaxation, or as a time for introspection, prayer, reflection, and self-discovery. We can frame the solo experience as a vision quest or a walkabout. We can speak of special places and sacred places. We might frontload the solo experience with an overview of the hero's journey or with reflections on solitude from hermits and monks. We may talk of the value of connecting with nature — emphasizing the psychological and spiritual benefits for humankind, and the ecological benefits for our planet. Whatever framework an educator chooses, time with solitude will be more meaningful for participants if we prepare them properly for the experience.

References

Allchin, A.M. (Ed.). (1977). *Solitude and communion: Papers on the hermit life.* Oxford, UK: S.L.G. Press.

Anderson-Hanley, C. (1997). Adventure Program Spirituality: Integration models, methods, and research. *Journal of Experiential Education,* 20(2), 102–108.

Baetz, R. (1997). *Wild communion: Experiencing peace in nature.* Center City, MN: Hazelden Press.

Bevington, M. (2003). *Solo: Roots in reflection.* Retrieved November 2003, from www.outwardboundwest.com/alumni/beyond

Buber, M. (1996). *I and thou.* New York: Simon & Schuster, Touchstone.

Campbell, J. (1969). *The hero with a thousand faces.* Princeton, NJ: Princeton University Press.

Cohen, M. (1989). *Connecting with nature.* New York: World Peace University.

Colegate, I. (2002). *A pelican in the wilderness.* Washington D.C.: Counterpoint.

Cornell, J. (1978). *Sharing nature with children.* Nevada City, CA: Dawn Publications.

Cornell, J. (1987), *Listening to nature.* Nevada City, CA: Dawn Publications.

Crystal, E. (2004). *Vision quest.* Retrieved January 2004, from www.crystalinks.com

Duncan, G. (2003). *The psychological benefits of wilderness.* Retrieved January 2004, from http://ecopsychology.athabascau.ca/Final/duncan.htm

Foster, S. & Little, M. (1983). *The vision quest: Passing from childhood to adulthood.* Covelo, CA: Island Press.

Foster, S. & Little, M. (1992). *The book of the vision quest: Personal transformation in the wilderness.* Covelo, CA: Island Press.

Frank, B. (2004). In M. Bevington, *Solo: Roots in the reflection.* Retrieved November 2003, from www.outwardboundwest.com/alumni/beyond./solo/html

Galland, C. (1980). *Women in the wilderness.* New York: Harper and Row.

Garofalo, M. (2004). *Walking*. Retrieved January 2004, from www.gardendirgest.com/quotations

Gibbons, M. (1974). Walkabout: Searching for the right passage from childhood and school. *Phi Delta Kappan*, May, 596-602.

Gibbons, M. (1984). Walkabout: Ten years later searching for a renewed vision of education. *Phi Delta Kappan*, May, 591-600.

Gomes, M., Kanner, A., Roszak, T. (1995). *Ecopsychology: Restoring the earth, healing the mind*. San Francisco: Sierra Club Books.

Goodwin, I. (2003). In M. Bevington, *Solo: Roots in the reflection*. Retrieved November 2003, from www.outwardboundwest.com/alumni/beyond/solo/html

Halliday, S. (2003). *Beyond the hero archetype: Exploring dreams*, Retrieved November 2003, from www.wildernessdream.net/DWW3D-Halliday

James, T. (1980). *Can the mountains speak for themselves?* Retrieved October 2003, from www.wilderdom.com/facilitation/Mountains.html

James, T. (2000). *Kurt Hahn and the aims of education*. Retrieved October 2003, from www.tj@kurthahn.org

Knowles, J. G. (1992). Geopiety, The concept of sacred place: Reflections on an outdoor education experience. *Journal of Experiential Education*, *15*(1), 6–12.

McGaa, E. (1995). *Native wisdom: Perceptions of the natural way*. Minneapolis, MN: Four Directions Publishing.

McIntosh, H. (1989). Re-thinking the solo experience. *Journal of Experiential Education*, *12*(3), 28–32.

Merton, T. (1956). *Thoughts in solitude*. New York: Farrar-Straus-Giroux.

Monaghan, P. & Viersek, E. (1999). *Meditation The complete guide*. Navato, CA: New World.

Mortlock, C. (1987). *The adventure alternative*. London: Ferguson of Keswick.

Mortlock, C. (2001). *Beyond adventure*. London: Cicerone Press.

North Carolina Outward Bound School (2004). *Unique course design*. Retrieved February 2004, from www.NCOBS.org./html

Perry, J. (2003). *Wilderness solo*. Retrieved November 2003, from www.janeproject.net/html

Rites of Passage, Inc. (2004). *Wilderness vision quest*. Retrieved January 2004, from www.ritesofpassagevisionquest.org

Rockwell, R. & Williams, R. (1983). *Hug-a-tree and other things to do outdoors with young children*. New York: Gryphon House.

Roszak, T. (1979). *Person/Planet: The creative disintegration of industrial society*. New York: Doubleday.

Sobel, D. (1992). *Children's special places: Exploring the role of forts, dens and bush houses*. Chicago: Zephyr Press.

Smith, T. (1977). Journal notes, Unpublished.

Smith, T. (1980). *Wilderness Beyond...Wilderness Within...* McHenry, IL: McHenry Press.

Snyder, G. (1990). *The practice of the wild.* San Francisco: North Point Press.

Spirit Quest. (2003). *The wilderness quest.* Retrieved November 2003, from www.spiritquests.org/html

Swan, J. (1992). *Nature as teacher and healer: How to reawaken your connection to nature.* New York: Villard Press.

Thoreau, H. D. (1970). *Walden.* New York: HarperCollins.

Thoreau, H. D. (1862). *Walking.* Retrieved December 2003, from http://eserver.org/thoreau/walking.html

Tim. (2004). *My special place.* Retrieved March 2004, from www.nexus.edu.au/projects/journey/tims

Tuan, Yi Fu. (1976). Geopiety. In D. Lowenthal & M. Bowden (Eds.), *Geographies of the Mind.* New York: Oxford University Press.

Van Matre, S. (1976). *Acclimitization.* Warrenville, IL: Institute for Earth Education.

Voyager Outward Bound School. (2004). *Chihuahuan desert backpacking ascent.*

Retrieved January 2004, from www.vobs.com/course./chihuahan

Winkelreid-Dobson, L. (1988). Meditation: Opening the door to true education. *Holistic Education Review*, Fall, 24–30.

Wolfe, L.M. (Ed.) (1938, 1979.) *John of the mountains: The unpublished journals of John Muir.* Madison: University of Wisconsin Press.

CHAPTER 2

The Mountains Can't Always Speak for Themselves: Briefing and Debriefing the Solo Experience

By Clifford E. Knapp

To come to terms with their vision experiences, novice visionaries sought the aid of older, experienced specialists to help them to integrate their individual experiences into the body of tribal ritual.

(DeMallie & Parks, 1987, p. 34)

Traditional Native people, commonly the North American Plains Tribes and the Northern Woodlands Tribes, have help in preparing for and following up their experience when they go on vision quests. Medicine people or elders usually provide this assistance. In modern terms, we might describe these people as solo facilitators or guides. These guides help vision seekers interpret and clarify their dreams and observations. They also provide support by conducting accompanying purification lodges, feasts, and other rituals. Many native people view the vision quest as a prayerful and solitary act, but also believe that it is a social gesture closely tied to their communities. The prayers often relate to how the vision questers can help the people by sacrificing physical comforts such as food, water, and clothing, and by remembering others in the community.

In contrast to the traditional way of having a respected elder assist a seeker of visions, some people believe that leaders should not mediate the experience by briefing or debriefing the solo taker, but "Let the mountains speak for themselves." According to what now might be urban legend, an Outward Bound Instructor named Rustie Baille coined the phrase "Let the mountains speak for themselves" as a reaction against pressures exerted by the Colorado Outward Bound School to verbalize student experiences and to use counseling techniques to manage the personal growth and group processes. Apparently Baille was not alone in his aversion to mediating the outdoor experiences provided in Outward Bound courses. According to Thomas James, "The debate began right after the first season in 1962, when there was a falling out about whether to instill an *intellectual element* in courses, and since then there have been plenty of historical examples of the rift" (1980, p. 1).

This paper outlines some thoughts about guiding others through their solo experiences. These solos need not be based on indigenous or land-based traditions, and can take any of the forms described in this book. The benefits of briefing (before) and debriefing (after) solos are founded in some basic assumptions about the process. After discussing some of those assumptions, clarifying a few definitions and providing a brief summary of cognitive research, this paper will outline six factors that can contribute to successfully facilitating the solo. These include: (a) committing to the central role of briefing and debriefing in experience-based learning; (b) deliberately planning for opportunities to brief and debrief; (c) realizing that a high level of facilitation skill is needed; (d) establishing clear intentions and objectives for the activity, in this case, the solo; (e) identifying the types of knowledge that the solo experience imparts; and (f) establishing a relationship with the vision quester based upon trust, acceptance, risk-taking, and mutual respect (Knapp, 1992, pp. 35-36).

Basic Assumptions

Those who help solo takers expand their meanings of the experience usually don't believe that "the mountains can always speak for themselves." Those who believe that the mountains are the only necessary mediators and that human facilitators are not important in the reflection process might want to approach their facilitation responsibilities for solos differently than this paper suggests. The author of this paper assumes that in most cases the role of facilitator is critical in helping others maximize what they glean from the solo experience.

According to recent research studies on cognition, past knowledge is essential for acquiring new knowledge. "All learning involves the ability to transfer knowledge from previous experience" (National Research Council, 2000, p. 68). Transfer is "the ability to extend what has been learned in one context to new contexts" (p. 51). When something is learned, it is dependent upon what already has been learned. Although another human is not always needed for this transfer to occur, a facilitator can be useful in helping learners by prompting and supporting them in some way. By applying competent facilitation skills, learning can occur more efficiently and be retained longer. The role of facilitators can be described as helping others with meaning-making. Briefing and debriefing, when done well, increase the value of the experience to the learner. The more skills and information a facilitator has about the goals of the solo, site location, and the person taking it, the better that leader will be able to guide the learner in making sense of the experience and in achieving deeper understandings. The key goal for the vision seeker is to know how to apply what is learned in the future. This paper is founded on these assumptions about helping others maximize learning from their solo experiences.

Defining Relevant Terms

To facilitate someone's learning is to help that person acquire knowledge more efficiently, understand it more deeply, and to draw more meaning from the experience. One who assists learners is described as a facilitator, teacher, or guide. Sometimes this facilitator can provide the vision seeker with some missing information, but most of the time the facilitator's role is more related to asking the questions rather than giving the answers. The drawing out of wisdom from within the learner is more in line with the original Latin meaning of the word, *educate*, which is "to lead out." This can be done with questions or structured activities that promote the replay, examination, and evaluation of a recent experience.

The word *brief*, according to Webster's, means to "instruct or advise in advance." In military terms, a briefing (the noun) consists of "the final instructions given to aircraft pilots and crew members before a flight or raid" (Funk & Wagnalls, 2000, p. 167). Priest and Gass (1997) suggest an instructional approach in which the facilitator directly frontloads the experience or highlights the projected learning prior to the experience. They also suggest that metaphors such as climbing a mountain, jumping a hurdle, or running a marathon can be introduced (isomorphically framing the experience) to help clients make connections between the adventure experience and their future lives at home. Steven Foster and Meridith Little explain how metaphors can be used to expand the meaning of experience on a vision quest:

> *He/she finds the self in a double-meaninged universe. An animal is both animal and spirit. A mountain is a mountain and a quest. A star is a star and an angel. A direction walked is a trail and a Way. A dream is a dream and a divine visitation. A mosquito is a pest and a messenger.*
>
> (1988, pp. 31-32)

The word *debriefing*, as used in the process of facilitating experiential learning, has several synonyms. These include: processing, critiquing, bridging, reviewing, thinking about thinking (meta-cognating), teaching for transfer, evaluating, and reflecting (Knapp, 1992). No matter what term is used, this word describes a guided activity involving a leader and at least one other person who has experienced an event such as a solo. The purpose of this structured activity is to help the participant transfer what is learned from one setting to another and to deepen the understanding of what is learned. Deepening understanding goes beyond just stating more facts; it includes knowing when, where, why, and how to use those facts in another setting. According to Jack Mezirow, "A defining condition of being human is that we have to understand the meaning of our experience" (Costa & Kallick, 2000, p. 15).

Considering Cognitive Research

The debriefing after the solo can be helpful for expanding the learning and considering how it will be transferred to other life situations. A growing body of research has focused on expert and novice learners and documented distinct differences in how they learn. For example, several key principles of how experts acquire knowledge have been identified (National Research Council, 2000, p. 31). A few of these include the following:

1. Experts notice features and meaningful patterns of information that are not noticed by novices.

2. Experts have acquired a great deal of content knowledge that is organized in ways that reflect a deep understanding of their subject matter.

3. Experts' knowledge cannot be reduced to sets of isolated facts or propositions but, instead, reflect contexts of applicability: that is, the knowledge is *conditionalized* on a set of circumstances.

4. Experts are able to flexibly retrieve important aspects of their knowledge with little attentional effort.

Although all of these findings do not apply directly to learning from the solo experience, a few do. By briefing and debriefing, facilitators can help novice vision seekers become more expert as learners. The American Psychological Association's Board of Educational Affairs and Board of Scientific Affairs developed a list of learner-centered psychological principles in 1991 and revised them in 1997. Their goal was to direct attention to the contributions of psychological research and to examine how these principles could enhance new designs for curriculum and instruction (APA, 2004). These 14 principles are divided into four categories: (a) cognitive and meta-cognitive, (b) motivational and affective, (c) developmental and social, and (d) individual difference factors influencing learning. The first two categories are most relevant to facilitating solo learning. The original text is paraphrased and condensed below for two of the four categories. A related question is provided for each principle to assist facilitators in conducting learner-centered solo programs.

Cognitive and Meta-Cognitive Factors

1. The learning of complex material is most effective when it is an intentional process of constructing meaning from information and experience. Question: How do facilitators help vision seekers remember what happened during solo?

2. The successful learner, over time and with support and instructional guidance, can create meaningful, coherent representations of knowledge by setting goals. Question: How do facilitators help vision seekers become aware of some of their short- and long-term goals for the solo?

3. The successful learner can connect new information with existing knowledge in meaningful ways. Question: How do facilitators help vision seekers discover their prior knowledge levels and help them make meaningful connections to the new knowledge gained?

4. The successful learner can create and use an array of thinking and reasoning strategies to achieve complex learning goals. Question: How do facilitators help vision seekers examine their thinking and reasoning strategies?

5. Higher order strategies for selecting and monitoring mental operations promote creative and critical thinking. Question: How do facilitators guide vision seekers in creatively and critically sharing their insights about the solo?

6. Learning is influenced by environmental considerations, including culture, technology, and instructional practices. Question: How do facilitators help vision seekers explore the associated environmental, cultural, technological, and instructional factors involved in the solo?

Motivational and Affective Factors

1. The quantity and quality of what is learned is influenced by the learner's motivation. Motivation to learn is influenced by the individual's emotional states, beliefs, interests, goals, and habits of thinking. Question: How do facilitators determine the types and levels of vision seekers' motivations and emotional states?

2. Intrinsic motivation to learn is stimulated by tasks of optimal novelty and difficulty, relevant to personal interests, and providing for personal choice and control. Question: How do facilitators determine vision seekers' thoughts and feelings related to task novelty, difficulty, personal interest, and degree of choice and control?

3. Acquisition of complex knowledge and skills requires expanded effort and guided practice on the part of the learner. Question: How do facilitators discover the vision seekers' levels of intrinsic motivation to learn and their perceptions about the relevance of the solo?

These psychological principles developed by educators for educators can have important implications for facilitators of the solo experience. By considering the answers to the suggested questions and others, facilitators can be more effective in guiding the meaning-making process.

Committing to the Role of Briefing and Debriefing

Without being committed to the importance of briefing and debriefing, facilitators will have limited effectiveness in preparing the vision seekers and in following up after the solo. The word *commit* carries several strong meanings, including "to do," "to place in trust" and "to devote, pledge, or bind oneself" (Funk & Wagnalls, p. 264).

The briefing is key because of the potential for critical health and safety issues. Vision seekers must know how to signal leaders in case of an emergency. Different types of security systems can be set up to assure that the solo will be a safe event. At a minimum, the facilitator should devise a way to periodically observe the vision seekers during their time alone. The possibilities of being hungry, thirsty, cold, wet, or sore should be considered and discussed. Vision seekers should be advised that unpredictable events may occur and that it is impossible to remove all the risks from the experience. In addition to health and safety factors, facilitators should consider the vision seekers' emotional and psychological well-being. If vision seekers are briefed about some of the feelings that may arise during solo, such as boredom, impatience, fear, nervousness, awe, wonder, and surprise, they are more likely to learn from such feelings if they occur. Similarly, if seekers are clear about the potential benefits of the solo and have set personal goals, they are more likely to emerge from the solo enlightened.

risk?

Deliberately Planning the Briefing and Debriefing

The plan for briefing and debriefing the solo can incorporate groups of people if the situation warrants it. There is value in preparing and following up with a small group of soloists because of the potential power that can come from sharing perspectives. Plans can include discussions and structured exercises dealing with anticipated problems and issues. Those who are doing a solo for the first time will have many questions about their abilities to complete the allocated time alone. Self-doubt may enter their minds about how well they will do. Other participants may be overly confident. Each way of thinking and feeling presents ample briefing and debriefing opportunities. Solo facilitators should consider some of the following questions in their planning of the debrief:

1. What happened during solo?

2. How did these events affect the vision seekers?

3. Which events seemed important and which seemed trivial?

4. Why did these events seem important or trivial?

5. How might these events relate to future use at home, on the job, or in school?

6. What barriers could arise when trying to implement life changes?

7. Did anything happen that was not easily explained? If so, what?

8. What questions arose at different times throughout the solo?

9. What was most surprising? … awe inspiring? … beautiful? … disturbing?

These questions indicate only a small percentage of those that may arise during solos. A simplified outline for debriefing first presented by Terry Borton in 1970 (Schoel & Maizell, 2002) consists of three basic questions: What happened? What is its importance? And, now, what is the relevance of this? If journals are permitted on the solo, they may be used to record events and associated thoughts and feelings for discussion in the debriefing session and for later personal reflection. The more experience facilitators bring through personal experience with solo, the better they will be able to anticipate the concerns and questions of the vision seekers.

Realizing the Need for a High Level of Facilitation Skills

According to Priest and Gass (1997), there are five phases of the process of facilitating adventure experiences: diagnosis, design, delivery, debriefing, and detachment. Diagnosis involves seeking information about the goals people set. Design involves planning how best to help people reach their goals through the experience. Delivery involves setting up the experience in a safe (physically and emotionally), environmentally sensitive, and educationally sound way by thoroughly briefing the vision seekers ahead of time. Debriefing involves guiding the reflection through structured activities, interviews, or questions. Detachment involves providing the follow-up support needed to help people reach a point of closure and transfer what is learned to other settings.

One of the greatest challenges for vision seekers is that they cannot rely on the social support of the group while participating in the solo. They are forced to rely on their internal strengths and face their shortcomings. Social support can be realized before the group separates and when it re-convenes following the solo. While alone, vision seekers face themselves directly and cannot lean on others for support. When they follow Socrates' dictum, "Know thyself," some may be uncomfortable with the person they are getting to know. This individual aspect of the solo experience creates a situation in which facilitators need to function at high levels in order to maximize the benefits. Facilitators must realize that being alone is not easy for some, as it is likely to be a time when vision seekers come face to face with their gods and devils.

Establishing Clear Intentions and Objectives

Because solos may be completed in a variety of ways, under various conditions, and for different lengths of time, the intentions and objectives must be clearly defined by the facilitators and participants. For example, beginners can find sitting alone outdoors for as little as 20 minutes at night extremely threatening. At the other extreme, even those with prior solo experience can find a four-day fasting solo in the desert psychologically and physically challenging. Facilitators should ask themselves, "What would I like vision seekers to gain from this experience, and what conditions should be established to increase the probability that benefits will be achieved?" Other sections of this book discuss some formats for solo. The following questions indicate a few of the many issues that must be defined before a solo experience is provided:

1. Will this be a walking solo or a stationary one?
2. How long will the vision seeker stay out?
3. What clothing and personal belongings will be allowed?
4. Will a tent, blanket or bedroll, poncho or other form of shelter and warmth be taken?
5. Will books or other reading material be taken?
6. Will food and/or water be provided, or will the vision seeker fast?
7. Can fires be built safely for warmth and companionship?
8. Will the solo focus on a particular objective, such as prayer, nature observation, wilderness survival, journaling, self-understanding, vocational clarity, problem-solving, a combination of these, or any number of other possibilities?
9. How will the vision seeker communicate with the facilitators in case an emergency arises?
10. What will be the consequences (if any) if the vision seeker disturbs others or decides to terminate the solo early?

The answers to these questions and others will influence the types of intentions and objectives that may be achieved by the vision seeker. In order to answer these questions in a consistent and logical fashion, it is essential that the facilitators and the institutions for which they work have a clearly written and consistent philosophy of solo-taking. Constructing this type of document is no easy task, but the benefits to the individual and the program are well worth the effort.

Identifying the Types of Knowledge Represented by the Experience

The solo experience can lead to valuable knowledge, primarily related to the intrapersonal area. According to Howard Gardner, "Intrapersonal intelligence involves the capacity to understand oneself, to have an effective working model of oneself – including one's own desires, fears, and capacities – and to use such information effectively in regulating one's own life (1999, p. 43).

Carl Rogers believed that significant learning occurred when people saw themselves more positively, accepted their feelings more fully, became more self-confident and self-directing, felt more like the person they would like to be, were more flexible and less rigid in their perceptions, adopted more realistic goals for themselves, behaved in a more mature way, changed some of their uncomfortable behaviors, were more accepting of others, became more open to evidence telling them what is going on outside and inside of themselves, and changed some of their basic personality characteristics in constructive ways (1969).

Although time alone can lead to knowledge about how to relate better with others, self-insight can be a direct benefit of the solo. Clearly, how people see themselves influences how they respond in groups. Facilitators can take clues from what vision seekers say about their self-perception and concept, and then draw them out through intense listening and questioning. In fact, there are no boundaries on the kinds of knowledge that can be gained through the solo. Facilitators can help vision seekers to sort and prioritize the types of knowledge gained without imposing their own values and ideas on learners.

Establishing a Compatible Relationship With the Vision Seeker

Although this topic is described last, it may be the most important factor in successfully facilitating the solo experience. Without an established relationship with vision seekers, the ability of the facilitator to help vision seekers develop and change is severely limited. Ideally, this relationship should be based on a high level of mutual trust, acceptance, and respect. The vision seeker should understand that taking a solo involves a certain amount of risk, especially during the debriefing phase of the experience. The facilitator must have the necessary skills and personality to create a supportive climate in order to ensure success. Without a supportive climate, very few of the facilitator's efforts will be effective.

Because this aspect of facilitating the solo is so important, facilitators should find out as much as possible about the vision seeker before they meet face to face. If this is not possible, the activities preceding the solo and the briefing time before it begins should be used to gain an understanding of who will be soloing. It is difficult to imagine a vision seeker meeting a leader and then immediately being put out on a solo. Some traditional Native Americans would ask that the vision seeker undergo an elaborate series of preparatory steps before accepting the responsibility of facilitating the solo for someone. In some adventure programs this type of extensive preparation is not deemed feasible, but the lesson of how indigenous medicine people view their leadership responsibility for a solo should be seriously considered.

Summary

If the role of the solo facilitator is seen as one of helping vision seekers make sense from their experiences and apply some of the knowledge gained to future settings and situations, they must have an understanding of how people learn and what effective teachers do to nurture that process. This paper examines some basic assumptions and definitions related to facilitating solos and provides some information derived from educational research. Two aspects of the process, the briefing and debriefing phases of facilitating, are examined in more depth. More importantly, this paper raises some questions for facilitators to consider as they design and implement solos by examining six factors that contribute to successfully facilitating the solo. The power of questions to promote learning should not be underestimated. When solo leaders think about and discuss these questions, the experience will, no doubt, reach a higher level of quality. Since this paper supports the idea that the mountains can't always speak for themselves, solo facilitators will have to interpret for the mountains as they enable vision seekers to clarify meanings and maximize learning.

References

American Psychological Association (APA) (2004). *Learner-centered psychological principles: A framework for school redesign and reform.* Washington, D. C.: Center for Psychology in Schools and Education. Retrieved May 11, 2005, from http://www.apa.org/ed/lcp.html

Beck, P. V., Walters, A. L., & Francisco, N. (2001). *The sacred: Ways of knowledge, sources of life.* Tsaile, AZ: Dine College.

Costa, A. L., & Kallick, B. (2000). *Assessing & reporting on habits of mind.* Alexandria, VA: Association for Supervision and Curriculum Development.

DeMallie, R. J., & Parks, D. R. (Eds.). (1987). *Sioux Indian religion: Tradition and innovation.* Norman: University of Oklahoma Press.

Foster, S., & Little, M. (1988). The fasting quest as a modern rite of passage. *Holistic Education Review, 1*(3), 30–35.

Funk & Wagnalls. (2000). *New international dictionary of the English language: Comprehensive millennium edition.* Chicago: World Publishers.

Gardner, H. (1999). *Intelligence reframed: Multiple intelligences for the 21st century.* New York: Basic Books.

James, T. (1980) *Can the mountains speak for themselves?* (Unpublished manuscript, Colorado Outward Bound School, Denver, CO.)

Knapp, C. E. (1992). *Lasting lessons: A teacher's guide to reflecting on experience.* Charleston, WV: ERIC Clearinghouse on Small Schools.

Mails, T. E. (1979). *Fools Crow.* Lincoln: University of Nebraska Press.

National Research Council. (2000). *How people learn: Brain, mind, experience, and school.* Washington, D. C.: National Academy Press.

Priest, S., & Gass, M. A. (1997). *Effective leadership in adventure programming.* Champaign, IL: Human Kinetics.

Rogers, C. R. (1969). *Freedom to learn.* Columbus, OH: Charles E. Merrill Publishing Company.

Schoel, J., & Maizell, R. S. (2002). *Exploring islands of healing: New perspectives on adventure based counseling.* Beverly, MA: Project Adventure.

CHAPTER 3

The Rites of Passage Vision Quest

By Mike Bodkin & Linda Sartor

Without vision the people perish.

(Proverbs 29:18)

Initiatory ceremonies, so common in traditional societies and which many argue are essential to the health of any society, have largely disappeared from our modern world. Historically, rites of passage represented the confirmation of movement from one life stage to another, accomplished by undergoing a test or ordeal that challenged body, mind, soul, and spirit. Even when society does not emphasize the importance of rites of passage rituals, people still feel a calling to mark their life passages in meaningful ways, often creating rituals and ceremonies for themselves without the support of teacher or tradition.

Rites of Passage, a nonprofit organization founded in 1977, has a mission to provide opportunities for people to undertake a classical rite of passage to mark and celebrate their transition from one life stage to another. One of the programs offered by the organization is a nine-day vision quest, so named for its indebtedness to the Native American vision quest. Both of us are wilderness guides and facilitators for the Rites of Passage program. In this paper, we provide a brief overview of the Rites of Passage vision quest, and share some of our personal strategies and experiences.

Steven Foster and Meredith Little, the founders of Rites of Passage, wrote:

> *We seek to provide ways in which young people and adults can celebrate or confirm their attainment of new life stages in a traditional fashion in the wilderness.*

> (1996, p. 2)

Although the need for rites of passage is not generally appreciated in Western culture, its absence in this culture often has community-wide destructive impacts. That is because people do not automatically grow from one stage of life to the next. Children will not grow into competent adults, nor will adults grow in their capacity to love and care for others and the earth merely by aging. In addition, many people face emotional turmoil in their lives, and time alone does not automatically heal all the psychological wounds. A meaningful rite of passage can help people define life transitions and offer psychological healing when it is undertaken with intention, clarity, courage, heart, and passion. Rites of passage can be especially important for adolescents as they approach adult life.

In modern life, we are aware of the hunger of our young people to grow up. Because the old tradition-based initiations are gone, they create their own non-intentional rites as they seek to initiate themselves. Again and again we see how they test themselves against the edge of death. The fact is, we all need to feel that edge, especially in our adolescent years.

Young people are drawn to challenges to find out who they are and discover their capacities and limits. Obtaining a driver's license, getting a job or graduating from high school are appropriate markers of adult status in Western society today. Some young people create their own, often less appropriate, rites of passage. These include getting drunk or stoned, driving fast, or engaging in promiscuous sexual experiences to represent the achievement of a peer-sanctioned status of adulthood. Young people's need for rites of passage is often also expressed in more destructive, sometimes violent or deadly ways through a pseudo-initiation. Examples include being "jumped into" a gang and participating in hazing rituals that involve dangerous or self-destructive behavior, such as rapid consumption (chugging) of large quantities of alcohol. Longing for the sanction of the elders may be behind many young men's vulnerability to these mock rituals, where older male peers assign the challenge that must be faced in order to be recognized as a man (as defined by the peer group). These peer-implemented rites of passage lack the critical elements of a genuine initiatory passage: elders to sanction and guide them, appropriate and genuine challenges by which the achievement of adult status truly may be measured, and recognition of the achievement of this status by family and the larger community.

Foster and Little (1996) took Arnold Van Gennep's (1960) three-stage model of traditional rites of passage and applied it to the modern experience of the vision quest. The three stages of the model are severance, threshold, and incorporation. In Rites of Passage, Inc., *severance*, or "dying to one's old life," begins when a person commits to the program and proceeds with a series of steps that move away from ordinary modern life — packing, saying goodbye to friends and family, traveling to a wilderness area (leaving home behind), walking into the wilderness to set up a base camp (leaving vehicles, the road and civilization behind), and finally departing base camp to begin the solo experience (leaving everyone behind). The *threshold* stage, also called the *liminal*, marks the time between worlds, between death and rebirth, between the old self and the reborn self. In our program, this is the time of being alone in the wilderness, which is similar to rites of passage of many cultures, including Native American, Australian Aboriginal, and indigenous African. *Incorporation* is the time of returning to one's community with a new status, carrying the wisdom and inner truth of the experience back into the world.

An age-old story is invoked: The hero or heroine leaves friends, family, and community behind (severance); travels to an unknown or wild place where he/she lives alone on the earth, faced with the powers of nature and thrown back upon him/herself (threshold); then returns to family and community, bringing back the sacred stories and lessons of the solo for the benefit of all (incorporation).

Transitions

While the circumstances of each person's rite of passage are unique, the transitions of our participants usually follow identifiable life cycle themes that can be categorized as:

1. childhood to adulthood

2. transitions of adult life

3. healing psychological wounds

The young people who participate in our vision quest program are in transition from childhood to adulthood. They may be preparing to leave family, friends, and neighborhood to attend college; seeking vocation to support themselves; planning to remain at home while defining a more adult status within their families; or struggling with negative influences of peer group. The core questions that must be answered during this transition are "Who am I?" and "What are my gifts?"

For adults, transitions can be more varied. Life cycle events that might be marked by an adult through a rite of passage include, but are not limited to: entering or leaving a marriage, becoming a parent, deciding upon or changing a career path, the death of a parent, and becoming an elder. There are also personal markers, like anniversaries, celebrations of sobriety, leaving behind an unsatisfactory job, ending a relationship, or just taking time to listen to one's inner voice. Many adults who have not made a conscious entrance into adulthood will seek rites of passage to claim their true adulthood for the first time, in much the same way youth participants do.

Some people come to us as a part of a personal program of psychotherapeutic growth and healing. We do not believe that our program is a substitute for psychotherapy, but we have seen that participation in the vision quest makes a significant contribution to people's progress in therapy. For example, a woman in her early 30s who had a history of sexual and physical abuse as a child came on the quest. She had dealt extensively with her pain in therapy, but as the quest approached she reported that images and feelings from her childhood were surfacing again. She was assured that she was not "falling apart" despite the violent nature of some of her memory images. During the quest, which took place in high desert country, where there were signs of mountain lions, she had a dream that a mountain lion came to her offering to replace her wounded child-heart with a new healed one. In her dream, she accepted this offer. She returned from the mountain full of radiance and inner peace, having finally put her childhood demons to rest.

Other people come to our program to claim their healing from illness or trauma, perhaps in conjunction with an important life transition: a midlife woman marked her being free of cancer for five years; a drug addict celebrated 10 years of sobriety; a woman who was sexually abused as a child claimed her strength and competence as an adult; a young father came to terms with the wounds of his own father's absence when he was a child and committed himself to being fully present for his child; a teenage girl claimed the inner power and adult strength necessary to confront a domineering teacher.

Whatever the marker or transition, we've found that participants in our vision quest draw from their inner wisdom and strength to affirm their own path in the world, and find the courage and energy to follow it.

Risk and Challenge

An element of risk or challenge is important to any initiatory rite. We cannot and should not eliminate all risks if we want to allow participants to find their edge and discover themselves at core level. The vision quest program we offer has three challenges that work equally well with youth or adults:

1. Solitude: The candidate must spend time alone in nature, without distraction. With only his/her own resources on which to rely, the quester discovers him/herself reflected by the natural world.
2. Fasting: The candidate goes without food during the solo period. If there are medical concerns, this regimen can be modified while maintaining the spirit of going without nourishment.

3. Exposure: The candidate faces exposure to the natural world, having a sleeping bag and a tarp (but no tent) to protect against the elements.

Severance: Preparation for the Solo

Preparation begins early in the severance phase. The first level of preparation is on the physical plane, with safety being a primary concern. Prior to arrival in the wilderness, participants receive a handbook that includes an equipment list and extensive information about safety issues. On our nine-day program, the first three days are used to prepare participants. Many participants have never spent time in the wilderness, have never spent time alone, and are unfamiliar with the desert environment in which we conduct the majority of our programs. Staff — who are guides, not therapists — review information included in the handbook through interactive discussion of the following topics:

1. Equipment and how to use it.

2. Flora and fauna of the wilderness area: poisonous plants, dangerous animals, and what to do if you encounter them.

3. Hypothermia, hyperthermia, lightning, flash floods, and other potential risks.

4. The *Buddy System*, a safety system allowing for participants to check on each other's safety while in solitude without compromising privacy. Paired buddies leave a marker at a shared stonepile each day.

5. First-aid procedures: how to take care of oneself and provide basic care to one's buddy in case of an emergency (how to stop bleeding, treat for shock, get help, etc.).

6. Orientation, or how not to get lost, and what to do if you do.

7. The physical and psychological effects of fasting.

Preparing for the physical challenges within the context of the rite of passage ceremony touches on every part of the psyche and becomes a metaphor representing how one lives his/her life. There are deeper meanings inherent in each *literal* situation, and the natural world can be said to *mirror* or reflect the inner life of the participant. Here are some examples of themes that may be explored with participants:

1. What does *getting lost* mean to you? What have you done in the past when you've been *lost*?

2. What animals do you hope to meet, or fear to meet? What meanings do you attribute to a deer, a mountain lion, a rattlesnake, a mouse?

3. How do you take care of yourself? What do you do when you're afraid? When you're lonely? Where do you turn for comfort?

4. What items do you need to carry into the wilderness? What do these represent to you about your life? What do you want to leave behind?

To help participants explore questions or themes during the preparation time, we introduce the *Ceremony of Council* (Zimmerman and Coyle, 1996), a form of group dialogue. In council, the group meets in a circle, and a *talking piece* conveying the right to speak is passed around the group. Participants are asked to follow four simple guidelines:

1. Speak from the heart.

2. Listen from the heart.

3. Don't rehearse what you're going to say.

4. Be lean of expression — don't drone on.

During the first council, we ask participants, "What is your purpose in undertaking this rite of passage?" Clarification of purpose for the quest, which is closely connected to a sense of life purpose, will continue right up to the group meeting on the final evening before solo.

We also explore fears in council. We believe that the more people learn to be with their fears, to "make friends" with their fears, and not be stopped by them, the more they are able to bring forth their full inner potential.

Participants bring their own spiritual ideas, traditions, and practices to the program, and we offer earth-based spiritual tools and ideas that are inclusive and can work with all forms of spiritual practice. Christians, Jews, Moslems, atheists, New Agers, Buddhists, and people who attend 12-step meetings are among those who have found these tools to be of value.

We teach the basics of self-generated ceremony, so that people can create their own rituals during the threshold period, drawing on their creativity and authenticity. For example, a person who felt burdened by the "shoulds" in their world might decide to write them all down, burn all the pages and scatter the ashes to the winds to symbolize the releasing of their power. We've found that enacting or symbolizing a situation or problem has a greater impact than just thinking about it. The tools available for self-generated ceremony are essentially limitless, encompassing elements of the natural world as well as items such as clothing, camping gear, fire, and water.

We also suggest the value of a ceremony called *The Death Lodge*. To enact this, the participant imagines that he/she is preparing to die and calls each important person from his/her life, one at a time, in order to express truths, listen, and find completion. In saying goodbye, people often deepen their sense of love and connection to family, friends, and community and feel gratitude for the opportunity to return home to them.

We accept and honor the consciousness and intelligence of the earth — all the animals, plants, rocks, clouds, or wind one encounters during the quest can be seen as teachers. Rather than relating to the earth intellectually, as an *it*, we suggest that people relate to everything they encounter as a *thou*. This brings the natural world to life and more fully opens the realm of intuition. A participant might have the experience of being perceived and known by wilderness itself. This point of view can be experienced directly by *speaking* and *listening* to the earth, and does not require *belief*. There is support for this approach in the pan-cultural mythology of Joseph Campbell (1988), in the eco-theology of Thomas Berry (1990, 1999), and in many Native American teachings (c.f., Mails, 1979; Black Elk & Lyon, 1990; Lame Deer & Erodes, 1972).

We also present an overview of the Medicine Wheel, a Native American model of human nature deeply rooted in the natural world. Rites of Passage was first introduced to that model in the early 1980s by Hyemeyosts Storm, a Northern Cheyenne teacher and author of *Seven Arrows* (1972). Modifications to the Medicine Wheel model, important to the Rites of Passage vision quest, have been made through the past 20 years by Steven Foster and Meredith Little (1996, 1998).

In its simplest representation, the Medicine Wheel takes the form of a circle divided into four quadrants — a cross within a circle — an image found in Celtic, Buddhist, and Native American iconography, among others. The circle is an ancient symbol of wholeness and unity. In 5th century B.C., Greek philosopher Empedocles stated: "The nature of God is a Circle whose center is everywhere and whose circumference is nowhere" (Partington, 1992, p. 16). The division into four parts is found pan-culturally in the four seasons, the four directions, and the four winds, for a few examples.

The four cardinal points of the compass can serve as a starting point for introducing this material. Each direction or *shield* is associated with a life stage, certain human qualities, a season, and an animal symbol from the natural world.

1. South Shield: Childhood, innocence and trust, blind emotions and needs, dependency, survival instinct, sensuality, body, midday, summer season. Animal: mouse.

2. West Shield: Adolescence, introspection or looking within, memories, dreams, deepening of feelings, encounter with the shadow, ancestors, soul, sunset, fall season. Animal: bear.

3. North Shield: Adulthood, give-away, wisdom, taking responsibility, rational thought, self-discipline, work, community, mind, nighttime, winter season. Animal: bighorn sheep.

4. East Shield: Elderhood as well as infancy, rebirth, creativity, vision, inspiration, illumination, spirit, sunrise, spring season. Animal: red-tail hawk or eagle.

The Medicine Wheel paradigm helps participants deepen their understanding of themselves and the meaning of the initiatory journey they are about to undertake. The child (South Shield) is the uninitiated person who must pass through the trial of the threshold passage (West Shield) in order to be reborn as a true adult (North Shield) and return to the community as one reborn (East Shield), carrying vision for the people. The child, adolescent, adult, and elder live within us all the time. Recognizing this, and all four directions of ourselves — body, soul, mind, and spirit — as reflected in the mirror of nature, is to discover balance and wholeness.

As we present the Medicine Wheel model, we engage participants in conversation and exercises to activate a relationship with each direction of the Medicine Wheel. Which direction feels closest to you? Which feels most foreign? Where would you place yourself on the wheel in terms of your purpose for the quest? How do you relate to the South Shield? What was your childhood like? What things of childhood are you leaving behind? What are your fears? How do you relate to the West Shield? What lies hidden in your inner shadow? Can you accept and love all of yourself? What parts of yourself do you have difficulty accepting? How do you relate to the North Shield? What were your parents like as models of adulthood? What do you think a true adult would be like? What are the markers of adulthood for you? What gifts do you carry, and who are the members of your community? Can you create ceremony for yourself? How do you relate to the East Shield? What is your relationship with spirit? To what higher power (however you think of that term) do you turn when you are low?

The Medicine Wheel can also serve as an assessment tool as we help ready people to undertake solo. Does this person seem out of balance in some important way? Does he/she seem stuck in any particular direction? Is there a direction that he/she is having difficulty accessing? If someone feels completely out of touch with one of the directions, this may indicate a potential risk. For example, someone who cannot relate to the South Shield might be overwhelmed during solo by a sudden flood of emotion. Will they be able to take care of themselves if this happens? Viewing participants through our understanding of the Medicine Wheel may lead us to suggest specific exercises designed to activate their involvement with one or more directions of the wheel.

The last activity of the severance stage is a group meeting held the night before beginning solo. At this final meeting, the staff engages each individual in interactive discussion, probing their readiness to undertake solo, asking them to again clarify their intents, and challenging them to affirm their readiness to claim the new status they are marking with the rite of passage. The specifics of each talk are unique, reflecting the circumstances of each person's life. "I'm claiming my readiness to be a good father," a young man might proclaim. "I'm leaving behind the abuse I suffered as a child and claiming my ability to have a healthy relationship with a partner," a 30-something woman may say. "I'm marking 10 years of sobriety, claiming my place as a responsible adult in my community, with gifts to give young people who are struggling with drugs and alcohol," a middle-aged man might announce.

Transition: Solitude

The middle three days of our vision quest program are given to solo, the transition. We do not have as much to say then, because this is when the participants leave the staff behind. We have done all we can to prepare each person for his/her unique experience — now we must let go. In the morning, we send people off with a special good-bye ceremony, a last severance from base camp and staff. Questers depart knowing we will be available in base camp 24 hours a day for the three days of the solo to respond to any crisis or need.

There is no "right way" to do solo, and all experiences are valid and worthwhile. Every story of the solo passage is sacred. Some people have marvelous dreams or have encounters with animals. Others talk to the wind. Almost everyone struggles with something — hunger, fear, loneliness, boredom. A few just hang on physically and emotionally for three days and nights, thinking constantly of returning. Some think of their families, and others cry a lot. Teens tend to re-evaluate their relationships with parents, perhaps recognizing that they have been thoughtless and lacking in appreciation, realizing suddenly how much their parents mean to them.

On the last evening of the solo, we suggest that each person construct a Medicine Wheel circle of stones, enter it at sundown, and then stay awake all night. This final challenge — for many the most difficult and rewarding of all they face on the vision quest — is literally and metaphorically a journey through the dark night, awaiting the rebirth of dawn.

Incorporation: Return and Processing

We mark the incorporation stage of the vision quest program with a series of steps taken over the final three days. For many, the incorporation — the return to community — is the most difficult part of the vision quest. We welcome questers back with a meal, prepared by the staff, to end the fast. We follow with three distinct council circles spread over the three days. After the questers have eaten and rested, we convene a council in which guides play the traditional role of *elders*. We listen to the stories of those who have been on solo and mirror aspects of the significance and meaning of the stories. Each person is honored for the unique, individual gifts with which he/she has returned. The mirroring can never be complete, because of the richness and myriad potential meanings inherent in the stories, but each staff person will add something unique and significant to understanding solo. This meeting is characterized by depth and openness, reflecting the newborn state of the returnees. Tears and laughter are usually present, along with a rich sense of community; they've been through this together, and can recognize and support each other now.

Reuniting with civilization is as challenging as leaving it at the start of the program and must be undertaken with care. On the second day of incorporation, we'll take another step back into the world by saying good-bye to our wilderness base camp, hiking out, and driving to a nearby campground. We'll also visit a local hot springs to wash off the dust and grime of the solo.

Our second council focuses on the return home. For most people, when they return to community — workplace, family, church, town — there is not the welcome that would happen in traditional cultures. They may even be met with indifference or outright hostility. For some, the return will be difficult because they will cling to the high feelings of their solo experience and the love they felt from the council. Some, of course, will return home full of excitement and inspiration but soon fall back into old patterns, losing confidence in what they accomplished and learned.

Yet the task of incorporation is clear: to return home with the gift and to share it with one's people. We spend time in council asking them what challenges they foresee for their return, what are their sources of support, and what commitments do they wish to make to embody the gifts of their solo? Participants state their gifts in many ways: "I'm bringing back a renewed sense of joy and aliveness, and a commitment to nourish this sense in myself and to struggle against the trap of feeling sorry for myself." "I have strong support from my family and close friends, and from people in this group, with whom I plan to stay in contact." "The biggest challenge I see is in my work with at-risk youth, which can be very draining and exhausting. It's not the kids so much as the administrators of the school where I work. I plan to stay with my job because I care about the young people and I think I'm making a difference, so I want to use the inner strengths I have discovered, as well as my support systems, to face the challenge of dealing with the administrators." "I want to commit to getting up every morning to watch the sun rise, in order to sustain my spirit."

At the final council on the last morning, the guides *resign* their positions and participate as group members. Each participant sits in council as an elder in support of the other participants. With this support and encouragement of the group, each must take on the responsibility for living the vision that he/she has received.

We believe we must be especially careful when preparing youth for returning home. When they are fresh out of the experience and have not yet faced the realities of home, they might deny that it will be difficult — yet the impact of returning can be overwhelming. Many years ago, Rites of Passage guided a group of young drug addicts on a vision quest. They were completing several months of residential drug treatment, and the vision quest was a culmination of their efforts. One young man had a profound spiritual experience during solo, which he summarized for the group as we met during incorporation: "Now I know I can never go back to using drugs." Tragically, only a month later, at a reunion meeting for the group, he was missing; he had gone back to shooting drugs on the streets. The transition from the vision quest, which also marked the end of the treatment program, was too much for him. His incorporation to home was inadequate, and we wondered whether we had sufficiently prepared him for the impact of returning.

What lasts from the experience is the story. The opening theme of each story is told during the preparation stage, as "I'm so scared of being alone," or "My wife died two years ago, and I haven't gotten over my grief," or "My mom is scared to let me grow up, but I think I'm ready." The story unfolds during the solo, then is re-told and mirrored at the council of elders, confirming its truths. The entire experience continues as a life-giving story in the memory of the person who has passed through the rite. Following is an example of two such stories.

Case History: Adult Participant

Vivian, a 41-year-old woman, came with us on a spring vision quest program to the Funeral Mountains of Death Valley. She had recently split up with her partner of 21 years and was dealing with grief, loss and a sense of dislocation. Before going out she clarified that she wished to say goodbye, face her fears, and reaffirm her life. As is true with many, her purpose became clearer while she progressed through her time alone. On the first day of solo, she wrote in her journal:

> *Why was I here? To learn that I could survive alone and not just to survive*
> *but to learn how to be happy with my aloneness. I was here to see what being*
> *alone might teach me. I was also here to face my other fears — the ending of*
> *my relationship, the endings of things and events in general, and the ultimate*
> *ending — death.*

She made a little hut, composed of rocks, branches and tarp, as her home, and she recognized one important lesson right away. She wrote of that lesson in her journal: "This experience gave me the confidence that I can create a comfortable home anywhere on this earth…. I felt like I belonged here. This was my place."

In the evening, it started to rain and she went into her hut, glad to be warm and dry. Then the rain came down harder, and her shelter began to leak. It was now dark, getting colder, and Vivian felt very scared. After "praying to God," she decided to stay put rather than risk hypothermia by leaving her shelter to return to base camp. Strangely, all her fear left her then.

> *I huddled in my hut over my backpack until I decided to just give up on*
> *fear…. I felt I had lived my life well and I was doing what I wanted to, which*
> *was to go on a quest and find the meaning of endings/death.*

Finally the rain stopped, and Vivian felt a surge of gratefulness for her life. She reflected that the rain had taught her to "weather the storm."

The good weather held on Vivian's second day of solo, but she was facing a new fear. She was deathly afraid of snakes, but she accepted the possibility of their presence and even named her site the "Valley of Snakes" — acknowledging the possible presence of these frightening creatures. Despite her fears, she allowed herself to walk around the open landscape of the desert mountains. Again, she made her own interpretation: "There may be snakes in life, but that doesn't mean I should stop exploring what the world has to offer."

At sunset, she called her ex-partner to her in spirit, and they "talked" about their relationship: "We offered our forgiveness and our love. It was a sad time for me. Tears fell, but afterwards I felt full."

What happened next was unexpected. Vivian describes it as a vision:

> *The sun cast out its rays in a very distinct radial pattern of about 12 arms …*
> *slowly they rotated outward and downward. The Crown of Glory appeared to*
> *me and as the Crown descended into the horizon, leaving one solid ray ascend-*
> *ing into the heavens, I heard the words: "Endings lead to heaven. It's okay*
> *when things end and turn into the night. The next day will be glorious. All is*
> *a cycle. I am always with you every step of the way … in Life as in Death."*

She cried then and waited until it was dark and the stars were shining before returning to her hut to sleep.

Her third day was marked by strong winds, but this didn't faze her. She called this day "Riding the Stallion." The night came on freezing cold, and she was bone-tired, but she survived it. She woke up eager to meet her buddy on the fourth morning, ready to return. She looked exhausted but radiant when we welcomed her back into base camp at the ceremonial circle. She told her story at the elders council, where we confirmed what she already had claimed for herself — that she had indeed looked deeply into endings and beginnings, and had returned with many blessings.

Case History: Youth Participant

John, age 17, attended a vision quest with Rites of Passage during the summer between his junior and senior years of high school. His stated intention was to enter manhood in a meaningful way, honoring his deep sense of spirituality and connection to others. During the solo, John thought a lot about his teachers, parents, religious values, and those he loved. He faced his biggest challenge on the last night, when he struggled against exhaustion and boredom to stay awake until sunrise. The story he told contained prayers, blessings, and a growing sense of his own capacity to give of himself to others. We confirmed that he had stepped into his manhood with courage and determination.

Nine months later, we received a letter from John telling us about the impact of his vision quest. He wrote:

> As I sit and reflect on what high school and senior year have been for me, the importance of my experience on the vision quest is immeasurable. I am writing you this email to thank you for the experience I was able to have of the vision quest and tell you, after a year, how much it changed my life.

His letter went on to mention several important changes in his life since the quest, which we excerpt here:

> It has given me so much more confidence and perspective in the way I treat myself and others. To know that I was able to persevere and then experience the illumination that I did on the last night has given me such a rock solid core of self-worth and confidence.
>
> The vision quest also gave me much more perspective on life. It is so easy to get wrapped up in the everyday details that it becomes easy to miss the big picture. For me the big picture is that I am part of a world far greater than me. The big picture is also the goals that I have set out for me in the future: to support a family full of love and happiness.

When I interact with others, all of those close to me tell me that they have noticed that I act with much more compassion.

After going on the vision quest, I developed a new understanding of what it means to be a person of faith.

John's comments indicate the potential for the long-term positive impact of the vision quest program for young people. He concludes his letter with, "I will never forget my vision quest."

Benefits

Participant feedback via informal conversations and letters usually received within a year following the program form the primary basis for evaluating Rites of Passage programs. Briefly stated, we've seen the following benefits:

1. Personal: Recognition of the accomplishment of a new life stage with a sense of purpose and meaning; healing; coming to completion, self-acceptance and/or forgiveness related to previous life situations, childhood issues, and/or relationship issues; increased self-confidence and self-reliance; deepening of spirituality and connection to the sacred; increased trust in one's *inner voice* of soul; and affirmation of one's life-path, including career choices.

2. Societal: Bringing communities together, especially in forging a bond between youth and elders; recognition by participants (both young and old), and by significant people in their lives, of their value and capacity, and of the gifts they take back to the community; increase in caring and acceptance between young people and their parents or guardians; increase in maturity and a sense of responsibility to care for others and for the larger community.

3. Environmental: A deepened sense of connection to the natural world; a heightened desire to protect and preserve wilderness; a desire to spend more time in the natural world; increased interest in contributing to the healing of the natural world (e.g., buying food grown without pesticides, driving a more fuel-efficient vehicle, constructing green housing).

Vision quest guides Marilyn Riley and John Hendee (2000) have co-authored a study of the reported benefits of the vision quest for adult clients. They identified a continuum of benefits, beginning with connection to self, leading to a sense of self-empowerment, and finally moving toward a sense of spirituality and connection to others. Key components of this continuum are as follows:

1. Connection to Self
   a. Self-connection/awareness
   b. Self-discovery/identity/purpose
   c. Self-understanding/clarity/insight
   d. Self-knowledge/acceptance
2. Self-Empowerment
   a. Self-confidence/reliance
   b. Facing fears/trusting nature
   c. Empowerment/strengthened
3. Connection to Other
   a. Connection to nature
   b. Spirituality/connectedness
   c. Healing/renewal
   d. Community

Considerations

A complex set of skills is required for effectively guiding rites of passage events. The leader acts as a combination of wilderness outfitter, counselor, educator, and ceremonialist. Perhaps the best overall description is *midwife* — helping people to birth themselves. As midwives, we recognize the earth as the real teacher in this work. Guides place the participant in the care of the earth, with as much attention to safety as possible, and then get out of the way. We encourage each person to connect with his/her own wisdom. We'll provide guidance and support, but each participant must find his/her own way through the program. We don't believe in gurus or spiritual authorities in this work, and we stand shoulder to shoulder with our participants — not above them.

In some ways a guide is similar to a therapist. Both therapists and guides must have excellent listening skills and be able to help clients clarify important issues. Both need to assess potential participant/client risks (physical and psychological), and be capable of intervening in crisis situations. Both need to be aware of power dynamics in relationships with participants/clients, especially potential abuses of power with vulnerable people. Guides and therapists both need to hold clear professional boundaries.

There are also important differences between guides and therapists regarding underlying assumptions and their effect. Guides carefully prepare participants, then release them to the care of Mother Earth. Implicit in this approach is a belief in the inherent power of ceremony that comes from the innate capacity of the client to discover new strengths, find healing and claim a new sense of self. Guides do not develop or implement treatment plans based on problems that have been identified.

As we've noted, risk is inherent in our work. We initially assess participants for physical and psychological risk, and once we've accepted them into the program, we must be willing to adjust the program parameters to fit the needs of each individual. For example, people with diabetes cannot fast but are capable of eating lightly as a way to honor the spirit of the *no food* injunction. We cover all that we know about safety and make recommendations about how to do the quest. Then participants have to make their own decisions about what does or doesn't work for them and how much risk to take. For example, people who show a great deal of fear of being alone at night can be encouraged to find a place close to base camp that is still far enough away so that they are on their own.

In summary, the Rites of Passage vision quest program provides participants with a modern-day ceremony to successfully pass through and mark significant life transitions. Our experience is that participants come into a better understanding of and connection with their unique core essences and life purposes through having the many facets of their lives reflected back to them by the natural wilderness where they spend an extended period of time. They return from their time alone with a narrative that confirms the value and meaning of the solo.

Questions we are working to improve our program include the following:

1. How might we better support our youth in staying strong in their newly discovered understanding of themselves when they return to their not-always-so-nurturing world of school and neighborhood?

2. How might we better integrate vision quest experiences into educational programs?

3. How might we develop human communities that provide the nurturing support to returning questers in ways communities of the past may have done?

References

Berry, T. (1990). *The dream of the earth*. San Francisco: Sierra Club Books.

Berry, T. (1999). *The great work*. New York: Bell Tower.

Black Elk, W., & Lyon, W. S. (1990). *The sacred ways of a Lakota*. New York: HarperCollins.

Campbell, J., with Moyers, B. (1988). *The power of the myth*. New York: Doubleday.

Foster, S., & Little, M. (1980). *The book of the vision quest*. Covelco, CA: Island Press.

Foster, S., & Little, M. (1996). Wilderness vision questing and the four shields of human nature. *Wilderness Resource Distinguished Lectureship*. Moscow: University of Idaho Wilderness Research Center.

Foster, S., & Little, M. (1998). *The four shields: The initiatory seasons of human nature*. Big Pine, CA: Lost Borders Press.

Lame Deer, J., & Erdoes, R. (1972). *Lame Deer: Seeker of visions*. New York: Simon-Schuster.

Mails, T. (1979). *Fools Crow*. Lincoln: University of Nebraska Press.

Partington, A. (Ed.) (1992). *The Oxford dictionary of quotations (4th ed.)*. Oxford, UK: Oxford University Press.

Riley, M. F., & Hendee, J. C. (2000). Wilderness vision quest clients: Motivations and reported benefits from an urban-based program, 1988 to 1997. *USDA Forest Service Proceedings*, RMRS-P-O. pp. 1–8.

Storm, H. (1972). *Seven arrows*. New York: Random House.

Van Gennep, A. (1960). *The rites of passage*. Chicago: University of Chicago Press.

Zimmerman, J., & Coyle, V. (1996). *The way of council*. Las Vegas, NV: Bramble Books.

CHAPTER 4

Growing and Deepening the Solo With a Creative-Reflective Journal

By William F. Hammond

[Drawing] has nothing to do with artifice or technique.
It has to do with aesthetics or conception.
It has only to do with the act of correct observation, and
by that I mean a physical contact with all sorts of
objects through all the senses.

(Nicolaides, 1941)

In the contemporary world of pre-processed fast foods, there is a rush and grind to acquire things we believe we really want, and connections into meaningful community relationships and political complexities are reduced to shallow sound bites. For the majority of North Americans, life has become a blur as people skim its surface without making time to dig deeper into rich options or to reflect. This social environment limits exploration into the inner self and nature, and implies that a solo experience is not on the horizon of possibility for most of today's population in North America.

Over the past 45 years, my experiences as a facilitator and teacher have shown me that although most people don't take the time to reflect on a daily basis, they are open to learning how. In the 1970s, I taught a course entitled "Don't just do something, sit there!" The curriculum was focused on the solo model of naturalist writer Ernest Thompson Seton. Seton would sit as still as possible for hours in a natural setting until wildlife simply saw him as a part of the background environment. Practicing Seton's method is a key step in learning to meditate, relax the body, and empty the mind of external and internal chatter, while focusing on becoming a keen observer of the beauty, detail, and small life forms in nature. Teaching that course was when I first learned that people genuinely want to be shown how to slow down, and that solos and journals are two of the best life-refocusing tools.

The peacefulness of a solo is a healthy, healing, and rejuvenating encounter. Using a creative journal to record one's insights and reflections in words, sketches, paintings, and meaningful artifacts (glued into the journal) melds a second powerful tool to the solo experience.

My own perspectives on solo experiences continue to evolve. Fifty-five years or so ago, I thought of solo as a time spent alone for hours or days camping, canoeing, or just wandering in the woods. My favorite was the quiet time early in the morning, when I would get up before others to wonder at the dew-mantled spider webs, hear the awakening of birds on wildflower-covered hillsides, and sit and watch the sun rise over the ridge at a little church camp in Hope, New Jersey. I have fond memories of quiet evenings spent by Little Silver Lake, watching the stars reflect on its mirror surface. Memories of wandering the forests, creeks, beaches, and salt marshes of Great Kills are still etched clearly in my mind, including the sights, sounds, and smells of each of those special places.

My most vivid recollection of a solo experience is as a young Boy Scout, when I was being inducted into the Order of the Arrow at Ten Mile Scout Camp in the mountains of New York. The experience included three days of service work completed in absolute silence and a solo camp experience for the duration of the trial. I still remember sitting alone in the evening by my tent, recording the insights and emotions in my field journal as I reflected upon the day's experiences.

In his work *Thunder Tree*, Robert Michael Pyle recounts the life-shaping experiences of his childhood, when he'd go wandering (sometimes alone and at other times with a small band of friends) through drainage ditches east of Denver, Colorado. He observes that the majority of today's children grow up without these experiences. Pyle recognizes this as the "extinction of experience" in today's young people.

During Boy Scout Jamborees and month-long canoe trips in the Adirondack Mountain lakes, I began keeping a journal and photo scrapbook. While the specifics of the times spent alone doing reflective journaling have faded, looking back through these entries makes me realize how important those moments were to me. These early journals are now treasures in my life. By taking time to sit alone and sketch, write, and photograph special places, I was gaining a powerful tool for introspection. This recognition built my connection to place and the ways of nature. I was creating a personal value set. I used my journal as an excuse to seek alone time away from idle camp gossip, trivial chatter, and busy work. I looked forward to the opportunity to debrief myself and harvest the images and feelings I had while experiencing awesome beauty, unique encounters with wildlife, weather, and my travel partners. Today, I seek a park bench, ground under a tree, a set of steps during breaks at conferences as mini solo-journaling places. I continue to be amazed by how a brief 10-minute solo journal experience can help me clarify, reflect, and make connections to the event. The investment in solo time and energy makes participating more productive.

A few years ago, after a period of not using a journal as a tool in my solo encounters, I rediscovered how important the journal is for clarifying the meaning of each experience. Now journals have become indispensable tools that support my work and creativity as an educator and community activist by stimulating insight and providing ways to harvest reflections.

Time and experience has also taught me that solo is about *alone time* spent anywhere — not only in the wilderness or pristine natural places. It is a habit of mind and soul that connects me to places, experiences, and interactions. Thus, the solo is about opening to feeling and connecting self to environment and environment to self. A solo place can be a bench or wall in the middle of a crowded inner-city, your yard, the hammock, on park trails or, indeed, in the deep wilds of mountains, prairies, water bodies and their edges. My tiny suburban backyard is my number one solo site.

How and Why Journaling Works

William Glasser (1998) makes a compelling case that people should spend at least half an hour daily alone in some reflective endeavor. At such times one may engage in journaling, painting, creative writing, running, gardening, a creative hobby, or essentially in any activity in which one loses a sense of time. Glasser has found that engaging in such a solo experience tends to make a person a better listener and a better communicator (possibly because she/he has listened to her-/himself and thereby served her/his personal ego). It also reduces mental and physical stress. These findings alone build a compelling case for making sure everyone includes at least 30 minutes of solo time every day.

If the solo experience entails introspection and connection to place, nature, and human relationships, then why is a journal an important tool in the solo-reflective experience? Research focused on human learning and how we construct personal knowledge suggests that most people benefit from access to cognitive maps that explain how a complex idea, process, or theory operates. Solos enhanced by reflection in images, both graphic and written, are highly personal. The process is influenced by the journal-keeper's emotions, whims, priorities, learning style, brain dominance patterns, motivations, and tolerance for creative risks. Both learning and building competence grow from experience. Every experience evokes an emotional, intellectual, and physical response. The transition from initial response to interactions with the experience, and then the transfer of what has been learned from the experience to new contexts is a process that demonstrates that the learner not only knows something new but also understands the meaning of the experience. This cyclical process is often called the cycle of learning.

Some generic elements to consider in framing the cycle of experience include the following:

1. Always begin with a sensory stimulus created by interaction with objects,

events, emotions, and places that stimulate emotional connection and reflection.

2. Interactions build from a flash of recollection of previous experience followed by the brain-mind system making personal meaning by melding one's prior and current experiences.

3. A response of attraction to the experience or a rejection and withdrawal follow as meaning is felt and valued positively or negatively.

4. The experience is reflected upon and often discussed or recorded in one's journal in a multimedia form.

This process affirms the response and tends to *fix* the core touchstones of the experience in context and personal memory. The experience is reinforced when the soloist shares the experience with others verbally, graphically, or in writing. Each solo experience builds upon previous solo experiences, creating the potential for a spiral of growth in insight and creativity.

This generic cycle of experience and growth is affirmed in current research about the workings of the human brain, learning styles, learning, and cognitive theory. The key to moving beyond awareness and knowledge to deep understanding is the act of transferring what has been experienced or learned to a new context. The journal is a tool that facilitates this process.

In his dissertation, David Pepi (1982) connects the conclusions reached by D. Bob Gowin in his book *Educating* (1981) with his own views of the thinking of naturalists such as Thoreau, Muir, the Comstocks, and many others. Pepi writes:

> ... *qualitative natural history as a form of nature appreciation in which thinking, feeling, and acting are integrated deliberately in order to obtain the richest experiences possible from natural objects and occurrences. The qualitative natural history approach involves relationships among four major elements: (1) an event or person experiencing a natural object or occurrence, (2) meanings, knowledge concerning the event, (3) feelings, emotions and sensations that attend the event, and (4) felt-significance, a culminating sense of warranted satisfaction (terms drawn from D. Bob Gowin).*
>
> (pp. 4–5)

In his text *Metaphoric Mind* (1971), Bob Samples made the case that one of the unique foundations of communication is the set of modalities that mediate both the input signals and output signals in communication. In addition to the long-established modalities of auditory (hearing), visual (seeing), tactile (touch), and olfactory (smell), Samples made the case that in a society of modern literate humans a fifth modality has emerged. He labeled the fifth modality as *symbolic-abstract* (communication through spoken and written words and abstract symbols).

Some estimate that people in the United States spend less than 10% (my college students average less than 5%) of their time in the out-of-doors. In a culture devoid of rich experiences in the out-of-doors, abstract and virtual realities define experience. Words, highway signs, books, emails, commercials, video games, TV, video, DVDs, texts, newsprint, memos, models, virtual reality technology displays, and rubrics have become the primary ways humans experience and understand their environment. Interpersonal relationships, politics, religion, and video games have become more and more virtual and are highly mediated through modern technologies of communication and information. As a result, much of what we know from experience is constructed from a base of pre-packaged, processed, man-made, and selected experiences and sensory inputs rather than through direct contact with the natural or cultural/social environment using our own senses and personal lenses. Modern research that meshes human brain function and the development of cognitive processes affirms that if we write, draw, and otherwise document important experiences, we are more likely to fix the experiences into long-term memory. When these experiences occur in an outdoor solo, all are enhanced. College students find half-hour to hour-long solos in the woods or a cypress swamp to be life changing. This is an affirmation that when we engage directly in solo experiences and write, sketch, diagram, paint, or otherwise record in multimedia forms of our own making, we enrich the experience in long-term memory and enhance its power for learning.

The tradition of the solo as a source of inspiration and enlightenment can be found in many of the world's leading religions. Moses went to the mountain, Jesus Christ often went into the wilderness, Buddha went on his quest, and Mohammed is said to have done the same. All went into the wilderness for solo time to gain insight and inspiration, which informed their teachings and writings. Similarly, many of those who have advanced human knowledge and understanding of the workings of the natural world used a combination of soloing and journaling to develop their theories. DaVinci, Darwin, Lewis and Clark, Thoreau, Carson, Edison, Burroughs, and Muir are but a few of the many who recorded their solo experiences in words and sketches as a means to think, explore, inquire, and reflect more deeply on new knowledge and understanding.

The journal can also be a powerful tool for stimulating metaphoric connections to other life experiences. Starting in his early years, Aldo Leopold was a devoted journaler. He held that the mark of a good observer was to accurately record what one saw, thought, and felt about the objects and events observed. Much of his *A Sand County Almanac* (1949) was written during pre-sunrise solo experiences at the "shack." In early-morning observations he made while others slept, Leopold recorded his perspective on that year's seasons, patterns of behavior, and noted changes in the place, as well as the state of politics, economics, property, and his sense of place. Uniting personal reflections, a record of the seasons, and events in a single journal, revealed patterns. Leopold created an almanac that provided a unique and insightful glimpse into Sand County's cultural and natural history, and became the foundation for his concept of a *land ethic*.

While developing a weeklong residential experience for upper-level corporate executives for Fortune 100 companies, Ned Herrmann (1989), former Director of Training for General Electric Company, conducted an international search relative to creative thinking. His research indicated that the single most powerful tool for assessing a person's deep understanding of a concept or experience is the person's ability to create a high-quality metaphor that links two unrelated concepts or experiences. Experience I gained at the GE Institute and from the hundreds of journaling workshops I've taught worldwide have shown me that people who have experienced solo during the workshops, even if only for a half-hour, are far more effective in producing metaphoric connections and harvesting them in their journals. A little guidance, some quality examples, and a solo experience of a half-hour or more can result in their ability to create both written and graphic metaphors.

Another value of journaling during and after solo time is that it helps people to define the most poignant and significant elements of their feelings, thoughts, and actions that grow from the experience. This process tends to build clarity about and sensitivity to one's inner self, feelings, beliefs, and linkages to the world. Often, it provides insight into simple, more positive behaviors and to the lifestyle changes a person wishes to make.

The journaling process works best when self-directed. Leading workshops is mostly about giving participants the permission to take risks, dig deeper into their emotions, thoughts, wishes, and needs, to stretch themselves just beyond their comfort zones to try new techniques, create new patterns, and use a variety of expressive media in a low-risk environment. My experience with the solo process is much the same. Providing participants with short (30–60 minutes), safe solo experiences with some meaningful (to the participant) purpose, followed by an effective debriefing, produces a positive response. With a positive first experience and some supportive mentoring, the solo can become a sacred part of a person's life experience. When we combine the personal creative journal with a solo, we provide an opportunity for the blending of a personal experience with the recording of its most important and meaningful attributes in a process of personally harvesting and making meaning. The journal record takes on evermore importance as it builds, and the soloist often tends to discern patterns of thought, feelings, values, and metaphoric linkages. The solo experience builds insight while the journal entries build a book of reflective meaning and reinforce its place in the soloist's long-term memory.

Journal Process and Practice

The journaling process is logistically simple. Merely gather a variety of writing and drawing tools (pencils, pens, watercolor pencils or pans, and brushes), 35-mm film canisters (they hold water for painting and travel well in a fanny or backpack), and a blank bound journal, either homemade or purchased.

I strive to improve two skills that are the foundation for *creative* thinking. First is *flexibility* of mind. Tools and format shape how you think and work. Flexibility is about using different tools (each tool shapes how you work and think differently). My rule for myself is that I can't use the same tool or media for more than four pages in a row. The second skill is *fluency* of mind. This skill is focused on journal regularity or sustaining a working flow. I start each new journal with a solo, and the title dedication page becomes my journal record of that place. This practice creates a bond between me, my journal, and the place where I inaugurated the new journal. The ritual provides both a clear new beginning and ending place. This tends to leave me with a sense of a new beginning, as well as a sense of closure. When the journal process is merely a continuation from one book to the next, I rarely feel a closure point. Closure of a journal book gives me a sense of accomplishment.

Many people ask if there is a prescribed way to organize journal entries. If the journal is to be a very productive and fun-filled tool, it is essential that you experiment, and play with various forms and formats of your own invention. It helps if you first think through what it is you really want to derive from your journal effort. My criteria are:

1. What I do must feel like fun and be fulfilling.

2. It should be productive to growing my thinking or ways of knowing or seeing something.

3. It should nurture both flexibility of mind and fluency of ideas.

4. It should serve as a *Think Pad* or place where I can observe my early undigested observations and thinking growth.

5. It should serve as a messing about place (without fear of judgment) with a wide variety of media, tools, and methods.

I carry my journal most everywhere I go, or at least 3″ x 5″ cards I can later glue into my journal (with a glue stick). I do not write in my journal every day or on any schedule — sometimes entries just flow and other times the journal is a good sit-upon in the field. Nevertheless, I always keep my journal nearby as the moment it is needed is rarely predictable.

The organizational pattern I have evolved for myself is like the transcontinental approach to railroad building. The first page(s) are bonding page(s) that bond me to where and when a journal begins. Then, working from front to back, I make entries that keep me deeply in touch with a sense of place and the big ideas or projects on which I am working. Simultaneously, I fill from the back cover forward with day-to-day meeting notes, sketches, scrapbook memorabilia, and artifacts; these entries provide context and help me keep track of the important elements that are shaping my thinking at any given moment. When the back-to-front daily records meet the front-to-back deep-thinking entries, the journal is complete. This approach to creating a creative-reflective journal has evolved over many decades and is the mode I've found works best for me. It is just one example of how to keep a journal. The creative-reflective journal process is about allowing yourself to create your own form, with tools most useful to you. This is a case in which "Just do it!" is a good slogan for beginning.

Suggested Methods

My advice to beginning journal-makers is to explore using all types of materials and perspectives in creating your entries. This approach keeps you from becoming bored or tired of using your journal as an integral part of your personal and professional development and work. Dating your entries is often helpful in retrospective examinations. Many people find that just sitting quietly is enough of a stimulus for finding what grows from the solo experience. Others find some type of stem as a starter to be helpful. For example, journaling with graphic entries such as small sketches made in place during a solo develops one's ability to create metaphors because it requires you to draw or paint what you see and feel. As you practice this form of journaling, you'll find that your observational skills improve. Like any other skill, the more you do it, the more proficient you get. You bring eye, brain, and hand into coordination as skill grows. The better you see, the better you draw, the better you draw, the more skilled an observer you become, and the more you observe, the richer your thinking is likely to be.

When I am facilitating solo-journal experiences, the first thing I do is ask participants to take a self-test by studying and drawing a leaf or other object. In this exercise,

I ask soloist-journalers to find a leaf, preferably one that's on the ground or in a place that will be pruned. They then study the leaf for a full three minutes, paying attention to the detail, veination patterns, edges, size, width, length, and color. Then the soloist-journaler places the leaf out of sight and reach, and from memory creates a line-drawing of the leaf in an exact 1:1 scale (life size). Once the participants have completed their line drawings, I give them a piece of clear acetate and a marking pen so they can trace their leaves. Then they lay the tracing over top of their drawing. Next, I ask them to write a brief critical analysis of what their brains, hands, and eyes were able to recall and replicate and what they failed to see or remember. Writing the analysis enables them to think about what they need to do to improve their observation skills, so that the next time they do the exercise they are able to more accurately reproduce the leaf from memory. It's an exercise they can do anywhere, anytime, and no matter how well they do on the first try, they'll notice improvement every time they repeat it.

Some people find using a frame helps delineate an image, whether it is an object on the ground or a vista. A 35-millimeter slide frame or a 5" x 7" index card with a 4" x 6" hole cut out of its center work well. Drawing is about seeing critically. The sharper you see and remember things, the better you will draw or paint them. Practice is the only way to build coordination between eye, hand, and tools. Withhold any criticism of your drawings. The exception is to occasionally compare your early images with your current work to review your growth. Remember, the purpose of the drawn or painted images is to recall, think, and reflect at a deeper level. It is not about creating artistic masterpieces!

Here is a list of other starter *stems* that can jump-start a solo-reflection:

1. What is going well in my life? What is not? What and how can I change what is not affirming?

2. What is my contribution to the quality and sustainability of life and living on this planet?

3. What is my favorite thing in life? What is my least favorite? How do I attain more of my favorites and reduce my least favorites?

4. How can I simplify my life? What priorities must change?

5. How precious is time to me? How can I make more time for me and those I love?

6. Who are the priority people in my life? How do I serve them better?

7. What do I want most from life today? In the next year? In the next five years?

On the solo journey, you can begin wherever your mind takes you and harvest what comes. Each element in the following list of journaling outcomes can also make a challenging prospect upon which to reflect during the solo period.

1. Becoming a more skilled observer

2. Deepening insight into culture and nature

3. Messing about with ideas and insights

4. Harvesting creative insights

5. Developing deeper insight into knowing deep ways of knowing

6. Training a keen memory

7. Making deeper connections with your emotional intelligence

8. Collecting artifacts to build a sense of context and place

9. Diving deeper into life and living

10. Having a private place to play with words, images, and creative insights — a place for discovery of new ideas, new ways, new products, and process

Conclusion

Just as the novice soloist may be uneasy without a Walkman or others to chat with, the journaler must overcome the perception blocks of rational messages that say to her/him, "I can't draw!" or "I can't write!" Most bookstores sell books that can guide you to improve your drawing or writing skills no matter what your current skill level.

The solo is an experience about the journey of life that makes life more meaningful, loving, thoughtful, introspective, more connected to the land, to the people in one's life, and to personal creativity. The creative-reflective journal builds an insightful record of one's feelings, thoughts, insights, actions, dreams, plans, wishes, values, and philosophy. Like any other skill in life, journaling improves with practice and the exploration of new tools and techniques. There is no best or most correct way to complete a journal — only the way that is meaningful for the journaler. For the journal process to be a positive element of a solo, you must stick with it long enough to develop a personal style and find comfort with the process. Once you fill a volume with your graphic images and written reflections, you will find journal-keeping fulfilling, and it will become a vital part of your way of knowing. Enrich your next solo with a journal experience. Just do it!

References

Bruner, J. (1985). *Child talk.* Scranton, PA: Norton

Glasser, W. (1998). *Choice theory: A new psychology of personal freedom.* New York: HarperCollins.

Gowin, D. Bob. (1981). *Educating.* Ithaca, NY: Cornell University Press.

Herrmann, N. (1989). *The creative brain: Applied creative thinking.* Lake Lure, NC: Ned Herrmann Group.

Leopold, A. (1949). *A Sand County almanac and sketches here and there.* London: Oxford University Press.

Nicolaides, K. (1941). *The natural way to draw.* Boston: Houghton Mifflin.

Pepi, D. (1982). *Regularities in exemplar cases of environmental appreciating.* Ph.D., Dissertation, Cornell University. (Xerographic copies available from University Microfilms International, 300 Zeeb Road, Ann Arbor, MI, 48106.)

Pepi, D. (1985). *Thoreau's method: A handbook for nature study.* Englewood Cliffs, NJ: Prentice-Hall.

Pyle, R.M. (1991). *The thunder tree: Lessons from an urban wildland.* New York: Lyons Press.

Samples, R. (1971). *The metaphoric mind — A celebration of creative consciousness.* Reading, MA: Addison-Wesley Publishing Company.

Bibliography

Dvor'rak, R. R. (1987). *Drawing without fear.* Montara, CA: Inkwell Press.

Hinchman, H. (1991). *A life in hand: Creating the illuminated journal.* Salt Lake City, UT: Peregrine Smith Books.

Johnson, C. (1990). *The Sierra Club guide to sketching in nature.* San Francisco: Sierra Club Books.

Leslie, C., & Roth, C. E. (1988). *Nature journaling: Learning to observe and connect the world around you.* Pownal, VT: Storey Books.

Leslie, C. W. (1987). *A naturalist's sketchbook.* New York: Teale Books, Dodd, Mead & Co.

MacIver, R. (Ed.) *Heron dance.* Middlebury, VT: Heron Dance Ltd.

Narale, A. (1994). *For the love of simple linework ... a diary of an artist.* Toronto, Canada: Creative Group 2.

Nice, C. (1999). *Creating textures in pen and ink with watercolor.* Cincinnati, OH: North Light Books.

Rico, G. (1983). *Writing the natural way.* New York: Jeremy P. Tarcher/Putnam.

CHAPTER 5

Wilderness, Solitude, and Monastic Traditions

By Andrew J. Bobilya

To understand true self — which knows who we are in
our inwardness and who we are in the larger world —
we need both the interior intimacy that comes with
solitude and the otherness that comes from community.

(Palmer, 2004, p. 54)

*T*hroughout my life, interaction with wilderness has provided me opportunities for self-discovery, camaraderie, and retreat from the urban world. The spiritual benefits of such experiences have been greatest when my thoughts were directed toward a *spiritual perspective* or a greater awareness and understanding of God.

These experiences have sparked in me a desire to learn more about the relationship between wilderness, solitude, and spirituality. I have become fascinated with the writings of those monks who practice solitude and silence everyday, as they seek a balance between work, prayer, and community. Their lives provide interesting insight into the world of solitude and the role it plays in communities throughout the world. As I learn more about the monastic way of life, I find myself comparing it with my experiences of wilderness solo.

What Is Solitude?

In our search for meaning, we often try to concretely define all aspects of our lives, but solitude, like many abstract phenomena in life, is an individual experience that cannot easily be defined. Maybe it is not so important to define solitude as it is to strive to understand the characteristics of the experience. As Koch (1994) appropriately reminds us, "It is important not to over-intellectualize solitude, as though only writers and philosophers belong there" (p. 15).

Solitude: Defined by Outward or Inward Dimensions

Many believe that the most important condition for solitude is separation from others and the distractions of the everyday world. While some say that distractions are solely caused by humans, others would include any outside influence (including animals, rushing water, or wind) that might separate a person from his/her sense of *aloneness*. "The less one hears of human noise, the more disengaged from people one is, and so the deeper the solitude" (Koch, 1994, p. 20). Such a definition suggests that solitude is an exterior-based event.

I believe there is also a sense of solitude that comes from within, regardless of surroundings. I suggest that separation from others and retreat to the wilderness does not guarantee solitude and that solitude cannot be achieved unless one is peaceful within. Conversely, if people are at peace within, they can experience solitude in the company of another or in the midst of a crowd (Bobilya, 2001).

The heart is where silence begins, and out of it comes the true experience of solitude. If one's heart is not silent, the act of removing oneself from her/his surroundings will only accentuate the "noise" inside. Likewise, not until we are at peace with the solitude within are we able to reach out and interact with others.

Nouwen (1981) wrote, "Silence completes and intensifies solitude. ... Silence is the way to make solitude a reality" (p. 29). In a society immersed in noise, this concept is somewhat foreign. There are many vocations in which the practice of silence is regarded as critical. On the other hand, for many *awkward silence* can be more intimidating than the familiarity and comfort found in noise. Master teachers know how to use silence as an effective communication tool and do not shy from the momentary awkwardness it can create. I believe that not only can one experience solitude in the presence of others, but that when solitude is shared, the experience can be even richer. Or, as Sigurd Olson wrote:

> One does not have to be alone to enjoy silence. It has often been said that the
> ability to enjoy it with others is the mark of friendship and understanding. ...
> When I have been alone in quiet places, I have often wished someone could
> share it and make the experience even richer and more complete.
>
> (1956, p. 133)

Similarly, one can be in the presence of others and still enjoy the peaceful feeling of solitude. As Emerson (1904) stated, "The great man is he who, in the midst of the crowd, keeps with perfect sweetness the independence of solitude" (p. 13).

While removing oneself to a remote wilderness setting eliminates much external man-made stimuli, there is no escaping internal stimulus. True solitude can only be enjoyed by those who are at peace within, indicating that there is a significant inner dimension to the experience of solitude. Koch (1994) suggested that in order for solitude to provide a stimulus for interior growth in the individual, the experience must be comprised of some or all of the following: (a) physical isolation, (b) social disengagement, (c) reflectiveness.

According to Koch, there are patterns of solitude where all of these conditions are not present, but at least one must be present if the experience is to be classified as solitude.

Solitude: Required or Chosen

The experience of solitude can vary greatly depending on the degree of individual choice involved. Historically, people have experienced profound moments when solitude was forced upon them (e.g. Victor Frankl in the Auschwitz prison camp [Frankl, 1963]). To make forced solitude a positive experience, one often has to push through the negative aspects of the situation to be able to embrace the solitude in a positive light. "Indeed solitude's ability to restructure time contributes so powerfully to the sense of freedom that it can even mitigate the anguish of solitary confinement" (Koch, 1994, p. 108). As such, the lessons learned in moments of forced solitude as a prisoner often come long after the initial imprisonment.

Research has shown that wilderness solitude is more productive when voluntarily chosen. In his book *Cognitive Dimensions of Wilderness Solitude,* Hammitt (1982) discusses the importance of the participant's control over the experience: "Wilderness solitude is not so much individual isolation as it is a form of privacy in a specific environmental setting where individuals experience an acceptable degree of control and choice over the type and amount of information they must process" (p. 492). Consider the monks of various monastic orders throughout the world. Monastic communities use the term *vocation,* and emphasize that a choice to enter into a life of solitude and silence is a choice toward a *life vocation.* Individuals interested in joining this way of life determine it is the right choice for them. The monastic system would likely fall apart if monks were forced to join and subscribe to the solitary way of life. One's perceived degree of choice to enter into wilderness solitude (solo) is important to remember when intentionally programming a solo experience.

Aloneness, Loneliness, and the Process of Transformation

An individual's search for solitude has often been likened to a transformative process during which the individual goes through many stages before reaching a desired state of solitude. These stages can vary and depend upon the individual's state of mind when entering the experience, as well as the surroundings in which he/she is placed. Combined, these factors will determine whether the experience is primarily one of aloneness, loneliness, or solitude.

Aloneness and loneliness are often confused with solitude because they imply some sense of being alone – either in spirit or body. Many people feel alone and yet they do not experience solitude. Distinguishing among aloneness, loneliness, and solitude often helps me understand the transformation of a negative experience of loneliness into a peaceful experience of solitude. Many writers use the term *aloneness* to describe a healthy state of withdrawal from others, but when aloneness takes on a negative tone it becomes *loneliness*. Regardless of one's understanding of these terms, it is clear that the transformation of feelings away from loneliness is where a fruitful experience begins. Richley (1992) stated, "We are predisposed to think of aloneness as undesirable and as necessarily leading to loneliness. However, solitude can be a time of reflection, rest, and self-renewal" (p. 6).

In a world that is attuned to external stimuli provided through technology, social interaction, and the busyness of our lives, it can be hard to see the benefit of making time to be alone. For others, a fear of loneliness is often the obstacle to committing to aloneness. Ironically, the opportunity to slow down and reflect in solitude is exactly what is needed to move beyond that fear and find internal peace. As such, it is important for those facilitating solo opportunities, as well as anyone interested in the pursuit of solitude in their daily life, to remember that one must move through loneliness to find the benefits of solitude. On the other hand, the distinctions among aloneness, loneliness, and solitude must be determined by the individual involved in the experience. Most of my personal solos have been marked by feelings of aloneness and loneliness as I worked to become more comfortable with being alone and eventually reach a state of peaceful solitude.

Solitude: Essential to Community

Many writers have noted the importance of solitude as a tool for successful interaction with others (Bobilya, Kalisch, McAvoy, & Jacobs, 2005; Bonhoeffer, 1954; Nouwen, 1975, 1979; Olson, 1977). If one is to become part of a community, he/she must first be comfortable alone. The cognitive and emotional experiences that take place when one is without the company of others makes the time spent in community much richer. However, if one spends all of his/her time in solitude and never has opportunity to interact with others, then the significance of the solitary life is lessened because of a lack of contrasting communal experiences. Nouwen (1979) stated:

> Solitude leads us to a new intimacy with each other and makes us see our
> common task precisely because in solitude we discover our true nature, our true

*self, our true identity. That knowledge of who we really are allows us to live
and work in community.*

(p. 29)

Once we realize that responding to our need for time apart can lead to growth
in community, we begin to understand fully our place among others on this earth. We
were not made to live alone; nor were we made to be in constant companionship.
There must be a balance. When asked during an interview if he had any advice for
teachers who experience a sense of isolation or lack of support, renowned teacher and
author Parker Palmer replied:

> *Two things have been helpful to me in times of despair. One is to set aside regu-
> lar time to search my heart, in silence, walking in the woods, maybe journal-
> ing, maybe reading a good novel or poetry — whatever it is that will help me
> feel more clearly what is going on inside. Teachers who are in tough situations
> need some form of creative solitude to tap the well-springs of their own courage
> and truth. Secondly, we all need community — and since community is hard to
> come by in this society, we need to find ways of gathering it unto ourselves.*

(Dougherty, 1998, p. 29)

Solitude is not only essential for personal growth but for the development of
the community at large. Solitude can help form a complete human being and complete
human beings are the foundation of a caring and productive society. These are important considerations as we consider the role of solo in an organized educational program.

The Wilderness: A Classroom for Lessons in Solitude

Solitude can be found in a variety of settings, but when one enters wilderness
there is an increased opportunity for the benefits of such experiences to occur. As stated
in the Wilderness Act of 1964, the opportunity to experience solitude is a legal
requirement of any federally designated Wilderness Area. Of course, defining what
constitutes true solitude is a bit trickier. Olson (2001) suggested that "real wilderness"
has space and solitude, implying that any wilderness without such isn't true to its definition. The opportunity for people to limit the amount of contact with others increases
their ability to experience solitude. The term *wilderness solitude* implies an opportunity
to be alone in a natural environment that is removed from man-made intrusions.

It is often said that wilderness solitude provides a chance to retreat or step
away from society and the pressures of everyday life in order to regain one's focus. The

search for such experiences has taken people into the far corners of the earth, but regardless of the location of their wilderness experience, many return claiming similar benefits. It is important, however, to remember that one does not have to enter the wilderness to experience solitude.

Speaking of the search for *alone contentment*, Buchholz (1997) reminded us, "... we must learn to locate alone contentment in our everyday lives and avoid the literal escape to wilderness proper as the only solution" (p. 54). I believe this is an important reminder, for one of the goals of time spent alone in the wilderness is to enrich our daily living — and for most people that takes place in a setting other than the wild. Just as the monk seeks solitude and silence in the midst of community, one should be encouraged to create solitude amid everyday life. The wilderness, however, does provide an environment that often makes the experience of solitude remarkably memorable because of its contrast to more familiar environments. Thomas Merton, a Trappist monk, highlighted the spiritual power of the natural environment:

> *The silence of the forest, the peace of the early morning wind moving the branches of the trees, the solitude and isolation of the house of God: these are good because it is in silence, and not in commotion, in solitude and not in crowds, that God best likes to reveal himself most intimately to men.*
>
> (1999, p. 38)

The wilderness has long drawn people for recreational pursuits, but more and more people are seeking out wilderness for its peace and quiet, and for the opportunity to remove themselves from the pressures of everyday life. In his writings about the North Woods of Minnesota, Olson reflected on his appreciation for the wilderness and the impact solitude in the wild can have:

> *Over all was the silence of the wilderness, that sense of oneness which comes only when there are no distracting sights or sounds, when we listen with inward ears and see with inward eyes, when we feel and are aware with our entire beings rather than our senses. I thought as I sat there of the ancient admonition "Be still and know that I am God," and knew that without stillness there can be no knowing, without divorcement from outside influences man cannot know what spirit means.*
>
> (1956, p. 131)

Being in the wilderness does not necessarily result in a greater sense of solitude. Thoreau stated, "Solitude is not measured by the miles of space that intervene between a man and his fellows" (1854, p. 128). Still, the search for solitude can be greatly enhanced by a wilderness experience — if one is ready for the experience and willing to set aside the things that consume the rest of life. The true search for solitude begins in the heart, can be enhanced by the surroundings, and is one of the few things that we regulate on an individual level.

Solitude: Lessons From Monastic Traditions

I have studied the monastic way of life to further my understanding and definition of an experience of solitude. My interest is rooted in personal experiences of solitude in the wilderness, but I believe wilderness solitude and the solitude monks experience in a monastery share many similarities. The key difference between the two experiences is that the monk has dedicated himself to a way of life, whereas one who seeks periodic solitude in the wilderness is usually participating in a short-term experience. Looking at a few prominent monastic traditions in Western culture provides an interesting perspective on the idea of solitude as a way of life.

Monastic traditions dedicated to solitude and silence date back to the aesthetics of the Egyptian desert and surrounding areas in the 4th century. This discussion will concentrate on the influence of St. Benedict, whom many consider the father of Western monasticism and some of the *orders* or types of monastic traditions that came forth from his influence.

St. Benedict

Western monasticism traces its history back to the influence of St. Benedict, a Roman who in the 6th century established the monastic life in Italy. He developed a *Rule* that laid the foundation for monasteries to follow and which was a summary of all of the accumulated wisdom of Eastern monasticism. St. Benedict never founded a monastery, but his influence through the writing of this Rule is the cornerstone upon which monastic life around the world is founded. This daily life is centered on a combination of reading and manual work (Merton, 1999). The amount of solitude and silence a monk observes depends on the order of which he is a member and that order's interpretation of the Rule. Regardless of their differences, all Benedictine monasteries have a "common Father and a common Rule" (Merton).

Entrance into a monastery is a lengthy process. Depending on the order one joins, there is a multi-year process by which the monastery and the postulant (individual interested in joining) determine whether the monastic way of life is the postulant's *true vocation* and one to which he is willing to commit. The prospective monk is introduced to a way of life that places emphasis on solitude, penance, silence, manual labor, and contemplative prayer. The life of the monk is immersed in discipline, a discipline designed to help the monk attain spiritual maturity. How strictly the elements of daily life are adhered to depends on the monastic order and its dedication to reproducing the original purity of the monastic life.

We often think of monasteries as being places set apart in the wilderness or remote locations where monks live a life of recluse. In fact, the Rule of St. Benedict emphasizes the importance of the communities both within and outside the monastery walls. A number of monasteries place great emphasis on reaching out to the community by maintaining a guesthouse for personal and group retreats, providing meals, encouraging others to attend their prayer and worship services, and offering spiritual guidance for interested individuals. While there are numerous other forms of outreach embraced by individual monasteries, it is important to note that monasteries exist first and foremost for the formation of Christ in the soul of the monk. "A monastic community may maintain a school, but it may never exist for the sake of the school it maintains" (Merton, 1999, p. 33).

Cistercian Monastic Order

On the foundation laid by the Rule of St. Benedict were built many other monastic orders. Each order's practices vary based on its interpretation of the Rule and the importance that it places on manual labor, silence, solitude, penance, and contemplative prayer. While some directly follow the Rule of St. Benedict and therefore fall into the Benedictine category, others have taken elements of the Rule and incorporated them into a unique way of life. The Saint Vincent Archabbey, founded in 1846 in Latrobe, Pennsylvania, is considered the oldest and most venerable representative of the Benedictine family in the United States (Merton, 1999).

Of particular interest with regard to this paper is the Cistercian Order, which was founded by St. Robert of Molesme who in 1098 left a Benedictine monastery and went to the woods of Cisteaux in order to follow the Rule of St. Benedict "to the letter" (Merton, 1999, p. 95). This order, known as the Cistercians, has since split into the Cistercians of the Strict Observance and the Cistercians of the Common Observance. The Cistercians of the Strict Observance are often referred to as *Trappists* because of their formation in La Trappe, France. The Cistercians believe in living in community, and those who follow the strictest rule combine periods of silence and solitude with communal worship and manual labor in search of holiness. The Cistercian monk finds a balance between solitude and community, knowing when to observe silence, when to speak, and how to serve God through a life of poverty and manual labor. Most of us think of monks as hermits who live a life of complete solitude and silence. While the Cistercians follow the Rule of St. Benedict to the letter, their way of life emphasizes the importance of a strict observance of solitude and silence within community.

Looking at solitude through the lens of a monk who has given his entire life to the pursuit of godliness through solitude, silence, contemplative prayer, manual labor, and penance provides interesting insight into the pursuit of solitude (solo) as part of a wilderness or other educational program. These men have chosen a way of life that focuses on the importance of solitude, and for them it is a major part of a monk's vocation. We can learn from the importance monks place on the personal choice to enter a period of solitude. Most of the orders, however, also see the need to bring the monks together in community. Similar to a group in a wilderness program, there is a *sweetness* in the experience of community when one has been without fellowship.

Monastic Retreat and Wilderness Solo: Personal Reflections

I have had the privilege of participating in a few short-term monastic retreats at New Melleray Monastery in Iowa. During these retreats I have often reflected on my experiences in the wilderness and compared the retreat to an organized wilderness solo. What follows are my comments comparing my monastery experiences with those I have had both as a participant and facilitator of multi-day wilderness solo experiences. Some might say that one cannot compare an experience at a monastery with an experience in the wilderness, but I would argue that there is no significant difference. My motive for the experiences was essentially the same — to withdraw from the pace of everyday life and spend time alone in reflection and communion with God.

When I first arrived at the monastery, I found it interesting that I felt a need to quickly orient myself. It is a phenomenon I have since observed in others while facilitating numerous wilderness solo experiences with adolescents and adults. I think that this behavior derives from one's initial need to feel safe and secure in a new environment. In both monastic and wilderness settings, one way of satisfying this need is to immediately identify available resources. This need is accentuated in wilderness settings because variables (animals, weather, etc.) exist that can drastically alter one's experience and even threaten one's safety. All of the wilderness solo experiences in which I have participated have ranged from 24 to 84 hours in length. These experiences were structured to provide participants the opportunity to focus on reading, prayer, and meditation, and to remove themselves from contact with others. Two of the first things I do in experiences of such duration are locate a water source and construct a shelter before dusk. This need to acclimate to my surroundings is similar to the desire I experienced to understand my surroundings, assess my resources, and get settled into life at the monastery.

I have also found the role of sleep in the solo experience to be quite similar at both the monastery and in the wilderness. Sleep is comforting, and when one enters a time of solitude, sleep can be a way of overcoming boredom. When I entered the monastery, I found I was faced with fatigue that had built up for weeks and months during my everyday life at home. The opportunity to step back and remove myself from my usual surroundings made me realize how tired I was. Without the stimuli that typically filled my day, the quietness of the monastery was the perfect place for a long-awaited rest. I gave in to the urge to rest because I felt I could not effectively spend time in reflection if I was struggling to stay awake. By comparison, I have often tried to override my need for sleep while on a solo in the wilderness for fear that the solo experience would be compromised if I slept the hours away. Awaking well-rested at the monastery left me refreshed, renewed, and eager to read and spend time alone in reflection. Having had both experiences, I now believe that a balance between sleeping and wakefulness maximizes the benefits of both experiences. Conversely, sleeping one's solo time away or denying the body's need for rest greatly compromises both experiences.

Most of my wilderness solo experiences have involved fasting. During my time alone in the wilderness, I spent a large part of my initial waking hours thinking about food. I believe this obsession with food distracted from learning and growth that could have taken place. I believe in the role of fasting in meditation, as a unique learning opportunity and as a form of identification with spiritual metaphors. Fasting, however, is not appropriate in all solo situations. It is important to set clear goals for the experience and assess the ability of the participants to facilitate their own learning through a time alone without food. This is difficult to do, and too often I have seen adolescents spend their entire time on solo sleeping and thinking about food. While at New Melleray Monastery, I found that following a reduced-calorie diet made study times fruitful because I was not so focused on my body's need for food. Like finding the right balance between hours spent sleeping and in wakefulness, eating just enough food can heighten the solo experience.

Finding balance in all aspects of both solo and monastic experiences seems to be the key to maximizing the opportunity for personal growth. While at the monastery I observed that times spent with others coupled with time spent alone enhanced both experiences. It made clear the importance of a free-flowing relationship between solitude and community. I still believe there is a place for complete solitude, in the wilderness or elsewhere, but through my time at New Melleray I saw the ability of community to facilitate the search for solitude. Upon my return home, the value of my time alone was even more accentuated, as I felt better equipped to enter into the relationships that fill my everyday life. This experience elucidated the impact of the intense community often cultivated when we work with groups in the outdoors and the need to offer participants regular periods of time alone.

I still look forward to moments alone in the wilderness, but short-term monastic retreats have shown me the search for solitude through another lens. I now give even more thought to the framing of the wilderness solo. As for my own search for solitude and silence, it continues throughout every day, whether I am alone or surrounded by people, whether inside the walls of a building or roaming the paths of a forest.

Conclusion

This paper has surveyed some of the themes that have emerged from literature, as well as my own experience with wilderness, solitude, and monastic vocation (as expression of spirituality). While people have experienced solitude in the wilderness and other settings throughout history, our understanding of the power of solitude is still quite limited. Recent research regarding the participant perception of the solo experience has begun to contribute to our understanding of the wilderness solo (Bobilya, 2004; Bobilya et al., 2005; Bobilya, McAvoy & Kalisch, in press).

I believe there is a need to further investigate this phenomenon. My hope is that in doing so, all of us who are interested in the programmatic use of solitude will gain deeper understanding and that that deeper understanding will lead to the continued enhancement of solo experiences. At the same time, educators must not forget the importance and practicality of the practice of solitude and silence in their daily lives. Richard Foster provided the following recommendations as steps in search of solitude:

> It is one thing to talk piously about "the solitude of the heart."... It is not enough to say, "Well, I am most certainly in possession of inner solitude and silence; there is nothing that I need to do."... If we are to succeed, we must pass beyond the theoretical into life's situations. The first thing we can do is to take advantage of the "little solitudes" that fill our day. Consider the solitude of those early morning moments in bed before the family awakens.... Slip outside just before bed and taste the silent night.... We can find or develop a "quiet place" designed for silence and solitude.... Four times a year withdraw for three to four hours for the purpose of reorienting your life goals. This can easily be done in one evening. Stay late at the office or do it at home or find a quiet corner in a public library. Take a retreat once a year with no other purpose in mind but solitude.
>
> (1978, p. 105)

My hope is that this paper helps in understanding experiences of wilderness, solitude, and silence, and in appreciating the history of monasticism and its influence on the human search for the *silent life*. More importantly, I hope I have raised questions in readers' minds about the relationship between solitude and wilderness as they pursue solitude in their own lives and with the programs they operate. I believe individuals should never stop the search for moments of solitude and silence and that further research can improve the quality of such programmed experiences. I conclude with a few questions recommended for those who use intentional solitude (solo) in a programmatic setting:

1. How can you assist participants in developing an inner sense of solitude and moving beyond loneliness?

2. Spirituality is often a dimension of the solo experience; how will you address spiritually related questions broached by your participants?

3. What can you do to assist participants in meeting their basic needs and acclimating to their surroundings while on solo so that they can move on to a more productive time of reflection?

4. How do you use intentional solitude in the development of community?

5. What is the ultimate purpose for the solo within the context of your program? If participants are not given a clear rationale, they will leave wondering why they have been intentionally isolated.

Author's Note: I would like to express my gratitude to all those — especially my parents — who fostered in me an appreciation for the relationship between wilderness, solitude, and my spiritual life. I am also thankful for my wife, Kirsten DeWitt-Bobilya, Dr. Leo McAvoy, Dr. Jasper Hunt, and Mr. Ken Kalisch, who have supported my research of solitude and silence. I look forward to continuing to understand the "intangible" benefits of wilderness and the search for solitude.

References

Bobilya, A. J. (2001). *An investigation of solitude and silence in the wilderness and the sacred.* Unpublished master's thesis, Minnesota State University, Mankato, MN.

Bobilya, A. J. (2004). *An investigation of the solo in a wilderness experience program.* (Doctoral dissertation, University of Minnesota, 2004) *Digital Dissertations,* AAT 3129201.

Bobilya, A. J., Kalisch, K. R., McAvoy, L. H & Jacobs, J. (2005). A mixed-method investigation of the solo in a wilderness experience program. In Paisley, K., Bunting, C. J., Young, A. B. & Bloom, K. (Eds.), *Research in outdoor education: Vol. 7.* Cortland, NY: Coalition for Education in the Outdoors.

Bobilya, A. J., McAvoy, L.H., & Kalisch, K. R. (in press). The power of the instructor in the solo experience: An empirical study and some non-empirical questions. *Journal of Adventure Education and Outdoor Learning.*

Bonhoeffer, D. (1954). *Life together.* New York: Harper.

Buchholz, E. S. (1997). *The call of solitude: Alonetime in a world of attachment.* New York: Simon and Schuster.

Dougherty, K. (1998). Seeking creative solitude and community: An interview with Parker Palmer. *The Active Learner: A Foxfire Journal for Teachers,* 3(3) 28–31.

Emerson, R. W. (1904). *Society and solitude.* New York: AMS.

Foster, R. J. (1988). *Celebration of discipline: The path to spiritual growth.* San Francisco: Harper San Francisco.

Frankl, V. (1963). *Man's search for meaning: An introduction to logotherapy.* Boston: Beacon.

Hammitt, W. E. (1982). Cognitive dimensions of wilderness solitude. *Environment and Behavior,* 14(4), 478–493.

Koch, P. (1994). *Solitude: A philosophical encounter.* Chicago: Open Court.

Merton, T. (1999). *The silent life.* New York: Farrar, Straus, & Giroux.

Nouwen, H. J.M. (1975). *Reaching out, The three movements of the spiritual life.* Garden City, New York: Doubleday.

Nouwen, H. J. M. (1979). *Clowning in Rome.* Garden City, New York: Image.

Nouwen, H. J. M. (1981). *The way of the heart.* New York: Ballantine.

Olson, S. F. (1956). *The singing wilderness.* Minneapolis: University of Minnesota Press.

Olson, S. F. (1977). *Reflections from the North Country.* New York: Alfred A Knopf.

Olson, S. F. (2001). *The meaning of wilderness: Essential articles and speeches.* (D. Backes, Ed.). Minneapolis: University of Minnesota Press.

Palmer, P. (2004). *A hidden wholeness: The journey towards an undivided life.* San Francisco: Josey-Bass.

Thoreau, H. D. (1854). *Walden.* Boston: Beacon.

CHAPTER 6

Reflections on Solo in Outward Bound

By Mary-Laurence Bevington

Solo is good. It provides guaranteed reflection.

(Bill Jacox, personal
communication, March 2002)

I first soloed on a school expedition in the Wind River Range of Wyoming. That experience involved an instructor escorting me to a small slab of rock overlooking a pristine lake. In the first hour, unsure of any objective, I amused my teenage brain by fixating on the lake surface rippling back and forth with the gentle winds. I wondered how much time had passed as I felt the impatient nudge a child feels on a long journey just before asking, "Are we there yet?" I had no idea that my journey was just beginning or that the next couple of days would enrich my soul. By the time my instructors came to pick me up, my boredom had shifted to a calm joy.

Some years later, when I was an intern at Wolfcreek Wilderness School in the southern Appalachians, I had the opportunity to facilitate my first solo as an instructor. Near the end of the course, a grueling 26-day expedition for adjudicated youth, we sent each student off to live in solitude for three days and nights. Together with the lead instructor, I kept watch over the students from a woodsy base camp. I expected that my students would return just as I did, peaceful and elated. But on the second day, when I visited some of them in their special places, I was surprised by their stories. One youth said he had cried all night and had nightmares about being alone. Another told of how he was sure his hair had been eaten by a mouse while he was sleeping. One student even showed me how he had kept busy by doing military drills with a stick as an improvised rifle.

I wondered if the solo experience was working for them. Then, at the group debriefing, as I listened to the youth share their insights, it seemed the solo had impacted every student in a profound way. Seeing such dramatic shifts in people over a relatively short period of time piqued my curiosity. I felt compelled to learn more about solo experiences and how they have come to be such a vital part of so many wilderness programs.

Roots of the Outward Bound Solo

Imagine being confined in a lifeboat for many days. Your hands grow raw from rowing all night, incessant ocean splashes irritate, and you sometimes have to vomit over the bow. A voice inside begs you to endure, but you know you cannot make it alone. It is imperative that you turn to your shipmates for support, so that you can muster the will to paddle to safe harbor. This paradigm of community coming together to surmount adverse conditions is seminal to Outward Bound (OB). In the middle of World War II, OB founder Kurt Hahn was hired by the Royal Navy to teach survival skills to sailors and merchant seamen. He found that small groups that act like a solid team through trust, communication, and cooperation were the most successful. He believed that united we stand, divided we fall. Fair enough, but then why is solo a part of almost every OB course? Where did it originate, and how does it brave time? Why is it marketed in the OB catalog as "the least understood element of the curriculum" and also "the highlight of the expedition"? In short, how does solo fit with the group process?

In 1999 I had dinner with Ernest "Tap" Tapley, the seasoned mountain man Chuck Froelicher recruited to help launch North America's first Outward Bound School from the Marble, Colorado, base camp. After Tap showed me a number of "trick" knots from his repertoire with a pocket cordolette, he started telling stories. When it came to my question about the origins of the OB solo, he claimed that solo was born out of a twist of fate, somewhere near the year 1962.

> *We had 40 students at the base camp and a flash flood had blocked the road*
> *with a landslide. The cook, Frank Menendez, got a call that the food truck could*
> *not make its delivery. Frank was frantic as he approached me. I told him the road*
> *would be cleared in two days and the time was right for a "Night Alone."*
> (E. Tapley, personal communication, April 1999)

In my continued exploration of solo, I have discovered that the legendary Tapley was standing on the shoulders of giants. Structured solitude has existed in innumerable cultures since time immemorial. History tells us that many great heroes, philosophers, artists, theologians and scientists sought time alone; Descartes, Earhart, Newton, Locke, Pascal, Nietzsche, Tubman, Kierkegaard, Dickinsen, to name a few.

Henry David Thoreau left his home for the woods because he "never found a companion that was so companionable as solitude" (Thoreau, 1971, p. 135).

The practice of taking time for oneself is a collective theme among world religions. The Taos Pueblo Indians traditionally spend long periods alone on Taos Mountain as they transition into adulthood. When in mourning, Orthodox Jews reflect at home for seven days, apart from daily visits to a synagogue. Catholics commemorate the 40 days and nights that Jesus spent alone in the desert before his crucifixion by sacrificing and taking more time to pray alone during Lent. The Dalai Lama advises every human to take time alone daily, because in Buddhism meditating by oneself is the way to the present moment. It is the path to the beginner's mind and emptiness. The Zen masters believe that "when you're completely identified with emptiness, you are always functioning in compassion, as pure and unconditional love" (Merzel, 2001, p. 137).

Perspectives From the Field

Since Tap Tapley made the defining choice to give his students a "Night Alone" more than 40 years ago, solo has taken its place at the center of OB programming. In an effort to delve deeper into the use of solo in adventure programming, I interviewed several OB field staff about their perspectives on the value of solo. Their stories all support an observation made by Kurt Hahn long before the first OB solo ever took place: "True learning requires periods of silence and solitude as well as direct activity" (James, 1980, p. 3).

While at first solo may seem the antithesis of the lifeboat model, the anecdotes shared by the following veteran OB field staff support the belief that solo and group process go hand in hand because humans are both social animals and solitary beings.

> *Reflection should be happening throughout course, but as we all know, all those great reflective and thought-provoking activities we had planned to do on day one are placed on the back burner to simmer some more. Except for solo! Instructors always seem to find time for solo when the students really think they need it, regardless of what day it occurs during the course.*
>
> *I have a little theory about solo. Unless you surprise your students with it, they always display behavior indicative of "just in time for solo" (i.e., selfish behavior and a lack of team consciousness). In other words, when students know solo is later that day, their brain is already in that "finally some time away from all this intense group process" head space.*
>
> (B. Jacox, personal communication, March 2002)

The solo is probably the most important event on an Outward Bound course. For most students it is the first time to truly experience being alone. It can be overwhelming, but it usually is an awesome experience. I think it solidifies the impression of both the immediate environment and the course experience for the student. For me, personally, solo has been a time for meditation and reflection.

(B. Frank, personal communication, March 2002)

In one of his many poems, the late Justin F. Kramer, a long-time OB instructor, gave a metaphorical nod to the importance of solo: "Our summers last as long as we are inspired, and our winters are the time to lay roots in the reflection" (J. F. Kramer, personal poem, unpublished, 1998).

Another OB field staff I interviewed was Maureen "Reenie" Kinney. Reenie summarized it nicely: "Solo is not just a good idea, it's mandatory for the soul" (M. Kinney, personal communication, April 2002).

When I spoke with Ian C.P. Godwin, OB field staff since 1993, he reflected on how his views of solo have changed.

Solo, like most things on an Outward Bound course, has developed more meaning for me over the years. The first courses it was more like: Yee-haw, the kids are going on solo. Three days to play or chill, whatever. This is what they will really struggle with so let's get them out there. Now I spend more time thinking about when the best time for them to be on solo will be. I try to do a better job framing the experience and taking into consideration the patrol and the individuals, and what they want or should try to get out of it. I'm also less concerned about what they can't take — or can't do, because I now believe that maybe if they are a bit more comfortable while they are out there, they will get more out of it. I now give students more information up front, if they ask. Ultimately it's about giving them the best opportunity to get the most out of the experience.

(Personal communication, March 2002).

During my 16-year career in outdoor education, I have heard many variations of the *solo talk* that is given immediately before students embark on their time alone. These briefings can range from the highly philosophical to the simply practical and informative. In their briefings, most instructors encourage students to become aware of their internal and external sensory experiences. Some instructors encourage students to create a sacred place at their solo site, where they will be free from social interaction and the temptation to visit other students. Often, instructors will share stories about their personal experiences with solo. The most memorable such story I've heard is one a lead instructor on a southern Appalachian trip told one of his groups:

> *I was 13 years old and my grandmother took me into the mountains. We walked for a day with our bedding, water, and a sack of bread on our backs until we came to a special place. She gave me a knife and some writing paper. "I'll be back to pick you up," she said. "Take care and cherish your time in the woods." One year later she returned to me. I had built a small lean-to and I was living off the land*
>
> (B. Luesing, personal communication, November 1993).

This is a wonderful story to tell, for students believe every word you say. And, as OB field staff Bill Bradley, a.k.a. "Butch Danger," used to say to me, "Why let the truth ruin a good story?"

When an OB solo ends, a debriefing takes place. I've noticed remarkable similarities in the more than 50 post-solo debriefings I have witnessed. They often begin with lots of complaints about being bored, food stress, and fear of wild animals. However, as debriefings continue, students talk about meeting one's authentic self, becoming aware of true needs, feelings and impulses, and finding some peace of mind. A few students even have claimed to have had fun on their solo.

I have also encountered those students who distrust solitude. They seem to associate it with abandonment, so instead of finding the mysticism in solo, they feel anxiety and loneliness. Even students who are fearful before and during solo, however, tend to work with that fear and find the strength to cope with being alone. When I have students who are anxious or who have an aversion to being alone, I place them in solo sites that are within sight of my tent and, if necessary, allow them to visit me in my base camp during solo. Properly facilitated, such situations can be empowering to students. As one OB instructor noted, these situations appeal to the duality of instruction: "...getting people to follow you where you want them to go, and going with them; while being sure they are really going where they want to go, alone" (Tyler, 1995, p. 4).

My most inspirational solo story is about my friend Curry Morris, a sometimes wilderness instructor and seeker. Curry helped intermittently on my first solo watch at Wolfcreek Wilderness School. He knew I was a novice at soloing and so, with his "N'Orleans" accent and a very serious expression, he liked to ask me: "Aren't you sca't out here alone Mary Bev? Aren't you sca't?" Then he would break into a wide, knowing smile. After I came to know Curry I realized how he was able tease me with authority. Curry understood the myriad emotions solo triggers through extensive personal experience with solo. He would ritualistically go on solos in the Blue Ridge

Mountains during fall, keeping a fairly standard procedure. He would secure a friend to drop him off and pick him up at a trailhead. From that point, Curry could wander to his sacred spot, set up his camp, build a small sweat lodge, and begin to eat less. After seven days, he would begin a 14-day fast in an effort to empathize with all the living beings that go to bed hungry. He would take a spiritual sauna in his sweat lodge as often as he could. And on Day 28 he would do a final sweat, pack up his belongings, erase his traces, and return to civilization (C. Morris, personal communications, July 1988, December, 1993).

Curry and I enjoyed a *graduation dinner* with a crew of youth on the last night of a course in December 1992. Curry had just returned from his isolation, looking thin but bright eyed. He sat next to me and waited until everyone was served. Then he served himself, prayed quietly, and began to savor his food. After a moment, he told me he was struggling with the hungry voice inside of him, the voice that "wanted more" as he put it. Then he smiled wide as we watched the food frenzy all around us. The students had not had an abundant meal in 26 days and their mad scramble to eat as much as possible was impressive. Clearly, Curry felt these same urges, but the presence of mind that his personal solo had deepened helped him maintain faith that there would be enough food. He stayed centered, ate consciously, and all our needs were met.

Perhaps the best summaries of the OB solo experience are those that have been recorded in the personal journals of participants. Consider these notes from the journal of an anonymous young woman, who was a participant on an OB course known as the John Wesley Powell Expedition, which traces some of Powell's river descents, when she recorded this entry:

> *When I woke this morning, from the last night of my solo, I felt such an incredible and exhilarating feeling of pride. I made it through the night. All me! I put the tarp up. I picked the spot. I laid down my sleeping bag. I didn't eat. I wasn't even hungry. But I could sleep! I may even take a nap today.... The silence here is incomparable to the busy sounds that we don't even think about back in our world. Nothing stirs except the wind, walking towards me. The sun beats down on my back. It casts its light over my home. In certain places the trees hold it in their hands and let the earth be shaded. What a beautiful friendship they have.... My heart feels so open. My body feels so alive and unique. I feel I am now part of something so beautiful. I'm now part of nature. I have become one with it. My skin has soaked in its color.... My earthly aroma matches that of nature's smell. I no longer smell of expensive shampoo and minty toothpaste. There is no soap to lather all over my body; just the sweat that drips down my back and falls off my forehead, and then evaporates into the hot desert air.*

Conclusion

Solo is a sacred time on an Outward Bound course. Throughout his teachings, John Dewey expressed that reflection is perhaps the most important aspect of an experience. The solo component gives participants time to reflect, allowing them to suck all the meaning out of the OB experience. It is a passage through which they can begin to know more and more who they truly are.

Prior to the experience, the prospect of solo yields universal questions: "What if I need to talk to someone?" "What if I don't know how to set up my tarp?" "What will I do with my time?" Afterward, it inspires and enriches the alchemy of a course. In every course I have worked, I have seen groups reunite after solo as a far stronger unit than they were before. Because the food rations slim down for solo, a feast is often prepared by the instructors to welcome the students back to their group. I like to tell select groups a fable about a place where people have inarticulate elbows, so they cannot bend their arms to reach their mouths to eat. I tell them to imagine their own elbows have fallen prey to this ailment, and before long the hungry students figure it out and start feeding each other. This is where the individual nature of solo meets the group process.

References

Merzel, D. G. (2001). *24/7 Dharma*. Boston: Journey Editions.

James, T. (1980). Sketch of a moving spirit. *Journal of Experiential Education.* 3(2).

Thoreau, H. D. (1971). *Walden*. Princeton, NJ: Princeton University Press.

Tyler, M. (1995). Ultimate instructing: Four tool boxes. *Internal Resource Article.* Leadville, CO: Colorado Outward Bound, Inc.

PART II

Research Results

CHAPTER 7

The Life Significance of a Wilderness Solo Experience

By Brad Daniel

You cannot harvest the lessons of life except in aloneness and I go to the length of saying that neither the love of man nor the love of God can take deep root except in aloneness.

(Kurt Hahn, cited in Miner, 1990, p. 62)

What is the long-term value of a wilderness solo experience? Is it significant over the course of one's life and, if so, why? This chapter presents the findings of a 25-year retrospective study conducted to examine the life significance of a spiritually oriented wilderness expedition. The purpose of the study was to discover what participants remembered of the trip, what they had learned during and as a result of the trip, and whether lessons from the trip had played a role in their lives. The study looked at two aspects of the expedition:

1. the significance of the entire expedition

2. the significance of its individual components

In this paper, I will describe the methods and data sources used in the study. Then I will discuss the results in relation to one key finding — although the solo was but one component of an expedition that also included backpacking, camping, canoeing, climbing, orienteering, and a marathon, it emerged as the most important and influential factor for the greatest number of participants. This paper will discuss various reasons for this finding derived from participant responses.

This study emerged from significant life experience (SLE) (Tanner, 1980)[1] research in which participants are asked to recount experiences of their own choosing. However, the Discovery study deviated from SLE research by focusing attention on one particular experience — the solo experience — that was shared by all participants. Because the study had its roots in SLE research, it used an SLE-oriented approach. Such an approach was appropriate because it "takes a life span perspective, seeking to understand how experiences that may have occurred 20 or 30 years ago continue to influence people's feelings or behavior" (Chawla, 1998, p. 385).

The study identified several characteristics that make life experiences significant. They are noted below.

1. An event may be classified as significant if it changes the participant in some way (i.e., perspective, behavior, or belief). This change may be mental, spiritual, physical, emotional, social, or some combination thereof.

2. An event may be classified as significant if it constitutes a new or extraordinary experience — outside the bounds of the normal routine.

3. An event may be classified as significant if it provides something useful for the participant in the future, such as a reference point or life lesson.

4. An event may be classified as significant if specific meaning is derived from or attributed to it.

5. An event may be classified as significant if one considers it to have been caused by something other than mere chance — God, a guiding force, or a higher power.

6. An event may be classified as significant due to its nature, magnitude, or timing.

(Daniel, 2003)

Program Studied

The program selected was the Discovery Wilderness Program offered by Montreat College in Montreat, North Carolina. Discovery is a Christian-based, Outward Bound-type wilderness expedition. The solo phase is one of the culminating activities of the trip, and it usually consists of two to four days and nights of solitude accompanied by fasting. The solo provides time for intense reflection, contemplation, and introspection. It typically follows a very strenuous part of the expedition, which means that the students have been pushed to their physical, mental, and emotional limits by the time the solo phase begins.

According to the *Discovery Wilderness Manual* (Fortson, 1988), the purposes of the solo are:

1. A time of fasting, reflection and rest.
2. A time to look back over the trip to see what has been learned.
3. A time to evaluate past and present relationships with Christ, family and friends.

(p. 57)

Students are encouraged to establish minimal camps, set individual goals, and record their thoughts in a journal. The instructors check on the participants every day.

Upon completion of the solo phase, the experience is thoroughly debriefed. Debriefing is essential because there may be a connection between spirituality, emotional intensity, and processing. Stringer and McAvoy (1992) have suggested that "by giving participants opportunities to focus on and process the intense emotional experiences they encounter on trips, leaders may help to foster spiritual growth" (p. 18). During the debriefing session, the group discusses how to transfer the lessons from the solo phase to their post-trip lifestyles, and the students set goals for reentering "civilization."

Data Sources

The study employed multiple methods and data sources. Primary data sources included self-administered participant surveys and focus group interviews. Secondary data sources derived from two pilot studies conducted in 1999 and 2000. The sources included written pre- and post-trip questionnaires, taped debriefing sessions, journal entry analysis, reflection papers, and instructors' observations and field notes.

Research Method

The sample involved 227 of the 446 individuals who went on the expedition at some point between 1976 and 2000. Multiple attempts were made to gather contact information on all 446, but this was not feasible. Contact information was obtained for 323 individuals; those with incorrect address information were eliminated, leaving a total of 291 potential respondents in the adjusted database. Many individuals participated in more than one phase of the study. The sample was a self-selected population. All years of the program were represented in the study.

Of this potential pool of 291 respondents, 227 people participated in this study. A total of 210 self-administered surveys were returned, yielding a response rate of 72.2%. Eighteen people participated in focus group interviews; 13 had completed the survey, while five of them (28%) had not and, therefore, represented new voices in the study. Individuals from 10 different years of the program were represented in the focus groups. Additionally, 41 people participated in pilot studies.

The primary research tool was a survey that was designed and administered following the guidelines suggested by Dillman (2000). The survey was divided into three parts.

Part 1 contained questions about pertinent background information, including the trip year and the respondents' gender, age, previous wilderness experiences, post-trip wilderness experiences, and religious orientation. Because background experiences can be very important in determining perception, it was necessary to obtain a detailed profile of each respondent.

Part 2 consisted of six open-ended questions about the significance of the expedition. The questions, shown below, allowed participants to describe the experience in their own words.

1. Why did you decide to go on the Discovery Expedition?

2. If a current Montreat College student contacted you to ask if you thought going on the trip would be a valuable experience, what would you tell him/her? Please explain.

3. What do you consider to have been your most significant experiences on the trip? What made them significant? Please explain.

4. Has your opinion of what the expedition meant to you changed or remained the same since completing the trip? Please explain.

5. Has the fact that you went on the Discovery expedition made a difference in your life in any way? Please explain why you think it has or has not.

6. If there is anything else that you would like to say about either the survey or your Discovery experience that you think is important, please do so in the space below.

Part 3 listed the individual trip components and asked respondents to rate their importance on a Likert-type scale ranging from 1 (not important) to 7 (very important). It is common for belief and attitudinal questions to rely on vague quantifiers (e.g., *strongly favored* to *strongly opposed*, *high priority* to *low priority*, or *agree* to *disagree*). Quantifiers that depend solely on numbers are considered even more vague. The vaguer the question, the vaguer the categories. Also, the more remote these items are from people's experiences, the more likely a question is to produce inconsistent responses if the same person is asked to answer this question at different times (Dillman, 2000). In an attempt to counter this, respondents were asked to comment on why they rated each component as they had. Lines were provided below each component scale for that purpose. Eighty-seven percent elaborated on their ratings, and their comments served as a valuable crosscheck for understanding why they rated the components as they did.

Procedures for Analyzing the Data

After the survey responses were typed and transcribed, a multi-layered approach was used to analyze the data. Although this study was predominantly qualitative, many aspects of the survey responses could be quantified based on the frequency, clarity, and context of keyword usage. This was done whenever possible.

In Stage 1, all 210 surveys received were read, the demographic data from Part 1 was tabulated, and the average rating for each trip component in Part 3 was calculated. Then, this process was repeated to ensure accuracy. The information was summarized in a series of data tables. The answers to the questions in Part 2 and the taped interviews were coded and analyzed for content. Surveys were sorted and coded by hand initially. The final layers of analysis involved coding using a qualitative software package that allows for a multiple coding of each passage. The data was analyzed for emergent themes using the *constant comparative* method whereby the researcher continually compares the emerging themes against new data (Corbin & Strauss, 1990). Making these comparisons assists the researcher in guarding against bias by continuously challenging concepts with new data. Such comparisons also help to achieve greater precision (the grouping of like and only like phenomena) and consistency (always grouping like with like) (Corbin & Strauss, 1990). Three additional researchers reviewed the data to confirm intercoder reliability.

Results and Discussion

The Findings in Brief

The essential findings are as follows:

1. Thirty-seven percent of participants in the two pilot studies said the solo was the most significant component of the trip.

2. Thirty-nine percent of participants in the main study said the solo was the most significant experience of the trip.

3. The solo was the only component deemed most important by at least one respondent from each of the 25 years.

4. The solo's role was described as significant in every focus group interview.

5. The solo averaged 6.20 on the 7-point Likert-type scale used to rate the significance of trip components.

The solo was described as the most significant trip component by a considerable margin. Thirty-seven percent of the 1999 and 2000 pilot study participants said it was the most significant experience of the trip. In the main study, the solo was cited as the most significant component by 81 of the participants (39%) that responded to the survey. For comparison, the next closest components of significance were rock-climbing and teamwork, each of which had 32 respondents (15%). The solo also was the experience mentioned most often by the focus group participants. The percentages of men and women citing the solo as most significant were almost equal —

33 men (38% of all males) and 48 females (39% of all females). The solo also was the only component classified as most significant by at least one respondent from each of the 25 years.

These findings were dramatic but were not necessarily unusual because the importance of solitary experiences has been reported in wilderness research. For example, Greenway (1995) reported one study in which 92% of participants cited *alone time* as the single most important experience of their trip. Bobilya (2004), Richley (1992), Brown (1989), Morgan (1986), and others have noted that solitude in remote outdoor settings can provide opportunities for self-exploration, reflection, and renewal — all factors that contributed to the significance of the solo for Discovery participants.

Factors Affecting the Life Significance of Solo

> *There are about four or five life experiences that I treasure as pivotal points in my personal and spiritual development. Discovery would rank in the top three.*
>
> (Discovery participant)

Informant responses indicated solo's significance to be a function of several identifiable factors. Focus group comments centered on solitude, challenge, reflection, and interaction with God as primary reasons for solo's significance. These ideas were echoed by survey participants. These factors can be clustered into several categories, which overlap and intersect one another. They are novelty, timing, challenge, spiritual influence, perspective, and setting. Together, they constitute an ecology of the solo experience (Figure 1).

The Novelty of Solo

> *[On the solo] I was alone for the first time for more than two to three hours, other than sleeping, in my whole life.*
>
> (Discovery participant)

The great majority of participants indicated that the solo was special because they had never had this type of life experience either before or after the trip. Katz (1969) and others have attributed much of the power of the solo experience to this fact. Do memories of unique experiences continue to be useful throughout life? This seems to be the case, for the importance of any one significant event is likely to be reinterpreted repeatedly as its role emerges in different contexts (Neisser, 1982). Neisser characterized those experiences that tend to endure in memory:

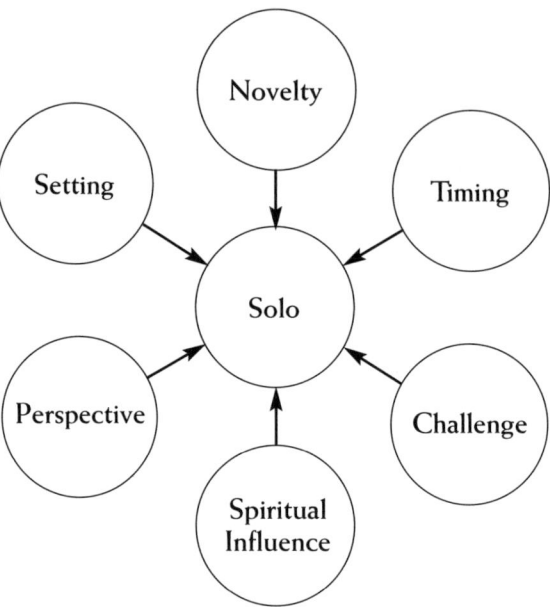

Figure 1. An ecology of the solo experience.

They are perceived as strongly emotional at the time. Life's subsequent course must make the target event focal in recall. The event must be seen as a turning point, instrumental in later activities. The event must remain relatively unique, its image must not be blurred by subsequent occurrences of similar events.

(p. 89)

The solo experience fulfills many of these criteria. Participants' reported experiencing a wide range of emotions due to the physical, mental, and emotional stressors encountered; the novelty of such stressors may enhance retention. The experience was rare or unique in the lives of most participants with the exception of those who went on one or more similar trips previously or subsequently. As a result, it held great importance for past participants.

Some experiences are considered more significant at the time they occur than when viewed in retrospect, because as the relative number of experiences increases throughout life, the significance of any one event can become diminished (Neisser, 1982). For the experience to remain meaningful, and, particularly, for it to become *more* significant, it must have had some extraordinary quality, some characteristic that separated it from the rest. The solo's novelty, not only among other trip components but also among other life experiences, accounted, in part, for why it was described as the most significant experience on the trip.

The Timing of Solo

> *We had finally made it to our destination after two days of arguing and thinking we were lost. We were all exhausted and tired of being around each other. What we didn't know was that we were about to go on Solo. Wow! I've never missed people so much in my life.*
>
> (Discovery participant)

While it is tempting to look at the solo experience in isolation from the rest of the expedition, we may oversimplify our understanding of its significance in doing so. Solo usually occurs at a time in the trip when many psychological defenses have been broken down by the cumulative fatigue of having met so many physical and emotional challenges. This occurs approximately two-thirds of the way through the course. Usually, it starts just after the group has traveled for one or two days without the instructors. Participants arrive at their destination exhausted, hungry, and sometimes a bit exasperated with one another; yet they must transition quickly from what usually has been a time of intense social interaction to a time of isolation, reflection, and fasting. The contrast between these states of being is dramatic and creates a dynamic tension that requires resolution (Doll, 1989). Participants must readjust to their immediate circumstances in order to strike a balance between them. Moreover, they must shift and adapt quickly. Luckner and Nadler (1997) and others have suggested that this tension serves as a catalyst for change because the more unknown, unpredictable, or unfamiliar the experience, the harder people work to make sense of what is happening to them. For many participants, the timing of the solo was as important as the uniqueness of the experience, and this may have enhanced its significance.

The Challenge of Solo

> *In some ways I longed for those three days. In some ways I dreaded them. In retrospect, that may truly represent my going through — and coming out of my dark night of the soul.*
>
> (Discovery participant)

No other trip component encouraged such an array of intense feelings as the solo. Participants faced many wilderness-related difficulties that produced anxiety, stress, fear, and dissonance. Being alone in wilderness while fasting afforded mental, spiritual, emotional, and spiritual challenges that had to be met and resolved. Participants cited fear, loneliness, boredom, hunger, and anxiety as feelings common to the solo experience.

Two aspects were mentioned most often as being the most difficult. They were solitude and fasting. Participants responded to being alone and hungry in a variety of ways. Many commented that they were bored and did whatever they could to fill up the time. Katz (1969) suggested that people usually try to impose order by establishing familiar routines when they feel they do not have control over their immediate circumstances. Discovery participants usually are given a list of recommended activities, such as writing letters, reading books, observing nature, journaling, or making a gift for someone; however, these activities only require a portion of the solo time, leaving sufficient time for participants to become bored.

Discovery participants commented that fasting was an important part of the solo experience because it broke down their defense mechanisms, thereby creating an openness to learning and growing. Brown (1989) and others have suggested that deprivation opens participants up to learning because the outer protective layers of the psyche have been stripped away. Similarly, fasting has been considered useful in many religious and spiritual traditions for experiencing the supernatural and for promoting spiritual growth because psychological defense mechanisms are worn down; this can lead to a state of brokenness, which can serve as a precursor to growth. As one participant noted, fasting contributed to that process:

> Solo was and still is one of the most significant times [experiences] of my life. I had never fasted before, or been left alone intentionally for three days. I felt closer to Christ during that time than any previous time in my life. My prayer time was constant and amazing, and the scripture I read sustained me. I did not feel hungry during the three days, and the presence of Christ was with me every minute! I learned during the rock climbing and solo that I could do all things through Christ who strengthens me.
>
> (Discovery participant)

One pathway through which personal growth potentially occurs is through the resolution of dissonance. Festinger's Theory of Cognitive Dissonance (1957) asserts that people change their behaviors, attitudes, or beliefs to alleviate the emotional state (tension, anxiety, stress) brought on by intellectual conflict. Similarly, Walsh & Golins

(1976) suggested that anxiety causes people to leave their comfort zones and to try new behaviors to reduce the anxiety, thereby adapting to resolve the dissonance.

Though most participants reported developing strategies for coping with the inherent difficulties of the solo, some were unable to do so. They noted that the solo was not a positive experience. This small group reported feeling overwhelmed to the point that it interfered with their learning. Martin and Priest (1986), Maslow (1968), and others have suggested that this is a possibility when participants are subjected to too much stress or risk. Katz (1969) remarked that "unfulfilled basic needs," such as those posited by Maslow in his *hierarchy of needs*,[2] "would interfere with the participant's ability to attend to higher order concerns, such as reflecting on religious themes" (p. 50). Clearly, this was the case for some Discovery participants. One participant commented, "I know [the solo] was really important to others in my group, but I thought it sucked. I was too physically and mentally drained. The solo was just too much for me."

Though the solo was by far the most significant expedition component, this finding explained why it did not receive the highest rating in Part 3 of the survey. Analysis of the ratings revealed that, although the average for the solo was high, it was also the component most often rated as a 1 (not important). The ratings for the solo, which was described as very significant in Part 2, was countered in Part 3 by extremely low ratings from respondents who disliked it; thus, the average ratings were lower than one might expect. Those who rated the solo quite low usually described their dislike of being alone, hungry, or both. This finding was interesting since the same factors, along with the natural setting, were also cited as primary agents of spiritual growth.

The Spiritual Influence of Solo

> The three day fast and being alone stretched me and my trust and faith in God. I felt his presence so near. The Bible was alive to me, I could not get enough. It strengthened my faith and trust in God as our provider.
>
> (Discovery participant)

Participants related spiritual growth to the solo more than to any other component of the trip, including the daily devotions and Bible studies. Often, they described spiritual growth in terms of an increased faith and trust in God. They cited solitude, prayer, meditation, fasting, scripture, journaling, and reflection time as factors that enhanced spiritual awareness and made them feel closer to God. Many said that solo was a time to be still and to experience God. Some mentioned that solo had helped them to experience God in new ways. One participant commented, "Solo made my spirit quiet. And I found that God really was interested in my smallest details."

Solitude in the wilderness has long been associated with spiritual growth (James, 1902). Many religious leaders, including Jesus, Buddha, and Gandhi, regularly spent time alone in nature (McDonald & Schreyer, 1991). Solitude and silence provided opportunity for reflection and interaction with God. Myers and Jeeves (1987) noted that, "Countless mystics, monks, hermits and prophets have found inspiration in times of contemplative silence" in the belief that "in times of silence and solitude, God reveals himself" (p. 61). James (1902) also noted that after periods of intense solitude in nature people often remark that they feel as if they are in the presence of something greater, whether conceptualized as God, Creator, or higher force. Participants in this study made similar claims, particularly when confronted with overwhelming beauty and physical hardship. The most common time when this occurred was on the solo.

Several participants remarked that the solo was a time to learn the secret of being content in any and all circumstances, a reference to Philippians 4:11–13 in the *Bible*. This passage is discussed often on the Discovery expedition. Many respondents remembered it as a part of the formal teaching of the program. They later used it to frame their understanding of what was happening both during the solo experience and in retrospect. These comments were usually about the value of learning how to transcend immediate circumstances by drawing closer to God. One participant noted,

> *By far, the most significant experience on the trip was my solo experience. Although I detested every lingering minute, the experience broke me in every sense of the word. I was physically and mentally drained. I was poor and broken in spirit. I felt helpless, hopeless, and at the mercy of the world. I had nowhere to turn, but to the Lord. Christ provided for all my needs as he always has and always will. Christ showed me what I was without Him, then He comforted me and showed me a life lacking nothing in communion with Him. I will never forget that experience.*
>
> (Discovery participant)

The solo included elements of a religious retreat — simplifying life in order to focus on the things of God. This was accomplished, in part, by detaching from external cares and concerns in order to have concentrated reflection time in solitude (Katz, 1969). The elements of a religious retreat — detachment, solitude, reflection, and simplification — were present throughout all data sources in this study, and the solo was the primary time when these feelings were most prevalent. One participant commented, "Solo provided lots of time for meditation and drawing closer to God — lots of time to reflect."

In summary, the primary time when Discovery participants experienced intense reflection and interaction with God was during solo. Many remembered the solo experience as a powerful spiritual experience.

The Perspective Afforded by Solo

> *The solo days were days that allowed me the space, focus, and clarity of mind to think about my future, what I wanted out of my life.*
>
> (Discovery participant)

Solo allows time for concentrated reflection, meditation, prayer, and decision-making. Life is reduced to the basics. Bobilya (2004), Knapp (1992), Horwood (1989), and others have proposed that the ideal environment for reflection involves solitude and silence — unfettered by busy schedules, deadlines, or interruptions. This introspection can lead to an increased insight into self. Experiencing solitude in the outdoors has the potential to empower participants because they must face their fears and be responsible for taking care of themselves during that time. In this way, wilderness solitude provides an optimal environment for an individual to become aware of his/her potential, capabilities, and talents as well as his/her natural surroundings (Swatton and Potter, 1998; Moustakis, 1956).

Hammitt (1982) noted that one of the chief advantages of solitude is that the individual has a measure of control over the type and amount of information s/he chooses to process. Therefore, for some Discovery participants, the solo was a clarifying experience in that it provided time for making personal and professional decisions. It offered perspective. One participant wrote, "By the third day my senses had cleared and my physical discomfort was gone — and so was my fear of being alone. This enabled me to disentangle myself from some unhealthy relationships in my life."

Discovery participants also commented that the solo provided time to process what had happened up to that point on the trip, time to digest the meaning of the experience. The solo days served as an incubator for ideas related and unrelated to the expedition. On solo, as well as the entire expedition, participants drew parallels between the wilderness journey, their life journeys, and their spiritual journeys. While the tendency to draw these parallels is relatively common on Christian-oriented, Outward Bound-type expeditions (Anderson-Hanley, 1997), the retrospective approach taken in this study revealed that participants continued to do so *long after Discovery was over*. The lessons learned from the solo experience were sometimes recalled in connection with other life events. For example, one participant commented:

Going into the trip, I was most nervous about the solo. The thought of spending the night alone outside terrified me. I wasn't sure that I would be able to do it but I did! I think back to that experience when faced with challenging situations today. Solo taught me to face my fears, not run from them.

(Discovery participant)

The Setting for Solo

Before the trip, I had never been camping or spent an extended period of time outdoors. Additionally, I had never sat quietly with nature and listened, observed or felt connected to the process of life. The Discovery Program gave me an encounter with the earth, water, wind and fire in a way that has changed, not only my hobbies (camping, hiking, etc.), but more importantly my way of life. Now, an escape to the mountains, deserts, oceans and farmlands are more than a vacation, but an opportunity to rest my soul and find myself in the big picture of life. This shift in world view has had profound implications on my personal, professional, and spiritual life.

(Discovery participant)

What is the role of the setting in the wilderness solo? Wilderness has long been seen as a place of renewal, inspiration, purification, trial, and testing in Christianity, a place where the outer protective layers are stripped away and we are humbled and broken (Garrison, 1995; McDonald and Schreyer, 1991).

Eleven percent of the survey respondents in this study said the natural environment was one of the most significant components on the trip. The natural environment emerged as an important trip component in all three focus groups for a variety of reasons. Of those who described the role that wilderness played in their experiences, the largest sub-group (65 respondents or 31%) went on to say that various features of the natural environment had been a tremendous source of spiritual inspiration. Three aspects were mentioned frequently — the *beauty* of the places, the *perspective* afforded by being on mountain peaks, and the *power* exhibited by natural elements, such as raging rivers or thunderstorms. One participant commented, "The beauty that God placed all around us let us take time out from the immediate and see the bigger picture."

As Fredrickson and Anderson (1999) noted, "Little is known as to how much of an influence the natural environment has on the individual's experience" (p. 22). Although spiritual experiences can occur anywhere (McDonald & Schreyer, 1991; Rosegrant, 1976), the power to encourage epiphany, healing, transcendence, enlightenment, restoration, renewal, and spiritual transformation has been ascribed to wilderness (Kaplan & Kaplan, 1995). To date, there has been relatively little research to support or refute this contention.

In the Discovery study, it is likely that the natural environment evoked deep reflection, in part, because it was interpreted as the creation of God by the majority of the participants; therefore, it was a source of great spiritual inspiration. The beauty and raw power of creation inspired participants to reflect on a Creator. This theme supports the work of Driver (quoted in McDonald and Schreyer, 1991), who noted that the spiritual significance of wilderness may derive from the idea that the least modified environments are the purest expression of God's power and glory ... wilderness acquires importance as a setting for answering the deepest questions of human existence, for celebrating the creative power behind life and things, and for understanding the unity of them all (p. 186).

All natural settings may not be equally inspirational. Rosegrant (1976) compared the experience of Outward Bound groups who soloed on a panoramic mountain peak with groups who soloed by a creek and found that those who soloed on the mountain rated the experience as being more meaningful. Fredrickson and Anderson (1999) compared two contrasting environments in terms of their ability to inspire — the Boundary Waters Wilderness Area and the Grand Canyon. They concluded that specific biophysical components, such as flora, fauna, and geomorphic features, contribute to a site being perceived as inspirational.

In this study, those environmental components described most favorably in relation to the solo included sunlight, running water, and trees. Environmental components mentioned in a negative context included snakes, mosquitoes, and spiders. One component — thunderstorms — was mentioned frequently in both positive and negative contexts.

In summary, the role of the natural environment in the solo's significance varied. Wilderness provided concurrent opportunities for solitude and reflection; for new experiences that tried patience and tested nerves; and for understanding, experiencing, and/or interacting with God in new and powerful ways. The results of this study suggest that, in a Christian context, wilderness did, indeed, provide a place for participants to experience "God's grace through trials and God's glory through creation" (Garrison, 1995, p. 3).

Conclusion

In silence, great things fashion themselves together.

(Thomas Carlyle)

The results of this study suggest that the wilderness solo is viewed in retrospect as an important life event because it incorporates many of the characteristics of significant life experiences. It was a new and/or extraordinary experience for most participants when they went on the expedition, and it was unique compared to other life experiences. It took place in beautiful, natural, and inspirational settings. Solo offered mental, physical, emotional, and spiritual challenges. Additionally, it allowed opportunity for reflection, introspection, and contemplation in solitude and silence. It offered perspective. It provided a reference point as well as one or more life lessons. The solo intensified the examination of the self in relation to the environment, to others, and to God as suggested by Katz (1969). Finally, the solo encouraged spiritual growth through prayer, meditation, and reading scripture.

Kurt Hahn, the founder of Outward Bound, once said that "you cannot harvest the lessons of life except in aloneness and I go to the length of saying that neither the love of man nor the love of God can take deep root except in aloneness" (as cited in Miner, 1990, p. 62). The findings of this study affirm Hahn's assertion and provide a basis for understanding why participants on this spiritually oriented expedition would consider an experience like solo to be significant. The participants in this study, all sojourners to the wild, looked back over the course of their lives and recognized the long-term value of the wilderness solo.

Footnotes

[1]Research into significant life experiences (SLE) derives from the work of Tanner (1980), who sought to learn more about those experiences that promoted concern for the environment. SLE research often involves asking participants to remember and describe experiences that have contributed to future decisions about environmental protection (Tanner, 1980; Palmer, 1993; Chawla, 1998).

[2]According to Katz (1969), Maslow believed that "the lower needs, such as a hunger, must be fulfilled before higher order needs, such as reflection, love, and transcendence, can become functional" (p. 50).

References

The Bible, New International Version (1986). Nashville: Holman Bible Publishers.

Anderson-Hanley, C. (1997). Adventure programming and spirituality: Models, methods, and research. *The Journal of Experiential Education, 20*(2), 102–108.

Bobilya, A. J. (2004). An investigation of the solo in a wilderness experience program. Unpublished doctoral dissertation, University of Minnesota, Minneapolis, MN.

Brown, M. H. (1989). Transpersonal psychology: Facilitating transformation in outdoor experiential education. *Journal of Experiential Education, 12*(3), 47–56.

Chawla, L. (1998). Research methods to investigate significant life experiences: Review and recommendations. *Environmental Education Research, 4*, 383–397.

Corbin, J., & Strauss, A. (1990). Grounded theory research: Procedures, canons, and evaluative criteria. *Qualitative Sociology, 13*(1), 3–21.

Daniel, B. (2003). The life significance of a spiritually oriented, Outward Bound-type wilderness expedition. Unpublished doctoral dissertation, Antioch New England Graduate School, Keene, NH.

Dillman, D. A. (2000). *Mail and Internet surveys: The tailored design method* (2nd ed.). New York: John Wiley and Sons.

Doll, W. E. (1989). Complexity in the classroom. *Educational Leadership, 4*(1), 65–70.

Festinger, L. (1957). *A theory of cognitive dissonance.* Stanford: Stanford University Press.

Fortson, M. B. (1988). *Discovery leadership manual.* Montreat: Montreat College.

Fredrickson, L. M., & Anderson, D. H. (1999). A qualitative exploration of the wilderness experience as a source of spiritual inspiration. *Journal of Environmental Psychology, 19*(1), 21–39.

Garrison, J. (1995). Encountering God along the Appalachian Trail. *Presbyterian Survey, 85*(1), 13–15.

Greenway, R. (1995). The wilderness effect and ecopsychology. In T. Roszak & M. Gomes & A. Kanner (Eds.), *Ecopsychology: Restoring the earth, healing the mind* (pp. 122–135). San Francisco: Sierra Club.

Hammitt, W. E. (1982). Cognitive dimensions of wilderness solitude. *Environment and Behaviour, 14*, 478–493.

Horwood, B. (1989). Reflections on reflection. *The Journal of Experiential Education, 12*(2), 5–6.

James, W. (1902). *Varieties of religious experience.* New York: The Modern Library.

Kaplan, R., & Kaplan, S. (1995). *The experience of nature: A psychological perspective.* Ann Arbor: Ulrich.

Katz, R. (1969). A solo-survival experience as education for personal growth. *Educational Opportunity Forum, 1*(4), 38–53.

Knapp, C. E. (1992). *Lasting lessons: A teachers guide to reflecting on experience.* Charleston: Clearinghouse on Rural Education and Small Schools.

Luckner, J. L., & Nadler, R. S. (1997). *Processing the experience: Strategies to enhance and generalize learning*. Dubuque: Kendall/Hunt.

Martin, P., & Priest, S. (1986). Understanding the adventure experience. *Journal of Adventure Education, 3*, 18–21.

Maslow, A. (1968). *Toward a psychology of being*. New York: Van Nostrand.

McDonald, B. L., & Schreyer, R. (1991). Spiritual benefits of leisure participation and leisure settings. In B. L. Driver, Brown, P. J., & Peterson, G. L. (Ed.), *Benefits of leisure*. State College: Venture Publishing.

Miner, J. L. (1990). The creation of Outward Bound. In J. C. Miles & S. Priest (Eds.), *Adventure education*. State College: Venture Publishing.

Morgan, O. J. (1986). Music for the dance: some meanings of solitude. *Journal of Religion and Health, 25*(1), 18–28.

Moustakis, C. E. (1956). *The self*. New York: Harper and Row.

Myers, D. G., & Jeeves, M. A. (1987). *Psychology through the eyes of faith*. San Francisco: Harper San Francisco.

Neisser, U. (1982). *Memory observed: Remembering in natural contexts*. San Francisco: W.H. Freeman and Company.

Palmer, J. (1993). Development of concern for the environment and formative experiences of educators. *Journal of Environmental Education, 24*(3), 26–30.

Richley, A. (1992). *A phenomenological investigation of wilderness solitude*. Unpublished Master's thesis, University of Alberta, Edmonton.

Rosegrant, J. (1976). The impact of set and setting on religious experience in nature. *Journal for the Scientific Study of Religion, 15*(4), 301–310.

Stringer, A., & McAvoy, L. (1992). The need for something different: Spirituality and wilderness adventure. *Journal of Experiential Education, 15*(1), 13–20.

Swatton, A. G., & Potter, T. G. (1998). The personal growth of outstanding canoeists resulting from solo canoe expeditions. *Pathways: The Ontario Journal of Outdoor Education, 9*(6), 13–16.

Tanner, T. (1980). Significant life experiences: A new research area in environmental education. *Journal of Environmental Education, 11*(4), 20–24.

Walsh, V., & Golins, G. (1976). *The exploration of the Outward Bound process*. Denver: Colorado Outward Bound School.

CHAPTER 8

Lessons From the Field: Participant Perceptions of a Multi-Day Wilderness Solo

By Andrew J. Bobilya, Leo H. McAvoy, & Kenneth R. Kalisch

There was just some pure connection with God and nature that I fell in love with all over again there.

(2003 High Road Participant)

There is no denying the impact of an extended period of solitude in a remote wilderness setting. This is why solo is a part of most traditional *Outward Bound-type* programs. It provides an opportunity for individual reflection on the lessons learned in the wilderness, as well as a respite for the staff and students. Previous research has shown that the solo experience is regarded as one of the most influential components of organized wilderness programs (Bobilya, 2004; Bobilya, Kalisch & McAvoy, 2005; Bobilya, McAvoy & Kalisch, in press; Daniel, 2003; Fredrickson & Anderson, 1999; Griffin, 2000; McAvoy, 2000; McFee, 1993; Sibthorp, 2000; Stringer & McAvoy, 1992; Williams & Kalisch, 1995). Yet there has been little research formally investigating this *black box* called solo. Daniel (2003) found solo to be the most significant part of a 21-day wilderness program by a two-to-one margin over all other course components in its contribution to a participant's life significance. In addition, solo was the only component classified as *most significant* from at least one respondent representing each of the 25 years investigated in Daniel's retrospective study. Solo continues to be a component of many wilderness experience programs, and it has the potential to have great impact on participants. Despite this positive evidence, solo is often given minimal attention during staff training and program planning. Perhaps this is due to the limited understanding of what happens during solo.

This paper seeks to provide insight into this prominent wilderness experience. It summarizes a research project undertaken with 126 first-year college students who participated in solos of various lengths (24-60 hours) as part of an 18-day wilderness program. The study methodology is briefly explained, but the main focus is to provide a summary of the participants' perceptions of their solo experience. The paper concludes with recommendations for program instructors and managers interested in using similar opportunities for creating intentional solitude within their programs, and offers suggestions for further inquiry.

The Study

This study was designed to investigate participants' perceptions of an organized solo within a wilderness experience program and the influence that the participants, the instructors, and the environment have on these perceptions. With a better understanding of participants' experiences during solo, program managers and instructors can determine what contributes to and hinders the solo as a tool for personal growth.

Program and Participants

The program studied, High Road, is a wilderness orientation program for freshman and transfer students entering Wheaton College. High Road is an 18-day wilderness experience program intended to prepare students for college. Similar to Outward Bound, High Road uses the small-group environment (8–10 participants) and the wilderness setting to provide participants with opportunities to stretch themselves physically, mentally, and spiritually. The explicit spiritual focus of the program supports the mission of Wheaton College and differentiates it from the traditional Outward Bound model. The High Road program includes a 24–72 hour solo experience with the option for participants to fast (take little or no food). The solo is primarily framed by the instructors as an opportunity for spiritual reflection and renewal.

The participants in this study included 126 of the 145 first-year students enrolled in the High Road Wilderness Program through Wheaton College during August 2003. Nearly half (46.8%) of the participants were male and 80.2% were 18 years old (age range = 17–21 years). Participants came from 33 states in the U.S., and four foreign countries (Brazil, Spain, Thailand, and the Czech Republic).

During this program 86.5% of the participants (16 of 17 groups) were on solo for two nights and one group was on solo for one night. All of the 126 participants chose to fast during the solo, but four participants decided to end their fast early due to health concerns. All of the participants' solo sites were located on the southern shore of Lake Superior in the Upper Peninsula of Michigan.

Summary of Data Collection and Analysis

In order to understand the participants' perceptions of solo prior to, during, and after the experience, four phases of data were collected.

Phase 1: All 126 participants completed informational surveys when they arrived at Wheaton College, prior to beginning the program. The questions focused on demographic data, and the students' prior experiences with and expectations for the solo.

Phase 2: All 126 participants completed surveys while alone on solo, prior to rejoining their expedition group. This survey asked them to describe their solo experience by answering various questions.

Phase 3: Group interviews were conducted with a total of 30 participants (three groups) after the wilderness expedition, but prior to returning to the campus. The questions prompted students to share what they recalled about their solo, the influence of fellow group members and instructors, and their receptivity to the experience.

Phase 4: Follow-up interviews were conducted on campus with 16 participants who were selected based on a theoretical sample (Patton, 2002). They were chosen because they had commented that they were anxious, bored, or peaceful during solo. The questions focused on the participants' perceptions of the solo experience, transfer of learning to life situations at home, and the cause of their boredom, anxiety, or peacefulness while alone in the woods.

Analysis of the qualitative data followed the constant-comparative method (Glasser & Strauss, 1967), in which recurrent themes were identified and direct quotations were used to support the themes. The quantitative survey data were analyzed, and descriptive statistics were produced. This analysis was limited to the data collected from July to December 2003 with participants in the High Road Wilderness Program. As with any primarily qualitative study focused on only one program, caution is warranted in applying the results to other programs.

Results

The Individual Participant's Influence on Her/His Perception of the Solo

This study provided insight into the participants' perceptions of the solo prior to, during, and after the experience. The results indicate that participants' expectations for the experience impacted their actual experience. This supports Hendee and Brown (1988) who stated, "Personal growth from a wilderness experience depends on the participant's receptivity. Do they want to go? What are their expectations? Are they ready to change?" (p. 10). Other adventure education literature also indicates that participant expectations may influence the outcomes experienced from adventure education programs (Hattie, Marsh, Neill, & Richards, 1997; McKenzie, 2000). Participants in this study indicated that they expected positive opportunities for spiritual growth, reflection, autonomy, and physical rest, but also had concerns about loneliness, uncertainty, physical weakness, inability to focus, difficulty journaling, and a lack of structure. They had high expectations for the solo experience, especially the opportunity for spiritual growth. For many, these expectations raised anxiety about whether or not they would "experience what they were supposed to" while alone in the wilderness. One participant stated:

> *I remember for so much of it [solo] being frustrated that there was something that I was supposed to be doing or something I was supposed to be experiencing that wasn't happening. .... The instructors, you know, they told me [that] for the first time in the program I didn't have a job to do, I didn't have someplace I had to go, I didn't have some work I had to do. I just remember for the first day and a half probably even just walking around, pacing around, thinking, "What am I supposed to be doing?"*

These participants were *receptive* to change and seemed to question the value of the solo experience if they did not experience change. Conversely, the sense of peace experienced by many participants was enhanced by a conscious effort to limit expectations for the solo.

In the participants' minds the solo was not an isolated course component; it was affected by the experiences that preceded and followed it. This finding was highlighted by the high percentage of solo participants who indicated that journaling (25.3%) and rest (24.3%) were the most enjoyable part of the solo. When asked what they *expected* to be the most enjoyable, only 8.8% mentioned journaling and 8% mentioned rest. Apparently, many students did not expect to enjoy the rest and journaling because they could not foresee the busyness of the whole wilderness expedition. In retrospect one student stated:

> *I particularly enjoyed being able to set my own pace for the day, taking all the time I wanted/needed to accomplish different activities. I enjoyed the lack of time restraint especially when I was journaling and writing to friends and family.*

Personal enjoyment of the solo was also enhanced by the contrasting nature of the experience. After the solo, it was apparent to the participants how much they had needed the physical rest and time to reflect. They indicated that they developed an increased awareness of themselves and how they interact with others through reflection. One student commented:

> *There are a lot of things in myself that I hide behind my busyness, but [after] three days and two nights alone they're hard to ignore. I grew, reflected, and set goals.*

This finding points to the importance of program design and sequencing of components within the program in order to offer participants the contrasting experience of wilderness solitude.

The solo also offered participants the opportunity to develop skills that were transferable to other settings. In particular, the solo provided them with a metaphorical challenge that they were able to refer to once they returned to their college campus. One student commented:

> *I think it [solo] taught me that ... if I can handle something like that I can deal with a lot of other things at school. I get a little nervous about school — being in a new environment taught me that ... I would be able to handle it.*

Participants indicated that the solo was something they were able to look back on, and the memory of it gave them hope that they could overcome other obstacles in their academic and personal lives.

The solo experience separated participants from each other in order to provide an opportunity for solitude not experienced during other components of the program. The experience of being alone, however, is not immune from the influence of prior experiences with others, nor is it isolated from potentially impacting group experiences that follow. The participants in this study reported that other group members had an influence on their solo experience even though they were alone. Positive interaction with one's group prior to the solo led to feelings of support, comfort, and safety while alone. Some participants felt as though they were not really alone in their solo experience because they knew others were also in solitude nearby. One student stated:

> *The group members that I could see around me during my solo were sort of a comfort and a distraction. I found myself often wanting to know where they were or what they were doing. It was also nice to know that there were people around me going through it [solo].*

Participants also mentioned the positive effects that the solo experience had on their group's cohesion once they returned from the solo. Many participants indicated that their time alone allowed them to appreciate their fellow group members in ways similar to their appreciation of family and friends. A participant stated:

> *I think the attitudes were a lot different when we came back together. We were
> all just a lot more appreciative of one another and just saw each other in a
> different light because of that experience.*

The influence of fellow group members was not positive for all participants. For some, the proximity of their solo sites caused frustration, because they found themselves distracted and wanting to compare their solo experience with that of others.

Participant comments in this study indicated that the solo impacted them physically, mentally, and also spiritually. This confirms previous research that has investigated spiritual development through wilderness programs and found that both intentional and unplanned moments of solitude in the wilderness contribute to one's spirituality (Bobilya, 2004; Bobilya, et al., 2005; Daniel, 2003; Fredrickson & Anderson, 1999; Griffin, 2000; Price, 1999; Stringer & McAvoy, 1992). Some participants commented that the solo was an intense time of personal evaluation, goal setting, and spiritual growth. When interviewed three and a half months after the program, one participant stated:

> *...but there was just some pure connection with God and nature that I fell in
> love with all over again there [during the solo]. ... I realize [by] talking to
> some people that I can't depend on a solo or being in the woods to foster spiritu-
> al thoughts and being spiritual ... but I do remember it [solo] as just a time of
> total connection with God and I really yearn for that sometimes because it is a
> lot more difficult here [at the college].*

These outcomes were enhanced through the use of journaling on one's life, relationships, and spiritual growth. Participants did not expect journaling to be as enjoyable as they found it to be, and their comments indicated the significance of it in fostering reflection on the *mental* and *spiritual* aspects of the experience.

In summary, the solo experience is clearly affected by the participants and their fellow group members. Participants in this study frequently commented on the impact of their expectations for the experience and the fear associated with not meeting those expectations. The impact of participant expectations for their experience is a key finding that emerged across all phases of this study.

The Influence of the Instructor During Solo

The role of the instructor in wilderness experience programs varies greatly depending on the program, instructor personalities, group dynamics, and other factors

(Kalisch, 1999). Regardless of program type and population, the solo is one of the few program components in which the participants have to construct their own experience without an opportunity for regular interaction with their instructor. Many instructors have historically "let the mountains speak for themselves" (James, 1980) and intentionally have not taken an active role preparing the students for their solo experiences, aside from providing information about safety and logistical concerns (McIntosh, 1989).

Preparation for solo. The instructor has the ability to influence the participants' expectations of the experience (McKenzie, 2000). This influence is similar to the emphasis the students put on their own expectations. Many participants discussed the impact of their instructors' comments about the solo on their understanding of the experience. They reported that some instructors intentionally left their students with expectations for a "significant" experience while others simply stressed the uniqueness of each individual's solo. This variation in participants' perceptions of their instructors' expectations is highlighted in the following statements:

> *[The instructors] told us that solo is unique for everyone, so toss out any preconceived ideas about solo that we might have had.*

Another student indicated:

> *They [the instructors] described it [solo] as something that could [be] life changing and could be a once in a lifetime experience.*

These participant comments indicate that individuals distinctly recall different aspects of the pre-solo briefing.

The instructor has the potential to impact the participants' understandings of the solo before they are separated from the group and begin their time alone. The framing of the solo experience provides an opportunity for participants to clarify the intent of the solo and any associated activities. Most participants found that they only remembered what was most important to them from the group discussion prior to the solo. For example, if they were concerned about how they would find adequate drinking water, they may not have paid much attention to the rest of the briefing — including the rationale for doing the solo. This can be problematic, because participants should have opportunity to clarify their understanding of the solo with an instructor prior to leaving the group.

Visit during solo. Many programs have avoided encouraging too much instructor intervention during the solo because of the potential disruption to the participant's experience (McIntosh, 1989). However, participants in this study indicated the importance of carefully planned visits by their instructors. For some students, the visit by their instructor was a turning point in the solo experience:

> *[I was] laying on my rock and just crying, "I don't understand this and I don't understand that and I don't get it" and my leader walked up and we just talked about a lot of the issues and everything was a lot more clear after I had spoken aloud to her.*

Discussions with instructors during solo allowed some students to clarify their experience and create strategies for the remainder of their time alone. Many students mentioned that they would probably have continued to be frustrated, anxious, and bored during the solo if there had been no visit from an instructor. McIntosh (1989) highlighted the importance of the *style* of the instructor visit during the solo: "If a facilitator is in tune with the student's needs, a visit should intensify the experience, not dilute it" (p. 30).

In contrast, some participants indicated that they preferred not to be interrupted by an instructor and were satisfied with just a quick check on their physical health. Furthermore, some participants raised concerns that the timing of the visit caused periods of anxiousness as they waited for their instructor to arrive. One student stated:

> *I felt like I had to have something to show my instructors — I didn't want them to find me sleeping all the time.*

These individuals mentioned that their day was marked by the instructor's visit and they did not feel "free" until after he/she had checked in. Participant comments also indicated that the middle of the solo was the most significant, because they were able to completely focus and not worry about "getting settled" or "preparing to leave." What seems important to the participants is the optional availability of an instructor to discuss the solo experience. The timing of the visit is important in order to provide students with uninterrupted alone time in order to focus and relax.

Solo debriefing. Participants indicated that their interpretation of the solo experience was affected by the structure and expectations of instructor-led group discussions at the end of the solo. Some participants indicated that while they were excited to rejoin the group, it was difficult transitioning from intense solitude to community again. One student indicated his desire for an opportunity to discuss his experience with an instructor prior to being expected to share in a group debriefing session after the solo:

> *I think one of the problems was that we sat in a circle after being alone for three days and we were just like, "What happened on your solo?" It was kind of a shocker to go from complete solitude into that. … I do think it's important to share with your group what happened. That was good for us, it was just kind of a shock, you know, to go from yourself to 10 people. I don't think we got that much discussed. …*

For some, the debriefing session was a concern because they wondered what they "should have experienced" and if they would have the "right" answers when fellow group members shared what they had learned. One participant stated:

> *There's part of you that's thinking while you're on the solo, "When this is done, we are going to sit around the fire and we are going to talk about our solo. What am I going to say when it is my turn?"*

Instructors had responsibility for clarifying the perceptions of the participants prior to and during solo, and they had an influence on the participants' final memories of the experience as drawn from the group debriefing session. Group discussion was enhanced when participants felt comfortable sharing the difficulties they encountered during solo and were able to acknowledge struggling to recognize what they had learned from the experience. Reflecting on her solo, one participant stated:

> *They [the instructors] even said that you may not feel like you got anything out of this; which is how I felt. "There may be months or a long time before you see any benefits or you may not recognize the benefits, but it [solo] will still have affected you somehow. …" so I guess [I would recommend] making sure students feel comfortable and not to feel like they have to perform. …*

Participants who admitted psychological struggles during solo were few in number. Only 13% indicated that they were primarily anxious or bored. Those same participants indicated that being able to share openly and learn from others without feeling pressure to have had similar growth increased the value of their experience.

This study reinforces that the role of the instructor is a key program element in all adventure programming. Instructors should be given ample training on how to frame, conduct, and debrief the solo experience. Participants in this study indicated the impact of their personal expectations for the solo, some of which were influenced by their instructors. The solo is one of few course components in which instructors have limited contact with their students and therefore their influence may be even more critical.

The Influence of Environment During Solo

The environment in which wilderness programs take place is another key element in participants' experiences (Bobilya, 2004; Bobilya et al., 2005; Daniel, 2003; Fredrickson & Anderson, 1999; Kalisch, 1999; McKenzie, 2000). The contrast between the wilderness environment and the participant's everyday life often intensifies the program experience. When placed alone in the wilderness, the participant's sensory awareness is heightened and he/she is presented with opportunities to increase his/her attunement with him/herself, others, and nature (Hendee & Brown, 1988). This study clearly indicates the influence of the environment on the participants' perceptions of the solo experience. When asked at the end of the solo if the environment played a role in their experience, 96% of the participants indicated that it did.

For many participants, the physical location of their solo site (on the shore of Lake Superior) contributed a sense of peace and awe as they considered the intricacy and beauty that surrounded them. After the solo, one student stated:

> *The sheer magnitude of Lake Superior and the overwhelming aspect of being alone in nature did add to the [solo] experience.*

The open expanse of the Lake Superior shoreline contrasted with the thick forests where the participants had been backpacking prior to solo. This contrast in environments encouraged participants to reflect on their role in the universe. The sense of power, mystery, and awe that participants reported experiencing was similar to that described by Unsoeld (1974) as having characteristics of mystery (*mysterium*) and power (*tremendum*). This mystery and power caused participants to be in amazement of the beauty surrounding them. Many indicated that the rising and setting of the sun were memorable in a way they had never experienced before.

This study also indicated that the remoteness of the wilderness setting affected the participants' perceptions of their solos. The removal of most other human contact and human-made distractions caused participants to look inward and reflect on their lives, their experiences during the wilderness program, and their relationships with others and God. The results indicated that the lack of physical demands and the remoteness of the setting influenced the participants' attunement to the natural world and the intricacies displayed before them. Reflecting on the role of the environment, one student stated:

The natural environment has few of the distractions that other environments create. The only noises that I heard were that of nature. There were no clocks, only the sun. This all helped me focus on what I was doing.

Students were able to closely observe the natural environment because of the time and space provided.

Some participants commented that while the location of their solo site was beautiful, they were also affected by concerns about the weather, the insects, and the discomforts they experienced from their surroundings. One student indicated:

The bugs during the night drove me crazy and kept me awake for a while. The hot sun felt oppressive and the waves made me fear a storm was coming.

When discussing students' abilities to utilize the solo experience, McIntosh (1989) stated:

Some students' low outdoor skill level results in them being physically uncom-fortable, others do not feel safe on their own. ... If these needs are not met, stu-dents definitely are going to have trouble getting on to higher level thinking.

(p. 28)

Students did not *expect* that the wilderness setting would be difficult and yet when asked about their *actual* experience, 14.4% indicated that the environment, particularly the discomfort of insects, was troublesome. The solo within this program was inten-tionally located on the shore of a large lake to provide a setting conducive to reflec-tion and self-evaluation. Many participants realized this outcome, but those who found the setting difficult were not able to move beyond their need for physical and emotional comfort.

It is clear that the environment plays a role in participants' perceptions of the solo experience and the choice of solo site may have a direct influence on their ability to use the time effectively. Some participants indicated that an area with a grand view had a positive influence on their ability to reflect and experience a sense of peace. The environment, however, was not perceived positively by all participants, especially those who felt unprepared for the physical demands presented by weather, insects, and the general unpredictability of the wilderness.

Recommendations for Program Managers and Instructors

The importance of the instructor prior to, during, and after the solo experience has been highlighted in this study. What follows are specific recommendations for instructors and those involved in their training, regarding the intentional use of solitude experiences as a part of a wilderness program.

1. The location of the solo must be evaluated in light of the participants and their abilities, the goals of the program, the weather, and many other human and environmental conditions. Participants in this study clearly indicated that the shore of Lake Superior was an ideal setting to engage in reflection. In general, similar solo locations that provide an expansive view of the environment may increase opportunities for reflection.

2. It is critical that instructors understand the expectations that students bring to the solo experience and assist students by providing ideas that can help them better use their time alone and/or alleviate any concerns they have. Participants need reassurance that their solo experience is unique, and they may need to set aside preconceived expectations for what they "should experience" while alone. The instructor's role prior to solo may be even more critical than for other course components during which they are able to monitor students throughout an activity.

3. The preparation that instructors provide students prior to sending them alone into the wilderness is critical. Instructors need to present a clear rationale for the solo and suggested activities (e.g. fasting, journaling, selected readings). Instructors should give students an opportunity to practice shelter construction, journaling, and other reflective activities prior to asking them to perform them while on solo. While instructors cannot prepare their students for every situation that may arise, an opportunity to practice the necessary skills prior to being isolated by oneself may increase the participant's learning. For example, if a participant is expected to write in a journal during solo, prior practice with journal writing may enhance the experience (McIntosh, 1988). *Mini-solos* of less than a day can be a great strategy to build up to a multi-day solo. With proper preparation, students will be able to utilize their time alone more effectively.

4. An optional instructor visit during solo can enhance the participant's experience. Talking with an instructor during solo can assist participants in drawing meaning from an otherwise confusing experience and can also help them create strategies for using their time alone. Instructors should

also facilitate one-on-one discussion time with students after the solo to assist them in processing their experience. Participants must be continually reassured that each individual's experience is unique and valuable.

5. Instructors must remember that for many participants solo is a time for rest, structured reflection, and learning. Instructors should carefully consider how group dynamics and prior program elements may affect the experience of the participants when they solo and, conversely, how the solo experience may affect the group dynamics and program elements to follow.

6. The solo experience can affect participants physically, mentally, emotionally, and spiritually. Instructors need to consider the impact of the solo experience beyond the physical effects of removing a person from the group. While the spiritual development of participants may not be in the mission of some wilderness experience programs, past research has shown this is often an outcome of wilderness solitude (Fredrickson & Anderson, 1999; Stringer & McAvoy, 1992).

Recommendations for Further Research

Past research has already confirmed the impact of the solo within the context of wilderness experience programs (Bobilya, 2004; Bobilya et al., 2005; Daniel, 2003; Fredrickson & Anderson, 1999; Griffin, 2000; McAvoy, 2000; McFee, 1993; McKenzie, 2000; Price, 1999; Sibthorp, 2000; Stringer & McAvoy, 1992; Williams & Kalisch, 1995). Despite solo ranking as one of the most influential components of wilderness experience programs, little research has been undertaken to investigate participants' perceptions of the solo experience. The following are directions for future research:

1. Investigation is needed to study the length of solo in relation to the age of participants, environmental settings, and other factors that may contribute to a positive solo experience.

2. Research is warranted to investigate outcomes of the solo experience in other program settings, including type of program (summer camp, formal classroom, rite of passage) and locale (mountains, desert, urban).

3. Replication of this study with a program that does not emphasize spirituality in its programming may further understanding of the inherent spiritual benefits of the wilderness solo. Participants in this study were receptive to spiritual development, and many commented that they grew in that domain. The questions that follow are: What about programs that are using the solo without a spiritual emphasis? To what degree are their

participants experiencing spiritual development? These questions can only be answered through the replication of this research with other programs of similar type but without stated goals of spiritual development.

4. Longitudinal research is needed to explore participants' transfer of learning beyond the solo experience and the wilderness environment, and the influence of solo on continuing personal growth.

5. Research needs to investigate those participants who struggle with the use of their solo time and who cannot wait for its conclusion.

6. Investigation is needed to understand the role of other variables (e.g. socio-economic status, previous wilderness experience, life experience) on one's solo experience.

7. Research is needed to better understand the influence of specific solo activities (e.g. fasting, journaling, suggested readings) on solo participant outcomes.

Conclusion

Most components of wilderness experience programs tend to be group-focused. The contrast solo time offers to group time is likely one of the reasons it shows such influence on participants. Careful attention regarding its programmatic use is therefore warranted. Instructors often provide in-depth, careful attention when instructing participants in the skills necessary to perform other program components (e.g. rock climbing, canoeing, backpacking). The same preparatory attention should be given to solo, which has the potential to significantly shape participants' lives.

In this study, the solo experience appeared to enhance personal growth and learning, and was accompanied by a sense of peace for many, but this was not the case for all participants. The solo is one of the few times during a wilderness experience program when the student is truly alone without opportunity for peer or instructor feedback or the support that comes from community. Therefore, the importance of preparation and management of the solo is obvious. These results call for an increased understanding of soloists' perceptions of their experience. This study begins to provide an understanding of participant perceptions of the solo experience and how other participants, instructors, and the environment influence that perception.

Author's Note: We wish to extend special thanks to the students, staff and faculty at Wheaton College's Northwoods Campus at HoneyRock who assisted in various phases of the project. We are also grateful to Dr. Jim Glover, Dr. Corliss Outley and countless other colleagues at Southern Illinois University, the University of Minnesota and Wheaton College who provided critical feedback throughout the research project.

References

Bobilya, A. J. (2004). *An investigation of the solo in a wilderness experience program.* (Doctoral dissertation, University of Minnesota, 2004) *Digital Dissertations,* AAT 3129201.

Bobilya, A. J., Kalisch, K. R., McAvoy, L. H & Jacobs, J. (2005). A mixed-method investigation of the solo in a wilderness experience program. In Paisley, K., Bunting, C. J., Young, A. B. & Bloom, K. (Eds.), *Research in outdoor education: Vol. 7.* Cortland, NY: Coalition for Education in the Outdoors.

Bobilya, A. J., McAvoy, L.H., & Kalisch, K. R. (in press). The power of the instructor in the solo experience: An empirical study and some non-empirical questions. *Journal of Adventure Education and Outdoor Learning.*

Cammack, M. W. (1996). *A rite of passage with Outward Bound: Transpersonal perspectives of the solo from 16 wilderness guides.* Unpublished doctoral dissertation, University of Victoria, British Columbia, Canada.

Daniel, R. B. (2003). *The life significance of a spiritually oriented Outward Bound-type wilderness expedition.* Unpublished doctoral dissertation. Antioch New England Graduate School.

Ewert, A. & McAvoy, L. (2000). The effects of wilderness settings on organized groups: A state of knowledge paper. In McCool, S. F., Cole, D. N., Borrie, W. T., & O'Loughlin, J. (Eds.) *Wilderness Science in a Time of Change Conference: Vol. 3. Wilderness as a place for scientific inquiry.* (pp. 13–25). Ogden, UT: U.S. Department of Agriculture.

Fredrickson, L. M. & Anderson, D. H. (1999). A qualitative exploration of the wilderness experience as a source of spiritual inspiration. *Journal of Environmental Psychology, 19*, 21–39.

Glasser, B. G., & Strauss, A. L. (1967). *The discovery of grounded theory strategy for qualitative research.* Hawthorne, NY: Aldine.

Griffin, W. J. (2000). *Effects of an adventure based program with an explicit spiritual component on the spiritual growth of adolescents.* Unpublished doctoral dissertation. University of New Mexico.

Hattie, J., Marsh, H. W., Neill, J. T., & Richards, G. E. (1997). Adventure education and Outward Bound: Out-of-class experiences that make a lasting difference. *Review of Educational Research, 67*(1), 43–87.

Hammitt, W. E. (1982). Cognitive dimensions of wilderness solitude. *Environment and Behavior, 14*(4), 478–493.

Hendee J. C., & Brown, M. (1988). How wilderness experience programs facilitate personal growth: A guide for program leaders and resource managers. *Renewable Resources Journal, 6*(2), 9–16.

James, T. (1980) Can the mountains speak for themselves? (Unpublished manuscript, Colorado Outward Bound School, Denver, CO.)

Kalisch, K. R. (1999). *The role of the instructor in the Outward Bound educational process.* Kearney, NE: Morris.

McAvoy, L. (2000). Components of the outdoor trip: A response to the papers. In Stringer, L.A., McAvoy, L. H., & Young, A. B. (Eds.), *Coalition for Education in the Outdoors fifth biennial research symposium proceedings* (pp. 12–14). Cortland, NY: Coalition for Education in the Outdoors.

McFee, M. (1993). *The effect of group dynamics on the perception of positive learning experience in the Outward Bound process.* Unpublished doctoral dissertation, Forest Institute of Professional Psychology, Wheeling, IL.

McKenzie, M. (2003). Beyond the "Outward Bound Process:" Rethinking student learning. *Journal of Experiential Education, 26*(1), 8–23.

McKenzie, M. D. (2000). How are adventure education program outcomes achieved?: A review of the literature. *Australian Journal of Outdoor Education, 5*(1), 19–28.

McIntosh, H. (1989). Re-thinking the solo experience. *Journal of Experiential Education, 12*(3), 28–32.

Morrison, J. (1986). *The wilderness solo: Solitude and recreation.* Unpublished master's thesis, University of Alberta, Edmonton, AB.

Patton, M. Q. (2002). *Qualitative research and evaluation methods.* Thousand Oaks, CA: Sage.

Price, G. (1999). *A study of career perspectives on facilitating spiritual development through outdoor education.* Unpublished master's thesis, Moray House Institute of Education, University of Edinburgh.

Sibthorp, J. (2000). Components of an outdoor trip: What really happens? Study 1. In Stringer, L.A., McAvoy, L. H., & Young, A. B. (Eds.), *Coalition for Education in the Outdoors fifth biennial research symposium proceedings* (pp. 2–6). Cortland, NY: Coalition for Education in the Outdoors.

Stringer, L. A., & McAvoy, L. (1992). The need for something different: Spirituality and wilderness adventure. *Journal of Experiential Education, 15*(1), 13–20.

Unsoeld, W. (1974, October). *Spiritual Values in Wilderness.* Paper presented at the Conference on Experiential Education, Estes Park, CO.

Unsoeld, W. (n.d.). *Wilderness and the sacred.* Unpublished manuscript.

Williams, B., & Kalisch, K. R. (1995, November). *What we think we have learned about change in one college Outward Bound adaptive program.* Paper presented at the International Conference of the Association for Experiential Education, Lake Geneva, WI.

CHAPTER 9

Coming Home:
Adolescents and the Nature-Based Solo

By John Maxted

*The tree had a firm grip on the earth and [Paul] longed
to share its feeling of committal to this place. It had a comforting
air of permanence, so different from the camp and the life he
knew. Yes, it would be his fine-day tree, when he didn't want
to swim or go walking. He would sit here and think and dream
and perhaps some of the tree's vitality would come through to
him; he would learn to share its feeling that this was his place
too, he would learn how to beat that sudden strange urge to hide;
and that would help him through the rough places.*

(Hillard, 1965, pp. 138–139)

7 I am fascinated by the influence of solitude and natural places in shaping the human spirit. One of my favorite books on this topic is Noel Hilliard's *Power of Joy* (1965), a Huck Finn-type story set in rural New Zealand during the depression years. Paul, the protagonist, should by most measures be an unhappy child. He grows up the mostly ignored only child of a dysfunctional marriage, living in rural squalor and poverty, and largely ostracized by his school peers. Yet Paul discovers a love for nature and for hide-away places where his imagination and creativity run wild. He finds solace while climbing trees and spending time in various secret natural places. When Paul moves to a new community with his parents, he scopes out new places, spaces, and trees well before attempting to connect with other kids his own age. For Paul solitude is a joy-ful experience, a *coming home* to nature and a time for re-creation and self-definition. Czech philosopher Erazim Kohak (1984) speaks of solitude as a gift and our need to reclaim that gift if we are to become fully realized humans. It is a gift Paul happily and innocently accepts during his growing years, one he leans on in times of adversity. *Power of Joy* is a celebration of the gift of nature-based solitude for young people.

When speaking of solitude, Kohak (1984, p. 39) refers to "the condition of being alone in the presence of a living, familiar world, being willing to listen to it, to see and to understand it ... sharing in its feel and meaning." This definition merges solitude and the human condition with the natural world and reflects my own passion and bias as an educator. Like Kohak, I believe that experiencing nearby nature as a "familiar world" is a key to the door of human and nonhuman re-connection. Solo can involve a process of coming to know nature as both self and home, but these psycho-ecological ends do not easily fit into what is deemed school curriculum. Nor do they reflect the typical objectives of most of the solo programs I have observed. Yet the notion of *coming home* to nature via solo is an exciting one.

In recent years I have been on a quest to examine the meaning and significance of solitude in the lives of young New Zealanders, and to better understand what adolescents might feel, think, and be when provided an opportunity for time alone in a natural setting. I know from my own experiences facilitating solo over the past decade, and from my personal experiences with solitude as a means of rejuvenating from the routines and demands of everyday life, that solos typically work for adults. When solitude is freely chosen, many adults revel in the opportunities it provides. But what of the solitude experiences of adolescents, especially when their experiences are not necessarily freely chosen?

The term *adolescence* refers to an ill-defined period between childhood and young adulthood. Those "puberty years" are characterized as a time of physical and emotional growing, and of a subtle or sometimes rapid maturation as an individual travels toward young adulthood. I acknowledge that the term *adolescent* may not resonate comfortably with individuals caught somewhere between childhood and young-adulthood and that it may possibly be construed as derogatory. My interest in utilizing *adolescent, adolescents,* and *adolescence* throughout this work is with exploring the experiences of these young people with deliberately structured periods of time alone in natural settings.

During the years 2000 through 2004, I examined the solo experiences of adolescents who were challenged to remain in solitude for two days and two nights as a component of two distinctly different outdoor education programs — one was a six-day school camp and the other a longer term residential program. I was given the opportunity to interview students prior to and after their solo, and to hear from teachers and instructors about the solo experiences of their students. I was fortunate to peruse student journals, creative writing, artwork, and letters to family and friends arising from their solo experiences. Visits to other outdoor education programs also provided insights to a variety of solo philosophies, management systems, and practices existing in the New Zealand outdoor scene. Finally, I looked for insights about adolescents and solo in the emerging literature on adolescent solitude. This paper discusses what adolescents might actually do, think, and feel on solo in relation to the program objectives set for them and also explores the potential fears, anxieties, and loneliness adolescents may experience during solo. My intent is not to diminish the power and richness of the solo experience for most adolescents. Rather I aim to present issues for teachers and facilitators of the solo experience to consider in their quest to better assist their adolescent participants in discovering the gift of solitude and perhaps awaken a *coming home* to nature.

Insights Into Adolescent Nature-Based Solos

In *Oh, the Places You'll Go*, Dr. Seuss's classic treatise on the journey of life from adolescence to adulthood (1990, pp. 38–43), he presents a fundamentally difficult, challenging, and solitary journey:

> *All alone! Whether you like it or not,*
> *Alone will be something you will be quite a lot.*
> *And when you're alone, there's a very good chance you'll meet things that*
>   *scare you right out of your pants.*
> *There are some, down the road between hither and yon, that can scare you so*
>   *much you won't want to go on.*
> *But on you will go, though the weather be foul.*
> *On you will go though your enemies prowl.*
> *Onward and up many a frightening creek, though your arms*
>   *may get sore and your sneakers may leak.*
> *On and on you will hike.*
> *And I know you'll hike far and face up to your problems whatever they are.*

Although the journey he describes is a metaphor for coming of age, Dr. Seuss could well be talking about the adolescent solo experience. A solo can reflect some of the issues and challenges adolescents deal with every day, and present difficulties and challenges that might at times seem insurmountable. I believe adolescents can cope with many of life's difficulties and challenges — some better than others — and that they have the potential to face up to problems whatever they are. During the solo experience adolescents are often challenged to draw upon personal resources, but with far more loneliness, fear, anxiety, and boredom than the traditional literature on solo suggests. For some adolescents, longer solos are not the romantic, spiritual-growth opportunities idealized by many adults but rather trials to be endured. There is a wealth of literature suggesting the many spiritual, existential, emotional, philosophical, interpersonal, and intrapersonal virtues of nature-based solitude. Collectively, outdoor education literature is upbeat and positive about the solo experience and generalizes solo as something of a universal experience for children, adolescents, and adults alike. Most writing and research reports on solo are centered on the experiences of adults, but I believe that the solo experiences of adolescents are different. I am intrigued by the observed gap between stated objectives for solo and the immense variety of student responses. A solo experience is always unique; I have not met two students who have had an identical experience. Therefore I am fascinated by the desire of some solo facilitators to draw collective meaning from what is essentially an individual experience.

Facilitating a multi-day solo that adequately protects the physical, cultural, and emotional safety of participants presents significant challenges. There are issues with respect to the assessment of student readiness for solo, the challenge of monitoring and communicating with students during solo, student basic living preparation, and safeguarding female participants (Kelk, 1994). The enormity of the early teenage years must be acknowledged, as must the fact that while solo can be immensely powerful for some, it can be inappropriate for others. Literature rarely points out the potential for things to go wrong during solo, nor does it acknowledge the difficulties and problems that participants or staff may face. A number of extended-duration programs regard solo as downtime for leaders — an opportunity for staff as well as students to experience a time-out. Yet discussions with solo facilitators reveal that things can and do go wrong, and that good programs need to keep a vigilant — while distant — eye on their students.

I believe that adolescents present special challenges for the solo facilitator. I question the sensibility of developing any solo program that is based on the "it worked for me, so it should work for them" premise. Some leaders appear uncertain as to why solo is part of their program beyond an historic rationale, and there are others who offer solo to adolescents primarily as a character-building exercise. I fear that placing adolescents "out there" under the assumption that they will be better people for the experience has risks of emotional and physical harm. I fear that insufficient attention is given to planning and preparation for the solo in some programs, and this includes a lack of adequate preparation of the leaders as well as the participants. Interestingly, longer term residential programs avoid many of these issues through program sequencing and by devoting time to adequately preparing and getting to know their students in advance of solo.

A common thread across the solo programs I have visited is the passion of the educators and instructors who facilitate solos and their collective tendency to wax eloquently when asked about the virtues of solo time. They have an intuitive belief in the power of soloing that cannot be discounted, despite the dearth of adolescent-specific nature-based solo research. I have enjoyed many wonderful solo stories passed on from leaders, and it is readily apparent that in their eyes something special occurs during solo. I believe we can draw from practitioners' writings to provide fascinating glimpses of what is in store for the adolescent soloist.

John Kelk is one such impassioned teacher. In his book *Soloing: Perspectives in Environmental Education*, Kelk presents insights he has gained through outdoor education experiences while facilitating solo for adolescent school students in southern New

Zealand. He promotes soloing as "one of the greatest experiences that teachers can give their students" (1994, p. 1). He advocates that being alone in nature is profound and has the capacity to teach self-reliance and address issues of awareness of self, others, and nature. Kelk promotes integrating solo into a number of curriculum areas and suggests that solo can be adapted to suit any student age or maturity level.

Colin Mortlock (1998) similarly attributes wide-ranging virtues to the wilderness solo, a perspective that comes from his experience as facilitator of hundreds of solo experiences for young adults in the United Kingdom over the past 25 years. He suggests that the potential benefit of solo comes from the contrast between solo and everyday realities and regards solo as a more intensive experience than wilderness camping. Mortlock recognizes that solo also has the potential to lead to increased self-centeredness, inflated ego, and even arrogance on the part of the soloist. He acknowledges the potential for the solo going physically and psychologically wrong, and suggests that students need to be mentally stable and personally motivated to undertake a solo.

Mortlock makes the important distinction between the expectancies and outcomes of *static* versus *dynamic* solos. The dynamic solo journey is more concerned with improving self-confidence, self-respect, and self-reliance, while the static solo is more about providing time and space for reflection and experiencing a special natural place. For Mortlock, the static environmental solo presents opportunities for connecting young adults to natural processes, which when properly reflected upon can lead a person to the realization of being intimately connected to nature. Most of the adolescent solos I have observed have been static and have emphasized a goal of re-connection with nature. Yet two women writer/practitioners (Harbott, 2001; Angell, 1994) are adamant that we should not discount the enhancement of self via a static experience, an opinion with which I concur.

In *The Bliss of Solitude*, Richard Gibbens (1991) utilizes sections of prose and poetry to craft an historic overview of solitude as a training or educational endeavor. Many of the examples presented highlight the moral, philosophical, and mystical/religious benefits of solo. He identifies the profound opportunities solo presents for discovering a oneness with the natural world and for better understanding the interrelatedness of all natural beings (including humans). Gibbens states that if solo is to be taken seriously as a training technique or educational activity, then it needs to be "far more than a self-indulgent or escapist interlude" (p. 22). He suggests the need for carefully crafted experiences, with participants well supported with pre-solo training and post-experience debriefing at an individual level. Like Mortlock, Gibbens is critical of the solo journey or expedition for young people, and believes that traveling alone can intensify fears. He advocates static solos where "physical and mental stillness provides the shelter in which the seeds of insight can grow" (p. 23). Unfortunately Gibbens, like most other writers, focuses on the bliss associated with solitude and draws heavily from adult solo insights. Like each of the practitioners mentioned above, he does not discuss in any depth many of the core issues with which typical adolescents struggle — boredom, anxiety, fear, and loneliness.

Solitude or Loneliness?

All beings need, deeply, the company of their kind. But as it takes darkness to understand the light, it takes solitude to realize how fundamental that need is.
(Kohak, 1987, pp. 35–36)

Larson (1997) reports that adolescents spend upward of 25% of their waking hours alone. Combine this alone time with sleeping alone time, which Buchholz (1997) regards as the ultimate solitude, and it is evident that western adolescents spend a lot of time in relative solitude. The meaning adolescents construct from time alone is deeply embedded within the associated norms and societal expectations of their culture. For example, the role of solitude in First Nation/Indigenous cultures is often emphasized in rites of passage for young people entering adulthood (e.g., the Native American Vision Quest and the Australian Aboriginal Walkabout). On the other end of the spectrum, modern day Westerners seem to place a less positive emphasis on solitude for our young people; being alone is rarely perceived as a desirable state or a healthy way of life (Suedfeld, 1982; Bucholz & Catton, 1999). Extended periods of time alone typically meet with social ("adult") questioning, if not censure. Associations are inferred between adolescent solitary time and unnecessary risk taking or antisocial pursuits for young people (Bucholz, 1997). Westerners have also integrated into the lives of our young various forms of solitude as punishment: Being sent to one's room, given time-out in a corner, or being otherwise isolated are regular forms of discipline in childhood. When the offenses grow serious, these minor time-outs can translate into solitary confinement in prisons. Thus, for some individuals, a solo might be perceived negatively and not as a gift or an opportunity for personal growth. Kohak challenges us to remedy such negative perceptions of solitude:

For most of us, even to think of solitude as a gift requires an effort. We fear solitude no less than we fear darkness, and have striven no less strenuously to banish it from our lives. We are convinced that truth is in communication.
(1984, p. 34)

Larson (1997) infers that solitude for adolescents is a more lonely experience than solitude for adults, which my own solo investigations corroborate. From early to late adolescence there is a developing affinity for solitude (Larson, 1997; Marcoen & Goossens, 1993) that is perhaps related to more advanced reasoning skills and a developing sense of self-identity. It is apparent, however, that adolescents' emotional states tend to be more negative during solitude than when they are with others, and that teenagers are more likely to feel lonely, weak, and unhappy when on their own. The prescription of a solo experience for adolescents might well bring about feelings of loneliness and not pure joy, especially if the experience is not freely chosen.

Teenagers tend to feel positively about themselves after freely chosen solitude experiences, but during their actual time alone they often experience unhappiness, weakness, and loneliness (Larson, 1997). Larson suggests that the adolescent solitude experience is in considerable contradiction to the "poetic image of healthy solitude as a blissful transcendental state" (p. 91). This is confirmed by Buchholz and Catton (1999) in their exhaustive analysis of the literature on aloneness and loneliness for young people. Despite their lengthy discussion on the virtues of constructive solitude, they reluctantly admit that alone time is not construed positively by many adolescents.

Researchers who have examined student reports of their experiences with time alone suggest that loneliness is an important issue. Loneliness and the fear of loneliness have also emerged as prominent themes in my studies of adolescent nature-based solos. Pre-solo interviews have revealed that most adolescents anticipate the possibility of feeling lonely as very real and potentially scary. In post-solo interviews, actual moments of loneliness were reported, as students told of the intense desire to meet up with others, lengthy periods of sadness and melancholy, conversations held aloud with self, and yelling out to try to attract conversation from other soloists. Student debriefings also have revealed that the rate of self-reported departure from one's solo site is significantly higher than the perception held by the staff. Adolescents do wander from their solo sites, and although boredom may be the primary catalyst, the desire to connect with others because of loneliness also comes up as an impetus.

Post-solo interviews have suggested that for many adolescents the pre-solo fear of loneliness was greater than the loneliness actually experienced during solo. In fact, some soloists did not experience any feelings of loneliness despite initial apprehensions. One of the students interviewed told of utilizing a meditation mantra to stay positive and focused on the tasks set for the solo. Previous experience with the mantra was an important precursor to its success, and this suggests that similar *centering* tasks and strategies might prove effective if integrated into the preparation phase of a solo. At the other extreme, one individual came to the conclusion that his solo site was inhabited by the ghost of his grandmother. It played upon his mind to the point that he left his solo site and returned to the safety of the outdoor center after less than a full day of solitude.

Solitude as Anxiety and Fear

As determined from post-solo interviews and conversations, New Zealand adolescent soloists typically under-reported their anxieties and fears prior to solo. The completion of the solo generally fostered a more relaxed (and perhaps relieved) openness with the sharing of information and stories. Post-solo there was acknowledgment of significantly more apprehension and fearfulness than revealed in pre-solo conversations. Perceptive staff who lead solo experiences mentioned that most students are far more scared than they let on. In two instances I have witnessed from afar the end result of physical skirmishes between young males prior to solo, situations their outdoor education teachers told me they thought reflected pre-solo apprehensions.

Students experience many moments of apprehension and fear leading up to their solos — fear of being attacked, fear of not knowing what will happen to them or how they might cope, fear of what others will think of them if they return early, and fear of failing the solo challenge and letting either the program leaders or themselves down. During solo there were also anxieties (acknowledged immediately afterward) regarding the adequacy of shelters in relation to wet weather conditions and the real likelihood of clothes and sleeping bags getting wet. There were many reported increases in heart rate and serious fears about personal safety in relation to sounds heard outside their shelter. There were also a number of significant reports of not feeling comfortable with the long dark nights. In numerous incidences I observed students returning early from their solo, reporting fear of the dark or strangers as contributing factors in their decision-making.

My interviews and observations immediately after solo provided brief glimpses and insights into the students' experience. They reflected a joy in reuniting with peers, and there was communal celebration about surviving the experience. This period saw the commencement of storytelling, with the stories becoming more exaggerated with time. Buccholz and Catton (1999) promote one of the important virtues of alone time as nurturing and strengthening relationships with others. Every soloist I interviewed acknowledged spending time thinking about peers and family during solo. When students returned from the solo, chatter was loud, smiles abounded, and stories were swapped. While the students were clearly excited to reconnect with their peers, I believe this intense celebratory "noise" can be attributed more to the relief of surviving the experience and having successfully coped with inward apprehensions than to reconnecting with peers.

Interviews conducted after the emotional highs of return had subsided but within a 24-hour period provided even deeper insight into the issues of fear and apprehension for soloists. I have categorized these fears into two main categories: (a) fears of the bush/nature/others, (b) fears of the unknown within and of not being able to cope with the challenge of being alone.

Fear of the bush and the creatures within it (including humans) was often very real, which is surprising in that the New Zealand bush is not inhabited by creatures that might be regarded as harmful in other places (e.g., there are no bears, tigers, snakes, or poisonous spiders). Some reported fears of being attacked by wild pigs and opossums. Jokes about lost and armed humans supposedly living in the bush were often shared in carefully veiled jest among the student collective but were taken as more real by some individuals. Fears of the bush also centered on wet and cold weather and their implications for personal comfort. A couple of soloists feared visits from others within their group, and pre-solo skirmishes and long-standing issues between some students brought out concerns for personal safety. While there has been little mention in solo literature of *stranger danger* (people from outside the adventure group) or *insider danger* (people within the solo group), I found this the most common concern for female soloists. Despite the potential remoteness of a solo site, it seems that adolescents cannot completely leave behind the fear of violence.

Lengthy solitude is not something most adolescents have experienced, so solo can bring forth internal feelings of inadequacy or a fear of not being able to cope. Most soloists seem to ponder how they might cope with being alone, and for some this is the biggest challenge of solo. Many students admitted that they worried about dealing with boredom and the long hours of nothing to do. These fears diminished significantly during the solo experience.

Because of the many anxieties and fears of soloists, some suggest that solo may be an inappropriate activity for certain students, in particular for at-risk or juvenile offenders (Gibbens, 1991; Mortlock, 1998). It has also been suggested that solos are not usually relevant for action-oriented or hyperactive youth, for whom responses to boredom often include departure from the solo site (McIntosh, 1989).

Solitude as Boredom

Adolescents are prone to boredom, and on solo this appears to be accentuated. Students interviewed defined boredom in different ways, including, "not using hands," "being quiet or still," "having nothing to do," and "frustration or annoyance at not having anything to do." Many adolescents do not have the ability to use their time alone adequately or constructively. Solo is typically viewed as a massive contrast to other outdoor educational activities, and the lack of activity, the stillness, and the lack of structure presents an interesting challenge for young people.

Some soloists appear uncomfortable with themselves, which results in a loss of identity when one is removed from the social and physical contexts that shape identity. It has been suggested that one of the constructive benefits of solitude is to stimulate people to self-examination, self-discovery, and self-reconstruction via introspective reflection. This may not be possible for adolescents who are typically without the skills to adequately facilitate their own self-examination, self-discovery, and reconstruction, although there are exceptions. Instead boredom results because their thought processes remain random, rather than focusing in a linear fashion on one or more aspects of self.

There is potential for the solo to lead to deep thinking if there is appropriate reflective skill-building prior to the solo. Educators have an important empowerment role in this regard. Self-reflective adolescents can achieve personal growth gains. It has been reported that adolescents who have reasoning skills that allow for deeper cognitive attention to the self may receive better gains from solo than pre-adolescents (Larson, 1997).

My investigations highlight that adolescents on solo do not spend much time completing written reflections, even when such challenges are given to them (e.g., writing a letter to self, journal writing, or specific reflective writing assignments, such as reflections on the course, personal goals, poems, or a listing of virtues of others). There are exceptions. One school incorporated reflective writing and journal work throughout all of its outdoor course elements, which appeared to enhance student literacy. Some student solo writings are without doubt profound and thoughtful, although most are typically developed *after* the students experience solo. Very few of the students I interviewed reported spending any serious time with the written reflection tasks that had been assigned. Perhaps writing assignments do not generally work to counter boredom for the adolescent soloist.

Most soloists reported personal strategies for passing the time. Sleep is a common strategy, with students reporting sleeping some 40% to 50% of their solo time (by post-solo recollection) and lying in sleeping bags awake for another 15% to 20% of the time. In one instance a student overslept beyond his solo endpoint, and when carefully awakened by a staff member he yelled and lashed out in a direct fear or fright response. He reported sleeping for almost his entire solo!

Other interviewees told me about novel approaches to handling boredom, including meditating to keep positive and repeating a line of curses to oneself. Cognitive activities, however, were not a strategy typically used to counter anxiety and fear. On average, students reported spending less time working on the reflective tasks set for them than the time they spent constructing their shelter from basic materials. These adolescent soloists spent more time actively doing things than in introspective reflection.

For some individuals the nature-based solo is perceived and accepted negatively despite the best briefing intentions of program leaders. Some adolescents cannot get beyond the socio-historical perception of solitude as punishment. They appear confused about what they should do on solo and why they might be doing it. The typical response of these individuals is to move away from their solo site.

My interview with a team of staff who facilitate solos for at-risk youth highlighted the frequency of participants leaving solo sites (self-reported) as being significantly higher than for standard groups. The frequency was higher than that perceived by staff until the issue was recognized and subsequently more closely supervised. Once they focused on this phenomena, they were surprised at the number of soloists who left their solo sites. As I interviewed that staff, they shared stories of soloists wandering miles from their sites. On one occasion, a soloist broke into a holiday home to ultimately consume alcohol. The potential negative ramifications were many: The public perception of wayward youth wandering about unaccompanied put the image and reputation of the program at risk. It was obvious that individuals moving from their solo sites presented risks to other soloists and to members of the surrounding community, especially when an individual might be predisposed toward petty crime or violence. These leaders soon determined that boredom was a significant issue for these youth and reacted by shortening the solo component and more closely monitoring the sites.

My interviews also provided opportunities for leaders, especially women, to acknowledge apprehensions regarding physical safety while undertaking routine solo welfare checks. I believe that facilitating the solo experience for at-risk youth or adolescent juvenile offenders is especially problematic. Carefully planning and managing appears essential not only in curbing the fears of participants and maximizing their benefits but also in protecting the safety of program and staff.

Breaking the rules is common among adolescent soloists, and this also seems to be linked to boredom. All multi-day static solos seem to have a list of rules for soloists that include prohibitions such as: No Tree Climbing, No Visiting Others, No Fires, No Candles, No Killing Living Trees, No Knives, No Swimming, Sunbathe Only If You Have Sunblock On, No Books Except Journals, No Watches. These rules are set to limit physical injuries and ecological harm, and in many programs have come about as the result of prior incidents. Yet youthfulness is hard to keep in check, and there are wonderful stories of adventures climbing trees, creeping up on other soloists, and carving initials into rocks or trees. Beyond promoting self-responsibility and common sense, the solo facilitator is somewhat powerless to prevent violations of these rules.

Some leaders complicate their situation by presenting an excessive list of "do-nots." Perhaps an overview of consequences rather than merely stating these rules might work more effectively? Tree climbing, for example, was reported as a highlight experience of the solo for a number of youth interviewed. Students who had climbed trees felt that they took no excessive risks and that they looked after themselves more carefully because they were on their own. Breaking the rules in those instances may in fact paradoxically have enhanced self-reliance to some degree.

Managing Solo Emotional Safety

Determining the readiness of students for solo should be an important consideration for solo facilitators (Angell, 1994; Kelk, 1994; McIntosh, 1989). McIntosh is especially critical of institutionalized programs not assessing the needs of students and placing them in the woods without regard for their ability to achieve program objectives. He reports that while many solo programs have moved their emphasis from *survival* toward *personal reflection*, they still continue to challenge participants with minimalist equipment and far too little food.

Kelk (1994) acknowledges the need to screen potential soloists and to provide leaders with strategies to manage apprehensive, distressed, or harmful students. He suggests that personality-type information (e.g., from a Myers-Briggs personality test) can be invaluable for solo staff not familiar with the participants. Such screening may appear impractical for most outdoor programs, but it must be acknowledged that there is significant value in knowing the participants and judging their readiness for solo, especially because provided data may be insufficient. For example, standard medical forms may not provide information regarding particular fears of the dark nor a history of sleepwalking. Many of the educational solos I observed were facilitated by teachers who knew their students quite well. As a result, nervous or distressed students were placed near staff or base facilities and were subject to additional checks during their solo.

When placing students at solo sites, carefully considering who should be placed where is critical. In programs that operate in areas familiar to the students, some degree of choice typically is given to students when assigning solo sites. The final decision on placement, however, must be left to staff, and experienced solo facilitators carefully map out exactly who goes where in order to avoid unnecessary problems. For example, leaders who work with coed university students have reported couples getting together during solo. This potential also exists with adolescents on solo, as does the potential for sexual harassment by fellow soloists. Well-prepared solo leaders tend to know their students quite well, including the dynamics between individuals, and so can manage situations and fears appropriately. The most important strategy in this regard appears to be with the deliberate placement of students in particular sites, making sure to separate at-risk individuals.

In terms of placement, consideration must also be given to the likelihood of students leaving their solo sites and returning to the base camp. A clear and relatively safe pathway to facilitate this should be determined. Conversely, leaders who know their students have challenged apprehensive individuals by placing them at greater distance from a base to limit the likelihood of a return. This strategy, coupled with a routine of welfare checks, has proved sound. Of course, all students need to know where and to whom they should report if compelled to leave their solo sites. I have observed significant personal counseling interactions unfold in instances when students have returned to base camp. The counselor/leader is critical in supporting the student and can provide opportunities for discussing fears or issues before re-establishing the solo experience. This can be a valuable experience, even if the continuing solo is offered in a modified format.

In all of the solo programs I examined there was an expectation for students to complete various reflective challenges. For some students these tasks were a natural extension of their pre-solo work and they were empowered to accept the challenge. Other programs presented such reflective tasks without the pre-solo training necessary to cultivate reflection skills. It seems clear that in order to reflect well a student needs to be adequately fed, warm, dry, and emotionally stable. For some students the best place for a solo may be back at base camp. There, on their own, they may feel secure enough to commence the desired reflective tasks.

In terms of welfare check systems, there are numerous wonderful examples of nonverbal and no-contact forms of communication between soloists and leaders. One involves a signal system using various symbols to share information. If the soloist sets up a symbol suggesting that all is not well, then the leader moves in for closer observation and interaction. I believe leaders should check students frequently and, in most instances, a quick visual check is sufficient. Checking on students is especially important at the commencement of solo, during the first (or only) night, and during periods of inclement weather. Quality systems have staff armed with additional food supplies, materials for shelter repairs, dry sleeping bags, and first-aid supplies. Solo is certainly not a time for staff to rest!

Coming Home to Nature

The realities of loneliness, fear, anxiety, and boredom in solitude might suggest that the adolescent solo is not conducive to *coming home* to nature. The establishment of a framework for physical and emotional safety, coupled with pre-solo preparation for meaningful reflective practices, can transform potentially negative solo experiences into significant growth opportunities. A successful solo experience can lead the individual to recognize solitude as an essential element in life. Appropriate management of the solo situation, combined with attention to potential fears, phobias, and apprehensions, can assist individuals in countering boredom and instead focus both inside and outside of self.

With respect to connecting with nature on solo, Kaplan and Kaplan (2002) suggest that adolescence is a period in the life sequence where interest in natural phenomena and motivations for connections with nature wane. I do not know whether this is true in the New Zealand context, but I have found that most adolescents are indeed interested in nature and natural processes. Whatever the veracity of this statement or the extent to which all humans are somehow separated from nature, there needs to be significant preparatory work before students can engage deeply with their surroundings. I observed some outstanding programs that used a sequence of micro-solos with specific ecological observational and reflective tasks before embarking upon the big solo. Others ensured that participants could identify the special features of at least one local tree and bird prior to solo. I also observed students setting off on solo armed with sheets for plant, animal, and bird identification, and with reflective and contemplative nature task sheets mounted on their clipboards.

The "let the mountains speak for themselves" (James, 1980) debate still exists with respect to the potential connection of adolescent soloists to their solo site. My observations and experiences tell me that adolescents need to be jolted out of potential solo boredom in order to connect with nature. Students going on solo need to feel safe, warm, and comfortable, and also need to hold a sense of nature awareness and appreciation. The greatest potentials of the adolescent solo must surely be a coming home to, and an understanding of, nature and a recognition of self as a part of natural processes surrounding the solo site. Solo facilitators can support adolescents in this regard — by exciting them to take note of that rainbow, the color and veins of that leaf, listening for the first birdsong of the morning, and reading the patterns of the stars. Moving students to then engage in these endeavors on their own during solo is a challenge, though an exciting one. As Paul discovered in *Power of Joy*, the journey from childhood toward adulthood need not be a lonely one — for there are rich rewards when one is intimate with the spirit of local nature.

References

Angell, J. (1994). The wilderness solo: An empowering growth experience for women. In E. Cole, E. Erdman & E. Rothblum (Eds.), *Wilderness therapy for women: The power of adventure* (pp. 85–99). New York: Hawthorn Press.

Buchholz, E., & Catton, R. (1999). Adolescents' perceptions of aloneness and loneliness. *Adolescence, 34*(133), 203–213.

Buchholz, E. (1997). *The call of solitude: Alonetime in a world of attachment.* New York: Simon & Schuster.

Gibbens, R. (1991). The bliss of solitude. *Journal of Adventure Education and Outdoor Leadership, 8*(1), 21–23.

Harbott, L. (2001). *Wilderness solitude.* Unpublished manuscript, University of Otago.

Hilliard, N. (1965). *Power of joy.* London: Michael Joseph Ltd.

James, T. (1980). *Can the mountains speak for themselves?* Retrieved October 2003, from www.wilderdom.com/facilitation/Mountains.html

Kaplan, R., & Kaplan, S. (2002). Adolescents and the natural environment: A time out? In P. J. H. S. Kellert. (Ed.), *Children and nature.* London: The MIT Press.

Kelk, J. (1994). *Soloing: Perspectives in environmental education 1.* Invercargill: Southland Education Centre: Te Whare o te Matauranga o Murihiku.

Kohak, E. (1984). *The embers and the stars: A philosophical inquiry into the moral sense of nature.* London: The University of Chicago Press.

Larson, R. W. (1997). The emergence of solitude as a constructive domain of experience in early adolescence. *Child Development, 68*(1), 80–93.

Marcoen, A., & Goossens, L. (1993). Loneliness, attitude towards aloneness, and solitude: Age differences and developmental significance during adolescence. In S. Jackson & H. Rodriguez-Tome (Eds.), *Adolescence and its social worlds.* Hove (UK): Lawrence Erlbaum Associates.

McIntosh, H. (1989). Re-thinking the solo experience. *The Journal of Experiential Education, 12*(3), 28–32.

Mortlock, C. (1998). *Solos: A discussion paper.* Paper presented at the Ara Matauranga: 3rd National Outdoor Education Conference Proceedings, Auckland.

Suedfeld, P. Aloneness as a healing experience. In L. A. Peplau & D. Perlman (Eds.), *Loneliness: A sourcebook of current theory, research and therapy* (pp. 54–67). New York: John Wiley & Sons.

Seuss, Dr. (1990). *Oh, the places you'll go!* New York: Random House.

CHAPTER 10

The Use of Solos in Canadian College and University Outdoor Education and Recreation Programs

By Tom Potter & Tim O'Connell

The first great thing is to find yourself and for that you need solitude and contemplation ... or at least sometimes. I tell you, deliverance will not come from the noisy centres of civilization. It will come from lonely places.

(Nansen, 1988, p. 3)

Canadian college and university outdoor educators generally search for wild nature (an area of few human constructs) within which they can educate their students, and in so doing expose them to the ways of Canada's well-storied landscapes — the landscapes from which tales of Canadian exploration and settlement begin. They expose students to environments where many of the Canadian icons originate — "the beaver, the canoe, the loon, the snowshoe, the majestic white pine, the open sublime space, the winter stillness" (Potter & Henderson, 2004, p. 85). It is here, in wild spaces, that Canadian outdoor educators strive to help the land echo with personal experience. They challenge students to find a personal and collective adventure — a real and metaphoric journey in pursuit of intrapersonal and interpersonal growth, and a re-connection with wild nature. Whether short or long term, experiences in the outdoors attempt to remove students from many of the human cultural constructs found in everyday life, consequently inviting them to be more open to experience and value the *wild* in their lives (Potter & Henderson, 2004).

One of the classic ways for outdoor programs to stimulate students' personal growth and learning is to facilitate experiences of solitude. The solo experience with nature can be magical and powerful. There is a long history of the use of solo experiences in Canadian college and university outdoor education and recreation (OE&R) programs. Our colleagues in outdoor-related programs across Canada share a strong belief in the value of solo as an educational activity.

This paper will provide a brief overview of OE&R programs at colleges and universities across Canada that incorporate solo experiences into their curricula. We will explore why and how solo is used, as well as the practice's intended outcomes and problems. A case study on the use of solo in our own post-secondary outdoor recreation program will then be presented, and we will conclude with visions for the future regarding the value and use of solo in Canadian academia.

In Canada, there are some three- and four-year OE&R university programs that put a more extensive curricular focus on theoretical foundations, and there are also many OE&R college programs of two-year duration that provide students with a broad range of theory and practice. In response to the popularity of nature-based and adventure-based tourism, many colleges have expanded OE&R offerings to include ecotourism credits. In the last five years, several Canadian colleges have opened new programs; unfortunately, during this same period, at least two foundational degree programs at the university level have closed (Potter & Henderson, 2004).

Although most Canadian OE&R programs use modern equipment for their outdoor activities, many still strive to incorporate traditional methods, historic equipment, and camp crafts in order to reconnect students to Canadian heritage and bring them closer (cognitively and spiritually) to the land (Potter & Henderson, 2004).

Theory and Practice of Solos in the Canadian Context

As varied as the OE&R programs are in colleges and universities across Canada, so too are the ways in which solo experiences are implemented. How a program embraces the solo experience is always impacted by that program's design and goals. In addition, the beliefs and experiences of faculty and field instructors at each institution affect the unfolding of the program. In an effort to uncover the diversity of approaches to using solo, we contacted colleagues at six colleges and universities across Canada that offer courses in OE&R.

We asked them if they use solo in their programs and, if so, to respond to a number of questions designed to help us understand, compare, and contrast the individual, programmatic, and curricular aspects of the solo experience. The questions were:

1. Why do you use solo?

2. What are the intended outcomes of solo in your program?

   a. How do you implement the solo experience?

   b. What are the preparation and the processing/debriefing like?

3. In what specific courses and year(s) do you use solo?

   a. What problems or drawbacks to using solo have you encountered?

   b. Do you have any thoughts on minimizing or eliminating these problems?

Our survey provided the information that we summarize and discuss in this paper. We extend thanks to Morten Asfeldt (Augustana University College), T.A. Loeffler (Memorial University of Newfoundland), Stephen Ritchie and Roger Couture (Laurentian University), Paul Lehmann (Canadian University College), Ken Wylie (University of the Cariboo), and Bob Henderson (McMaster University), who were generous with their time and contributed their experience regarding solo.

The survey confirmed our prior knowledge that Canadian colleges and universities use solo in a variety of formats and lengths, as well as a gamut of expected curricular outcomes and impacts.

Formats range from the impromptu *teachable moment* style of solo, as in 30 minutes of assigned solitude during hikes or campouts, to more formalized two- and three-day traditional solo experiences. In Laurentian University's Outdoor Adventure Leadership Program, students are required to complete a number of expeditions, and some students choose to complete one or more of these in solo. Other colleagues reported that they often assign students to solo sites (special places) for some of their regular hour-long classes. In any case, in the context of field courses, solos may last from a few hours to a few days.

From a curricular standpoint, solo is used in anywhere from first-year (freshman) to fourth-year (senior) courses. We also found that solo is used in a variety of courses. For example: (a) Introduction to Outdoor Recreation and Education (School of Human Kinetics and Recreation, Memorial University, Newfoundland); (b) Adventure Programming (School of Human Kinetics and Recreation, Memorial University, Newfoundland); (c) Natural History (University College of the Cariboo); (d) Wilderness Survival (Laurentian University); (e) Stress and Leisure (Department of Outdoor Pursuits, Canadian University College); and (f) Practicum Seminar Leadership (Department of Outdoor Pursuits, Canadian University College).

On the practical side, some Canadian OE&R programs use solo as an opportunity for students to rehearse survival skills in real-life situations. Solo provides opportunities to hone basic outdoor skills such as shelter construction, fire starting, collection and preparation of food and water, dressing for changing environmental conditions, orienteering, navigation, route planning, and general logistics. The significance of traditional skills and equipment can be emphasized through solo camping, and this can bring students to a keen appreciation of their Canadian heritage.

Our colleagues noted that they use solo at different points during a program. Some offer it at the beginning, as a means of "cleansing the mind" (B. Henderson, personal communication, May 7, 2004). Some use it in the middle, to stimulate special growth and learning, and still others see value in implementing solo near the end of a course or program sequence to bring closure to the experience. No matter when a solo is conducted, the process of preparing mentally and physically for what happens is important. Appropriate preparation can lead to greater understanding of what has happened after solo is finished.

By far the most commonly cited motivation for implementing solo experiences is the reflective component of the exercise.

> *Solo, quiet time apart from others, can offer the most powerful form of private reflection. Severed from external constraints, habitual patterns and usual significant others, the immersion into a novel, refreshing environment can provide treasured opportunities for introspection.... For many, the mini-solo experience is an opportunity to slow down and simply notice, perhaps for the first time, the wonders of nature. For others, this time allows one to reflect upon the trip, the environment, oneself and others.*
>
> (Potter, 1992, p. 96)

Reflection, especially in solitude, is a difficult task for many people in Western society. The frantic pace of our everyday lives and the value that Western society ascribes to this *busyness* seldom encourage us to slow down and invite contemplation. Relaxation in daily routine is too often sought through passive entertainment. The television is an excellent example of a convenient time filler that poses a temporary escape from everyday life — for some, the TV is a part of everyday life. Young people spend much of their time in the presence of others (Larson, 1990), and many have become quite reliant on this companionship. Solitude can be a frightening thought to them.

However, being alone on a solo experience offers students the opportunity to "take a break" from others, from the rigor of an intensive outdoor adventure, and from the need to maintain their public persona. As noted by Larson, "The freedom from social regulation provided by solitude presents an opportunity to concentrate deeply and feel less self-conscious" (1990, p. 176). The potency of education through the wilderness solo lies in the temporary severance from modern conveniences and other people. Dislodged from everyday life distractions, students on solo in the wilderness are presented with an incredible opportunity for reflection, self-discovery, and connection with the natural world.

Unfortunately, many teachers and students fail to fully grasp the power of this educational opportunity. Fortunately, our colleagues do understand and successfully use solo to teach their students to value time for reflection, for *re-acclimatizing* with the natural world, and for making connections between the theoretical learning that occurs in the traditional classroom and the reality of lived experience.

Reflection may take different forms during the solo experience. Some Canadian university and college educators told us that they require their students to write journals to record observations, perceptions, interpretations, thoughts and feelings. In fact, the task of journal writing is sometimes considered to be a solo experience in itself; one colleague notes, "The students have to become quite introspective in order to complete a high-quality logbook entry" (S. Ritchie, personal communication, February 20, 2004). Journaling on solo can also be used as a means of encouraging "spiritual connectedness" (P. Lehmann, personal communication, May 6, 2004) and to "re-establish a sense of power in the Natural World" (K. Wylie, personal communication, April 28, 2004).

As diverse as the reasons for using solo are, so too are the expected outcomes from the solo experience. When polled about what these outcomes might be, our contemporaries overwhelmingly indicated self-learning and personal understanding as two key results of a solo. Not only are students expected to recognize what they have learned, but it is hoped that the solo germinates the desire to act on that knowledge in the future. Additional outcomes include problem-solving, organization of thoughts, thinking about the future, completion of a novel activity, and a renewed sense of place. Solo also provides a chance for relaxation — "taking a nap in the sun," (B. Henderson, personal communication, May 7, 2004), and relieving stress. Furthermore, many students will use solo with their own clients and students, so they are expected to learn through personal experience about the mechanics and risk management aspects of conducting solo, the *helpfulness* of solo, and the possible negative aspects of solo.

Our colleagues employ solo in a spectrum of styles, from the highly planned and organized to the spontaneous and flexible. Whatever mode of solo they use, these educators share a basic framework in their approach to implementing solo experiences. All advocate *framing* and information-sharing before the solo, and some sort of debriefing after the solo. The Department of Outdoor Pursuits at Canadian University College in Lacombe, Alberta, provides a good example of a highly organized solo program. Their one-hour and three- to four-day solo experiences include the following components:

1. pre-solo lectures and readings on meditation, and on fasting if that is to be part of the experience

2. pre-solo discussion of the rules and parameters of the experience and the meaningfulness of solitude

3. pre-solo instruction on the use of a flagging system for communication

4. plans for limited use of supplies and equipment

5. preparation for leaving the solo site and the pick-up by staff

6. leader preparation for risk management and procedures for intervention if necessary

7. post-solo debriefing of individual students before they rejoin the group, as well as group debriefing experiences

8. post-solo care and choice of food eaten at the end of solo by those who have fasted

(P. Lehmann, personal communication, May 6, 2004)

Other examples include the Program in Outdoor Adventure Leadership at Laurentian University (Sudbury, Ontario), which requires logbooks be completed in every activity course. The logbooks are read and evaluated by faculty. Students in the Adventure Programs Department at the University College of the Cariboo (Kamloops, British Columbia) must plan and execute their own two-day solo. They must give instructors a route plan before their solo trek, and are required to write about the experience in their journal. Students in the Department of Kinesiology at McMaster University (Hamilton, Ontario) reflect on their experiences through journal writing as well. Most of our colleagues note that they often use solo spontaneously along a hiking route and have found the practice quite successful.

We asked our colleagues about the problems, barriers, and drawbacks of using solo with their students. A common response was that many students are unsure of the value of solitude and are often reluctant to participate. One colleague remarked that many students initially perceive the solo as "hokey [sic]," but that many of those students still have "valuable and worthwhile experiences" (K. Wylie, personal communication, April 28, 2004). This confirms our own experience with the students' negative reaction to the process of reflection in general. Many students feel that the value of processing or debriefing is overrated, and that they spend too much time engaged in dialogue and interactional discussions designed to elicit new perspectives and learning. Then, with time and experience, most of those students come to truly appreciate (and demand) time for both group processing and solitude.

Other barriers to solo's effectiveness noted by our colleagues included the lack of time to conduct longer experiences of solitude, the interference of inclement weather, problems with wildlife, conflicts with hunters, general safety of the soloists, medical conditions (e.g., diabetes, hypoglycemia), and the absence of appropriate locations. All of our colleagues recognize these barriers and drawbacks, but they continue to confront and overcome them because they firmly believe in the positive benefits of solo. They have witnessed many students initiate solos with apprehension and negative attitudes and watched them emerge transformed, having had significant experiences despite negative pre-solo attitudes.

Our examination of solo use has revealed many common threads that connect the colorful mantle of Canadian OE&R academic programs. Students are encouraged to make the critical connection between theory and their lived experience through reflection. They are offered the opportunity to sense the power, beauty, and sublime character of nature, and are able to practice essential outdoor skills. They are afforded the chance to escape the pressure and drama of everyday urban life with others. Influenced by Canadian history, and sensing the connection of the land and personal experience, our colleagues take advantage of the multitude of benefits presented by solo experiences.

Case Study

To gain a perspective on how solo is typically used in Canadian college and university OE&R programs, we offer a case study based on our own program. The School of Outdoor Recreation, Parks, and Tourism (ORPT) at Lakehead University, in Thunder Bay, Ontario, is located on the north shore of Lake Superior.

> *Fairly isolated from other large urban centers, the area is rich in cultural heritage and surrounded by numerous protected areas, vast tracts of crown land (publicly owned), and an abundance of lakes, rivers, and picturesque natural features.... The program offers a variety of social sciences and professional preparation courses that emphasize the study of recreational activities and leisure pursuits related to and dependent upon the natural environment. The out-of-doors serves as a critical medium for the teaching, learning, and application of theories, knowledge, and skills.*
>
> (Cuthbertson, et al., 2003, p. 79)

The school of OPRT has about 350 students, and many of the school's courses involve experiential learning. Field trips vary in length from half-day and whole-day outings, to two- and three-day and even two-week excursions. The shorter trips frequently include 35-40 students who are divided into small groups of 7-10 people for experiential activities. Of the 46 courses offered over the four-year honors program, 21 (46%) involve some direct experience with the outdoors. (Cuthbertson, et al., 2003). Seven or eight of those courses sometimes involve solo experiences. Courses in which students spend solo time in the wilderness include: Environmental Issues; Outdoor Skills and Theory I & II; Ecological Literacy; Field Explorations, Advanced Outdoor Adventure Leadership; and Therapeutic Recreation and Adventure Therapy.

While the School of ORPT would seem a prime venue for the extensive implementation of solo, this is not the case. In most of these courses, solo is used to a limited degree, contingent on student numbers, student interest, available time, available solo sites, and environmental conditions. An influential factor in determining how much solo is used is the personal experience of both faculty and staff with solo, and the general value they place on solitude as a teaching methodology. If leaders do not have personal experience with solo, they usually don't advocate its use for their students.

All of the aforementioned courses use experiential learning techniques in which educators purposefully engage with students in direct experience and focused reflection in order to increase knowledge, clarify values, and develop skills (Association for Experiential Education, n.d.). According to Sugerman, Doherty, Garvey, and Gass (2000), learning from experience is dependent on integrating the experience with reflection. In the School of ORPT, solo serves as one of the several methodologies used to foster reflection. A description of how solo is used in the two Outdoor Skills and Theory courses of the School of ORPT follows.

Outdoor Skills and Theory I and II (OSAT) are required second-year courses that provide an experiential and theoretical basis for a wide variety of outdoor pursuits in autumn and winter environments. Weekly two-hour lectures are combined with one-, two-, and three-day field trips throughout the semester. Two sections of each course are taught each semester, with about 35 students in each. Both courses integrate a wide variety of activities. Stationary solos are used minimally in OSAT I and II to facilitate reflection, because large classes, the variety of activities offered, the demanding curriculum, and weekly excursions to fairly remote locations necessitate a heavy emphasis on logistics and risk management.

An additional complicating factor is location. On the north shore of Lake Superior, hiking trails are few and long. As a result, it is challenging to have multiple groups in the field simultaneously, and keep them moving and distant from one another. For example, a group on a three-day trip must travel a distance to complete a circular route; the use of solo for more than 30 minutes would most likely compromise a desirable route. The staff must make the decision to balance solo opportunities with shorter routes, or sacrifice the traditional solo to travel longer, more desirable routes. In meeting the objectives of OSAT I and II (e.g., navigation and leadership development), the opportunities for traditional stationary solo experiences are minimal. Therefore, rather than offering traditional two- to four-day solos within this context, we focus on other types of reflective activities, such as group debriefing, journal writing, and other creative expressions of experiences. Groups on a two- to four-day hikes incorporate what we have come to consider *solos on the move*. This may involve a half-day exercise in which students navigate on their own with map and compass through challenging terrain, including dense broad forest and swamps. In this case the students are alone and must rely on their skills and intuition to successfully reach their destinations.

Another application of solo experiences involves students who are divided up and spread out to hike a marked trail on their own, with instructions that they should not converse with anyone until a specific destination is reached. This practice involves a semblance of solo even while the group is progressing to their destination.

Building on OSAT I and II is the two-week tandem wilderness canoe trip, Field Explorations I, a third-year course designed to foster opportunities in which students can learn and practice outdoor leadership. For many students, this course may be their first extended experience in close contact with wild nature. Within a specific framework, we offer students choices in designing their curriculum to meet their needs and interests. Examples of these choices include route selection, distance to be traveled, and personal and group objectives. Within this student-driven model, many groups choose to conduct solo experiences, some short, others lasting up to 24 hours.

Group commitment to the solo idea is necessary in order for a 24-hour solo to take place. Typically, these groups paddle more than 130 miles, so they must be meeting all timelines in order to take an entire day out of their paddling regime. On such trips, solos occur after students have been traveling for at least a week and have begun to feel more comfortable in the wilderness and to consider free-nature as home (Cuthbertson, et al., 2003). For these traveling groups, the hours leading up to the 24-hour solo bring great anticipation, nervousness, and a sense of true adventure.

For reasons of safety and convenience, the choice of location is critical. Typically, the instructor chooses the location with the students. This is in an area that is fairly controlled (such as on a small lake), and where students can be relatively close to one another, even while in solitude. One of the reported instructor highlights is watching students divide the required gear before the solo. There is much discussion and sorting when equipment and food are negotiated and the balance is cached. Frequently heard comments include: "You take the tent-fly and the pot, I'll take the pot lid and use an overturned canoe for shelter." Some students are noticeably nervous about the solo endeavor, while others are "chomping at the bit" to get going. Some wish to camp near peers, while others want to be more isolated.

The following day, post-solo, the students are usually excited by the whole experience. They have had a chance to rest, reflect on recent experiences, be introspective, ponder their futures, and think about what they will do when they return home. Some may have had several critical revelations or made important decisions about how they will change their life course. No matter what their attitude is upon completion of the solo, most students develop an appreciation for the experience.

Visions for the Future

Bombarded and distracted by technology, many young people are spending less time alone with their thoughts than previous generations did. In fact, as stated by Suzuki (2004), in our everyday life experiences "we now have to make an effort NOT to be in touch with other people" (p. A7). Two of the major benefits of the outdoor solo are that students may counter this modern trend by taking opportunities for soulful reflection and encouraging independence through outdoor skills. We believe that more training and awareness of solos by students and instructors will lead to solo becoming more mainstream in the post-secondary curriculum. Perhaps professionals in OE&R need to employ a *solo across the curriculum* approach, in which solo becomes an integral part of most courses throughout a degree program.

As the OE&R industry has grown increasingly aware of safety and risk management concerns, instructors should take heart when considering the use of solo. As with most outdoor activities, the actual risk associated with solo may be reduced through proper planning and execution. Experience has taught us that attention must be paid to both physical and psychological risk. Properly preparing students for the solo experience can prevent negative outcomes and enhance positive outcomes. At the very least, solo may be used as a way to encourage students to get in touch with their local environment. We are amazed that students are often unfamiliar with the natural and cultural history surrounding their institution at the end of their college or university tenure. Canadian outdoor educators strive to use their unique heritage and connection to the local land to create meaning and context for students. Solo presents a unique opportunity for students to reconnect (or connect for the first time) with the natural world in meaningful ways.

The required change of thinking about solo by college and university faculty can be facilitated by having more discussions and readings about the educational potentials of solo. Furthermore, we believe more research is needed on the pedagogical uses of solo and the methodologies teachers use to affect the most meaningful experiences through solo. We should explore alternate solo formats, such as urban experiences, or introducing photography, art, poetry, and song into the solo process.

We suggest that OE&R professionals offer more opportunities for solo experiences to their students. After all, capturing the magic of solo is not difficult. As Sigurd Olson reminds us:

> *Everyone needs such quiet times, some solitude to recoup his [sic] sense of*
> *perspective. One does not have to be in a canoe or in some remote wilderness.*
> *I find such times at night when I do much of my reading, but to me when*

> solitude is a part of wilderness it comes more surely and with greater meaning.
> Since the time when man often traveled alone, hunting and foraging, all this
> became part of him. It is easy to slip back into the ancient grooves of experience.
>
> (Olson, 1976, p. 34)

References

Association for Experiential Education. (n.d.). *What is experiential education?* Retrieved September 22, 2004, from http://www.aee2.org/customer/pages.php?pageid=47

Association for Experiential Education (2002). *Frequently asked questions: Experiential education.* Retrieved February 11, 2002 from http://www.aee.org/resources/faq.html#ee

Cuthbertson, B., Dyment, J., Curthoys, L., Potter, T. G., & O'Connell, T. (2003). Engaging Nature: A Canadian case study of learning in the outdoors. In H. Crimmel (Ed.), *Teaching in the field: Working with students in the outdoor classroom* (pp. 77–98). Salt Lake City: University of Utah Press.

Henderson, B., & Potter, T. G. (2001). Outdoor adventure education in Canada: Seeking the country way back in. *The Canadian Journal of Environmental Education, 6,* 225–242.

Larson, R. W. (1990). The solitary side of life: An examination of the time people spend alone from childhood to old age. *Developmental Review, 10,* 155–183.

Olson, S. (1976). *Reflections from the North Country.* New York: Alfred A. Knopf.

Potter, T. G. (1992). Large group and weekend outdoor experiences: Finding meaning — nurturing growth, pp. 91–98. In Glenda Hanna (Ed.). *Celebrating our tradition: Charting the future. Proceedings of the 20th International Conference of the Association for Experiential Education* (pp. 91–98). Banff, Alberta, October 8–11.

Potter, T. G., & Henderson, B. (2004). Canadian outdoor education: Hear the challenge — Learn the lessons. *The Journal of Adventure Education and Outdoor Learning.* 4(1), 69–78.

Sugerman, D. A., Doherty, K. L., Garvey, D. E., & Gass, M. A. (2000). *Reflective learning: Theory and practice.* Dubuque: Kendall/Hunt.

Suzuki, D. (2004, May 16). Harnessing the power of stuff. *The Chronicle Journal,* Thunder Bay, ON.

PART III

Leadership in Action

CHAPTER 11

Leadership and the
Wilderness Vision Quest

By Burke Miller

*Leadership is a sacred calling to make a life-enriching
difference in the world.*

(Cashman, 2003, p. ix)

Paul (all names are aliases) emerged from the stand of sage as the sun's early morning rays hit the floor of the canyon. His face had an expression of timeless peace mirrored by the towering red rock walls on either side of him. A gentle flood of emotion and gratitude rose to the surface as he set down his backpack, marking the completion of three days and nights alone in the Colorado canyon wilderness. As Paul spoke about his experience later that morning, he described being gradually permeated by a feeling of oneness with everything around him. At first the plants, soil, and insects annoyed him and set him on edge. But something changed on the second day. A fly landed on his arm, and instead of brushing it off, Paul got curious. Looking closely, he started to appreciate its beauty. He even decided to speak to it. And then what felt like a small miracle happened — the fly sat still and allowed Paul to stroke its delicate wings.

Paul's encounter with the fly was one of many experiences with life in the wilderness that altered his perspective, and thus his perception of things. This altering of perception is the heart of the vision quest. The term *vision quest* literally means a seeking for new vision — in other words, new perceptions or ways of seeing. But what does the vision quest and perception have to do with leadership? Actually, the correlation is striking. When we look closely at leadership, we find that perception is the very ground on which the leader walks. The decisions and actions of any executive leader are an outgrowth of his or her perceptions of self, others, the organization, the economic environment, and the future, and larger questions of human purpose and values.

Paul is one of a growing number of corporate and nonprofit leaders who come to the Spirit River Institute for an Executive Vision Quest. He is CEO of a multi-million dollar consulting company. Paul was called to the vision quest by a strong intuitive sense that making the leap to the next level — both for himself and for his company — would require a bold, fresh perspective. One of the hallmarks of a great leader is knowing there is a "next level" to move to and then seeking it. Paul had the humility to claim that, despite his success, there was room for growth, and he felt an imperative to grow. It is that hunger that led Paul to the vision quest.

The Executive Vision Quest is typically a three-month process designed to be both a catalyst for and an affirmation of growth into a new stage of life and leadership. It begins with six to eight weeks of one-on-one pre-solo coaching sessions to clarify what this next level of being is about and what attaining it requires. The solo usually involves three days and nights of camping in the wilderness with water but no food. After the solo, we continue one-on-one coaching to begin applying the insights and lessons from the solo experience to daily challenges.

The vision quest works on leaders and their perceptions. Time and nature, as experienced alone in the wilderness, are like huge hands massaging the soul and the mind, altering perception like a good massage therapist alters the condition of muscles. The solo experience massages several levels of being at once: (a) self-concept, (b) life orientation, (c) evocative relationship, and (d) strategic mastery. These are all critical aspects of world-class leadership.

Self-Concept

When we consider how we approach our activities, interact with people and make decisions, our behavior is largely based on who we know ourselves to be. This self-concept has a lot to do with our attitude as we live our lives. It can empower us as leaders. It can also get in our way. When we consciously develop our sense of self in alignment with our highest wisdom and deepest desires for ourselves and the world we influence, we create a powerful reservoir of personal qualities and attitudes. If we are alert, we can bring these aspects of character to whatever opportunities and challenges we face. Instead of merely reacting out of our old habits to events and people around us, we can consciously respond by being more of who we want to be.

The ability to consciously respond rather than habitually react is supported by a mature self-concept. This is not merely bravado or merely self-confidence. A mature sense of self combines humility with conviction. Jim Collins, in *Good to Great* (2001), believes this combination is what defines a "Level 5 leader." Leaders with a mature self-concept are respected and trusted for their authenticity, courage, and integrity. Their presence inspires people to bring more of their own strengths and passion to the work of an organization. The vision quest is a powerful tool for activating core aspects of a mature self-concept, namely values, purpose, and vision.

Values

Values are fundamental to leaders' sense of self — and to their impact on others. We all know leaders who don't seem to stand for anything in particular. It's hard to read them and to know whether we can safely align ourselves with them. Conversely, we know other leaders who express their values clearly and act on them. These are the leaders we trust, even when we don't always see eye to eye.

Taking a stand for values is different than taking a position on an issue. Positions are negotiable. Core values are not. Foundational values are the intangibles you must have in your life. Values are like beacons, calling us to the highest expression of ourselves. They are the intangibles, like love, fairness, honesty, connection, peace, or passion. They are the guideposts we know must be expressed to reach our potential in life — and leadership. Strip away the titles, achievements, frenetic activities, and material possessions that too often define the self, and we are left with values and the ways we live them. The vision quest experience strips away all the veneers of identity so we can see and be with what's at the core.

Tony is a vice president and marketing director for a multi-national corporation. On the second day of his vision quest, seven deer wandered very close to where he was sitting in an open meadow. He watched in awe for about an hour as they grazed, every once in a while looking up at him. The deer seemed to speak to him and welcome him into their midst. Tony had longed for more trust, a personal core value, in his business relationships, but had not been able to create it. His experience with the deer showed him a way to build trust in his life. The lesson came in the form of insights and, perhaps more importantly, in the form of an in-the-body experience of trust that he will never forget.

Tony took this vivid lesson in trust back to his leadership work. The image of the deer kept playing in his memory as he began making small changes in the way he related to others. Over time, he created an atmosphere of trust that was absent before. The memory of the deer is there to remind him when he forgets. The vision quest works this way. It is much more than a one-time experience. It becomes a living catalyst in the psyche of the leader.

Purpose

Why am I here? Who am I to be? What am I here to contribute? These are the kinds of questions that lead us to a sense of our core life purpose. When we know our unique reason for being, our knowing becomes a compass. Knowing our purpose doesn't guarantee we will live by it, but it does help us align with something deep and true. In everything from major decisions to small interactions, we ask ourselves, "How can I express my purpose here?" This kind of attention to purpose is essential to effective leadership. It lays down the track on which the train runs, keeping the leader focused on what is truly worth doing. It keeps us clearly focused on the impact we have on people and events around us. It prescribes a way of being that feels deeply satisfying because it is the expression of authentic selfhood.

Paul is the CEO who had the close encounter with the fly. That and other experiences on his vision quest led him to see his life purpose in a new way. He began to understand his purpose as manifesting the Eastern concept of namaste — the God in me sees and honors the God in you. He found himself directing that spirit of appreciation to the fly and felt it reciprocated. When Paul returned to his company after his vision quest, he brought this deepened sense of purpose to all his interactions. It had an immediate and positive impact on his relationships with his business partners — helping to diffuse some areas of longstanding conflict. It also took his work with clients to a new level, because his thoughts toward them began to more consistently reflect his purpose of holding an attitude of namaste. Paul experienced what every conscious leader knows — our thoughts and perceptions of others have a major impact on how we interact with people and how they respond to us.

Vision

In the mature sense of self, purpose answers the question of why. It is our reason for living. Values answer the question of what is most important. A third component, vision, complements purpose and values by giving us a tool to help create what we want to experience in life. Vision is a widely used word in the arenas of human development and leadership and has a range of meanings. It most often refers to a way of picturing or describing outcomes we want to *achieve*. I use vision to mean a way of picturing or describing the kind of person one wants to *be*. It is a picture we hold in our imagination of how we want our purpose and values to be expressed through our behavior.

Ron is an account executive. On the first day of his vision quest, he set up a circle of stones that was 10 feet in diameter and marked the four cardinal directions — south, west, north, and east. He used each of the four directions to symbolize an important aspect of who he was becoming as a person. Acquainting himself with the four directions, he had discovered that developing these four aspects of his character could be a powerful path to creating wholeness and balance in his life. On his wilderness solo, from the middle of his circle, he ventured out daily into the landscapes of the four directions. He used his body and senses to create sounds, movements, and visual images that helped him gain insight into the essential characteristics of each direction and how they applied to his life.

One of the things he saw in the north was a bee pollinating flowers. He absorbed that image as a reminder of how essential the acts of giving and receiving are to his life. He identified with the bee and developed a metaphor around it, coming to view the diverse individuals in his life and work as flowers to whom he contributed; in return, he experienced fulfillment. The industriousness of the bee, and its thirst for the nectar of life, flamed Ron's own personal desire to give of himself with greater passion. When he turned to the south, Ron saw a place in the stream with seven small waterfalls. The sight took his breath away. Much of his experience in that direction helped him see more clearly a way of living for which he had been yearning — to create his life as a work of art. In the south, Ron rediscovered his artist self, and saw how he could bring his creativity more forcefully into every aspect of his life, from his parenting to his work with clients.

Ron's vision quest gave him many images and experiences that he now holds as a vision of who he can be at his best. Ron says:

> *I re-experience my solo every morning. When I sit still and breathe gently, I am actually present in the center of my circle and the four directions of my solo site. The feeling is so deep in my bones that I never lose it completely, even after a couple of years. It brings back clarity about who I am, which is especially welcome when I'm feeling lost or confused.*

Life Orientation

Self-concept is *who* we know ourselves to be. Orientation is *where* we know ourselves to be, mentally and spiritually, in relation to life around us. It is how we view the world and our place in it. When someone says, "I need to get oriented," they usually mean they need to find where they are in relation to a physical place, a community, a technology, or an organization. On one level, orientation refers to how we perceive the world and what we understand life to be.

Einstein once said the central question of human life is whether we see the universe as a friendly place or not. We all know people who live as if the world is out to get them. They are convinced that their gain requires someone else's loss. They see problems everywhere. Conversely, we know others who consistently see their "glass" as half full, rather than half empty. They are oriented toward cooperation rather than competition. They help themselves by serving others.

Peter Senge, author of *The Fifth Discipline* (1994) and a pioneer in the leadership development field, uses the term *mental model* to talk about the ways we orient ourselves in the world. Others talk about *framing* something, which means to see an issue from a certain perspective.

On another level, orientation refers to how we see and experience ourselves in relation to the unseen universe of spirit. Do we believe in God or an all-pervasive spiritual force in the universe? If we do, what is our relation to that higher power? If not, what is the larger context of our lives?

How we orient ourselves in this world and in relation to spirit is a critical component of leadership. Along with values, purpose, and vision, our spiritual orientation generates our attitudes and guides our decisions. Our orientation has a lot to do with how we treat people and whether or not we inspire and bring out the best in them.

A vision quest can powerfully deepen and affirm our orientation. It can also set in motion significant changes. We are asking the largest questions of existence and meaning when we ask ourselves the really big questions and stay still long enough to hear the answers.

Scott, a professional coach and consultant, intuitively knew there was some important awareness awaiting him in the wilderness. What he found was less about specific insights into his life and more about his general orientation. His solo experience awakened an awareness that was deep inside him. He remembered his intimate connection with all life. Every person who goes on a vision quest has an experience that to some degree matches Scott's. This awakening to one's connection to all life is at the core of the kind of humility that Jim Collins (2001) says is a part of Level 5 Leadership. Humility comes from a sense of being part of something much bigger than oneself. It enables a leader to be effective in relationships and get out of people's way.

Perhaps the most obvious way the wilderness vision quest helps leaders shift their orientation is through powerful metaphor. Most of us are not aware that we tend to see the world and our own lives through metaphors. For example, we may believe that most people are "sheep." Or, we see our organization as "a ship," with a "captain and crew." Or perhaps we view our family life as the place where we are deeply and securely "rooted," the way a tree is rooted in the ground. When on a vision quest, we start asking questions about our life orientation, and our answers often come as metaphors. Ana, a department head for a Fortune 500 company, was looking for insight into that fiercely mothering part of herself that nurtures her child and also her team at work. She chose a place to camp beneath what she called the "mother tree." That tree taught her many lessons about her mothering qualities.

Evocative Relationship

The self-concept and life orientation leaders bring to organizations are the mental and spiritual forces that drive their relationships with others. Those forces can tend to evoke more passion and contribution from others — or less. What we believe to be true about the world and ourselves affects how we think and act toward the people with whom we work. If we believe that people are basically lazy and motivated primarily by money, we will treat them differently than if we believe they are basically energetic and primarily motivated by a desire for creative expression, fulfillment, and opportunities to serve. If we believe that we have little to offer, we are usually uninspiring and incapable of evoking the greatness in others.

There are three core skills of evocative relationship — deep listening, system awareness, and appreciation. Underlying these skills is a fundamental attitude of believing in people and expecting the best from them. We have all been around people who expect others to show up at their worst. They treat people with mistrust. They micro-manage them. They overlook strengths and successes, and focus on weaknesses and failures. A few leaders blatantly exhibit this behavior, and many are guilty of it to some degree. Tony was one of these leaders. His experiences as a child, and throughout much of his adulthood, led him to believe that people are basically untrustworthy. He carried this pattern of thinking into his role as a leader, fostering an atmosphere of mistrust around him. His vision quest brought about a change in perception. He now chooses to believe that people are naturally trustworthy and expects them to be that way. He is not naïve, just expectant, and he is seeing a change in his relationships because of it.

Deep Listening

The ability to truly listen is essential to an evocative relationship. The kind of listening that evokes the best in others begins with actively seeking to understand what someone is trying to communicate. Most people are familiar with the basic skills of active listening, reflecting back what we've heard, and asking clarifying questions. Deep listening includes these skills and goes further. Deep listening includes the ability to sense the emotions present in a conversation — it includes empathy. It also includes an active curiosity about the communicator. What values are expressed? What emotions or unspoken assumptions are influencing the communication? What is the request that lies behind the complaint we are hearing? This kind of curious listening reflects a desire to understand and respect the person behind the communication. Most people are rarely listened to in this way. When they are, they feel affirmed and empowered. The experience of being fully heard touches that part of us that wants to express ourselves more and be seen for who we are, not just for what we produce. It evokes more of the personal qualities in us that add value to our work and our relationships.

Inner stillness. The wilderness vision quest is an invitation to deep listening that evokes more in others. By being alone in a wild place, with nothing to read and no to-do list, a profound stillness is available. Executive questers return haunted, in a good way, by the quality of stillness they experienced around and inside them. This stillness is essential to deep listening. From a place of inner stillness, the sound of a bird and the soft rustle of leaves actually register. Slowing down and becoming still allows us to focus on what's most important. We actually become more efficient listeners. We begin to access a quality of mind that enables us to find calmness in the daily storms the work world brings. It's never easy to maintain this stillness in the world of business, but once it has been deeply experienced, we can access it when we really need to tune into an issue, situation, or person.

Curiosity. Another aspect of deep listening that can be fostered by a wilderness immersion is curiosity. With few outside distractions, we can simply wonder about the world around us. On a quest, we may wonder about a rock formation, the exquisite form of a flower, or the birdcall we are hearing. We may wonder what there is to learn from the pattern of lichen on a tree or the sighting of an elk. This same curiosity can show up at work. It may take us to a place of wondering if there is something more we might learn from an interaction, instead of seeing it as a nuisance or something to check off a list. Or we might ask ourselves what information essential to an important decision is available by just digging a little deeper.

Receptivity. A third essential component of deep listening is receptivity. Without receptivity, the qualities of stillness and curiosity lose their potency. Stillness and curiosity bring us to the table. Receptivity is what enables us to actually take in what is there. We are all naturally receptive. Our bodies and minds are amazing receptors to all the world has to offer, and yet we have forgotten how to use them. We are taught to defend ourselves, to prove we are right, to take what we want. We have lost much of our ability to let in the gifts that others offer us — from a word of praise, to a helping hand, to an important piece of feedback. Alone in the wilderness, we are continually showered with gifts that awaken our receptive nature.

By the end of the second day of her quest, Laura, a partner in a successful consulting firm, had gone through all the core issues of her life and created some clarity. She wondered what she would do during the third day. It seemed she had already received that for which she had come. Then, on that third day, she opened to receive a big vision. She received a clear message in a waking dream state about the direction of the next phase of her life. When she let go of the image of how her vision quest was "supposed" to unfold, she opened herself to receive something entirely unexpected. We can do that with the people we lead, freeing them from limiting expectations and opening ourselves to be surprised by their gifts. This way of being in relationship evokes more from them.

Deep listening also acknowledges the interconnectedness of things. When we listen deeply, we can listen for context as well as content. We can listen for how things fit together rather than for isolated pieces of information. We can listen to many people and many sides of a situation before making a decision. The wilderness exposes us at every turn to interconnectedness. Seeing synergies and patterns in the natural world sensitizes us to them in our work world.

System Awareness

A second major aspect of evocative relationship is system awareness. System awareness is a crucial leadership orientation. When we are aware that our actions take place within a complex web of interrelationships, our thinking changes. We think about our organization as a system that is bigger than the sum of its parts. We also know that this system is interwoven with the wider world of customers, vendors, investors, and markets. For many leaders, this is not news, but it remains an abstraction. To make it real, we need to start asking ourselves questions: What is the system trying to create? How does the system want to grow? What is needed to provoke the system toward an innovative breakthrough? These are questions few leaders ask, and they can lead to very different actions and highly innovative results.

When we start to think about our organization as an entity with a life and designs of its own, we stop trying so hard to control or manage things and begin looking for ways to evoke the potential in the system. We become aware that the system wants to live larger, which leads us to seeing individuals as part of the expression of the life of the system. This shift in perception causes us to become curious about how each individual's ideas or perspectives are indications of something trying to happen in the larger system. We may realize that a "problem employee" is really a source of information essential to the organization's growth. When we perceive people differently, we treat them differently.

System awareness causes us to lead in a new way. We no longer see our role as the puppeteer pulling strings. We become relationship builders rather than people movers and problem solvers. In her book *A Simpler Way* (1998, p. 67), well-known business consultant Margaret Wheatley writes: "This is more than an observation. It is a crucial leadership characteristic. It focuses the work of leadership on strengthening the relationships that constitute the system."

Executives on a wilderness vision quest are immersed in interdependence. They cannot help but be aware of themselves as part of a much larger system of life. This not only fosters humility but also lays the groundwork for a leadership style that is focused on evoking rather than controlling. On a wilderness vision quest, we can learn to let go of our controlling tendencies.

We see that there is a much larger system of weather and time that creates the context of our solo, conditions over which we have absolutely no control. The sun takes its own time to move across the sky, and the weather is what it is. When we let ourselves sink into the natural rhythms and elements, instead of getting anxious and trying to swim upstream, we feel more centered and peaceful. We can apply that metaphor to our work by becoming aware of the natural rhythms present in our organization and flow with them instead of against them.

Appreciation

A third major component of evocative relationship is appreciation. On one of my vision quests, I noticed that I was feeling irritated by the barren landscape of the desert. After a couple of days, I decided to appreciate each small flower in the surrounding space. The first thing I realized was that there were many more flowers than I first thought, and a much greater variety. I looked closely at them and marveled at their intricacies. What was once a barren place became full of beauty, simply through the act of appreciation. The act of appreciation also changed my frame of mind from being irritated to being inspired.

When we bring genuine appreciation to the people around us, they bloom. Their performance tends to rise to meet that appreciation. Acknowledging good work invites more of it. When we look for people's strengths and passions, our expectancy evokes their expression. When people feel welcomed and valued, they not only perform better but also communicate more, which spawns innovative ideas and smarter decisions.

Appreciation also tends to open up our minds to the ideas that will take an organization forward. When we are unappreciative, or overly judgmental, we tend to close ourselves to new information. On my vision quest, changing my orientation to one of appreciation actually changed how the landscape appeared to me. This can happen in the business world as well. Instead of seeing problems everywhere, we can see possibilities and opportunities. That change of perception can affect what actually shows up.

Strategic Mastery

The wilderness vision quest can have a powerful impact on the way leaders think and act. We've touched so far on three foundational aspects of leadership — self-concept, life orientation, and evocative relationship. Strategic mastery is a fourth. How could spending time alone in the desert, mountains, or woods possibly impact the strategic decisions one makes in a business or organizational setting? The wilderness is about as far removed as we can get from the world of phones, email, and conference rooms. As strange as it might seem, this removal is exactly what makes the vision quest a powerful catalyst for strategic thinking. The vision quest creates time and space for the mind to wander. Our minds get stimulated by foreign scenery, which allows us to escape the habitual patterns of thinking that are reinforced by our familiar urban/suburban surroundings. The wilderness landscape stimulates parts of the mind — the inner landscape — that may lie dormant. This helps us "think outside the box." It helps us bring fresh perspectives to challenging situations and decisions.

Sean undertook his vision quest as part of a three-month sabbatical from his leadership role in a thriving nonprofit organization. He knew he would have to make a major career decision upon his return. He would have to decide whether to take a more senior position, where he could have greater impact on the direction of the entire organization, or stay where he was and continue to have a more hands-on and localized impact through the programs he led. The solitude and stillness of the vision quest helped him tune into his inner wisdom and get clear about the kind of relationship he wanted with the organization. It helped him create a framework to guide his ultimate decision.

Sean's experience is an illustration of system awareness overlapping with strategic mastery. Understanding our organizations as systems leads us to ask important questions about our strategic roles as leaders. How does our leadership style fit with the system? What would we have to change about how we lead in order to have a greater impact? Where are the leverage points in the system to make the most difference through our actions? What leadership role is most appropriate for us, given the makeup of the system and our strengths as a leader? Sean saw that his leadership style is best suited to a particular role in the organization. That insight helped him make an important strategic decision.

Clearly identifying what the resources are and knowing how to marshal them is an important aspect of strategic mastery. In our fast-paced work lives, it's easy to keep our heads down and stay busy putting out fires. We need to lift our heads once in a while, take a look around, and remember where we're going and how we're going to get there. The vision quest is a powerful opportunity to take that look around. When Ana went into the mountains for her quest, she was feeling reluctant to lead her department. She had become overwhelmed by bogged-down projects and didn't remember if or why her work mattered. Her solo rekindled her enthusiasm and helped her see new ways to move her team forward.

Conclusion

Kevin Cashman, author of the corporate executive best seller *Leadership from the Inside Out* (1998) and *Awakening the Leader Within* (2003), defines leadership as "a sacred calling to make a life-enriching difference in the world" (p. ix). More and more leaders, from corporate CEOs to nonprofit executives, aspire to this kind of leadership. These are the kinds of leaders who are attracted to the vision quest. They know their lives have a deeper purpose, and they want to be more plugged into it. They are not forsaking the bottom line for a monk's robe, but they want their contribution to the world to be something larger and more meaningful than good-looking financial statements. They are doing the work of improving their self-concept and shaping their life orientation in ways that make them more powerfully adept at evoking great things from their organizations and bringing wisdom to their strategic thinking and action.

References

Cashman, K. (1998). *Leadership from the inside out*. Provo, Utah: Executive Excellence Publishing.

Cashman, K. (2003). *Awakening the leader within*. New York: John Wiley and Sons, Inc.

Collins, J. (2001). *Good to great*. New York: Harper Business.

Senge, P. (1994). *The fifth discipline*. New York: Currency, Inc.

Wheatly, M. (1998). *A simpler way*. New York: Berrett-Koehler Publishers.

CHAPTER 12

Erazim, Sigurd, My Students, and Me: Thinking About Solo

By Bob Henderson

Standing there alone, I felt alive, more aware and
receptive than ever before. A shout or a movement would
have destroyed the spell. This was a time for silence,
for being at pace with ancient rhythms and timelessness,
the breathing of the lake, the slow growth of living
things. Here cosmos could be felt and the
true meaning of attunement.

(Olson, 1956, p. 130)

I am feeling quite old-fashioned at the moment, for I propose to write an essay, a rumination of sorts, in the form of a letter to a close friend. I have a few friends in mind. I am hardly a man of letters. My email correspondence is always brief and to the point, and my letters are scratchy and too often composed of superficial thoughts. Not here! Sharing these musings will satisfy my urge to discuss with some depth the matter of solitude and solitude's relationship to community. My aim is to share some long-saved thoughts that have arisen during my decades as an outdoor educator. A few are my own, others are those of my students, and the underpinnings of most have been culled from literature I have read throughout the years. My hope is to show that solo experiences need not be long in duration or remote in location to be strong in influence, for there is much to be gained from solo time, be it with wild earth or city parks.

The works of two writer-philosophers have illuminated my explorations of solitude. They are Erazim Kohak, a Czech philosopher I understand only in joyous bits (*The Embers and the Stars*, 1984), and Sigurd Olson (*Reflections From the North Country*, 1998, reprint). Through their writings I have come to know these two authors as friends. Erazim and Sigurd have accompanied me on several travel experiences, both solo and with small groups. Their books were the only ones brought along to enlighten and set the mood for contemplation. It seems right to focus on them now, as they make good traveling companions.

I will write this essay in a few intense sessions. I have placed myself in a favorite therapeutic solo place, a writer's retreat: no phone, lots of birds, and much fresh air to breathe deeply. I write as a student, an outdoor educator, a travel guide, and a university classroom teacher. I write as someone who consciously seeks out solitude in my daily life; from a quiet donut and coffee at midday to five-day solo canoe trips here and there. I write as a teacher who tries to bring moments of solitude into the classroom curriculum and the outdoor adventure experiences of my students. I know that a significant part of education is getting people to do things they wouldn't plan to do themselves but that given the opportunity to do they would really enjoy and benefit from.

Solo as Teaching Tool

Key words rise to my consciousness: *solitude, loneliness,* and *community.* When I find myself being overcome by the social and community side of family and work life, I find a way to "take off." It might be a jog in the woods, a quiet evening with a guitar or book, a morning paddle, or, if I'm lucky and time allows (or demands), a few days of canoe tripping. My longest solo trip has been six days; not that long, but just right for me. Solitude feels like a gift and embraces my whole being. I bask in it, take it in like a sponge, let the land envelope me and free my mind. Then I wander about with my soul at the forefront of consciousness. Well ... that's what I hope for when I pause to think deeply about it. Sometimes I satisfy the deepest cravings of my soul (or psyche). Sometimes I simply break the tension caused by too much "in-your-face" social-community life in both leisure and work. The jog in the woods might do it sometimes, but I often need those days of solo camping or *retreating* to an isolated cabin.

I do not always venture out alone. As Sigurd says, there is a charmed solitude in the company of another. Not a contradiction I think; solitude can involve the best of quiet company.

> *Only when people are strangers do they feel obliged to be entertaining. Where there is agreement and appreciation, silence is no bar to mutual enjoyment. When I have been alone in quiet places, I have often wished someone could share it and make the experience even richer and more complex.*
>
> (1956, p. 133)

I have noted that students often start into solos seeking settings in pairs of comfortable friendships — a delightful and decided step taken. There is always that greater enterprise out there and in here. Sigurd hopes we can be in pace with ancient rhythms and feel the cosmos. Erazim hopes we can "recall the ageless rhythm of nature and ... the moral law which our bodies and spirits yet echo beneath the heavy layer of forgetting." (Kohak, 1984, p. x)

If solitude, even in fleeting moments, is about seeking one's soul or inner psyche, then it is also about absorbing the love or alluring presence of the universe and seeking the source of life, of self, and of all. All this, with a jog in the woods, a few days alone traveling in a canoe with tent, or even a quiet pause with donut and coffee? Absolutely! Too many human artifacts and human constructs interfere with this alluring consciousness toward the greater enterprise of life. Nature, the more-than-human, is paramount in our lives. Without it we are too easily a very lonely lot. Solitude and nature go together for me.

Erazim speaks to me of loneliness and "the gift of solitude."

Loneliness: a condition of feeling abandoned amid an alien world, cut off from communities.

[Solitude] is the condition of being alone in the presence of a living, familiar world, willing to listen to it, to see and to understand it ... sharing in its feel and meaning.

(1984, pp. 39–40)

Strangely though, when I do get the opportunity for a longer solo, I soon feel satiated. Then, once the tension is eased by a few days alone — and I begin to crave community again, with all its associated commitments and responsibilities — I easily find tolerance for the compromises community requires. It isn't loneliness that draws me back so much as readiness to return to community. And just as going out on solo doesn't guarantee solitude, nor does surrounding yourself with people guarantee community.

Hmmm ... I do not think I am so unique. I'd say, in fact, that I am downright ordinary. Unique would be my friend Herb Pohl, who throughout the 1980s and 1990s traveled solo through canoe routes in Labrador and the Northwest Territories for up to six weeks at a time. Unique as well might be those socially oriented folks who never feel the need, or have never satisfied the craving for solitude.

In Western culture there is an emphasis on community. Such an emphasis does not negate the importance of solitude but rather elevates its importance. There is a tension between solitude and community. They are co-dependent — you cannot have one without the other. Olson put it this way: "Wilderness can be appreciated only by contrast, and solitude understood only when we have been without it" (1998, p. 35).

I would suggest that my students and I have too much community, or, dare I say, too much community that may look like community but is superficial and lacking substance. As Erazim writes:

We obliterate solitude with electronics and blind ourselves with the very lights we devised to help us see. There is nothing wrong with our artifacts; there is something wrong with us.

(1984, p. xii)

I fear many are lonely even when in community — but that is another essay, one that is very complex, and that I am not prepared to tackle at this moment.

Horizontal Growth and Vertical Growth

Eliezer Shore refers to our need for community as "horizontal growth, as our lives touch and are touched by others ... [this] fosters in us a greater compassion and awareness of the human condition" (1992, p. 18). He suggests that solitude represents "pure vertical growth," for it allows us to transcend the mundane realities of the every-day world and begin to travel with our inner spirit.

Thinking of outdoor education as a starting point for such a journey is much more compelling than teaching the *J-stroke* in canoeing or helping people develop a specific character skill such as perseverance. When one works on the axis of horizontal concern about the human condition *and* the axis of vertical alignment with the spirit, one is engaged in the eco-psychological pursuit of healing self, others, and the planet. When the outdoor educator is drawn to facilitate beauty, adventure, and truth in community *and* in solitude, what s/he teaches transcends basic skills and provides transformational skills for self and all humankind. If you are inclined toward the lofty aspiration of healing, it makes sense to focus on solo experiences.

Through the Eyes of Students

Tea and Lanterns in the Wilderness

My students live in the city. Each day we all go to school. We are intensely scheduled; we have deadlines and demands. We juggle multiple interests and, within all of this, most of us are rushed. Perhaps the difference between my students and me is that I know I need midday solo time or an end-of-term canoe trip. So, working from the perspective that my own needs mirror those of like-minded others, I seek a balance of solitude and community for my students too. Years in outdoor education have taught me that many people discover the gift of solitude as a revelation. In the role of outdoor educator, I introduce those who are ready to understand the balance of solitude and community. Of course, the Buddha knew this long ago: "When the student is ready, the teacher appears."

And so, on the first night of a nine-day canoeing trip, I ask students to sit quietly for a time to consider our place, socially and geographically. Now is the time to be still, to hear what Sigurd called the great silence, the old silence, and the creative silence. Now is the time to find our place amid this particular geography. We gather in the darkness around a kerosene lantern and a *billy* of tea. We walk to a quiet spot in our surroundings and sit in a circle around the lantern and the teapot. The tea is distributed in silence. People soon relax in the circle and are ready to receive a friendly invitation from the woods to be there by themselves. It is a friendly start.

I first learned of the tea ceremony from one of Steve Van Matre's acclimatization lessons (1974). Rich in simplicity, I thought at first, not initially realizing the complexity of the experience. Now I know students cull personal meaning from the exercise. Their journals never cease to affirm the ritual's power. These excerpts, from two of hundreds of student journals collected over a 22-year period, reflect what most students feel following the tea ceremony:

> *The tea and lantern ceremony. This event had a great effect on me as a person, as I am sure it has on everyone else. I think that this type of event was unexpected by the vast majority of the group and was viewed at the start as something very strange. It was bizarre to be told to "stop talking" and to become serious after an afternoon and evening of fun and games. Many strange looks passed between everyone with a few stifled giggles and looks of suspicion. As we separated into four different groups, we followed only the light of the lantern to a secluded area. I found myself surrounded by six other people all sitting in a circle on the dock with the dim glow of the lanterns. In silence, tea was passed out to each member and we shared the warmth of the beverage together. The night air was warm and the sky was filled with a multitude of stars. As the time passed we began to feel more comfortable in the group and relax and enjoy the beauty of the evening. The silence accentuated the tranquility and peacefulness that the surroundings were providing. With everyone lost deep in their own thoughts it provided the opportunity to really feel the love for nature. One is not often given the chance to sit back and marvel at God's creation. Sharing these few brief moments in nature had a major impact on the outlook for the trip. Each aspect of nature was given the attention it so rightly deserved after this session. All of a sudden the trees, water, fish and sky became all that was important. Preserving these creations and respecting their place in God's plan is what is important. Thanks to a few moments of getting in touch with reality — which is really nature — it created an atmosphere for learning and caring about what happens to our land and our lives.*
>
> (Mary)

Take your tea in silence
Won't you listen to the night.
Take the time for peace of mind,
Soaked in lantern light.
Get in touch with things out of sight.
Bask in moonlight shining,
Down on feeling fine.
Emotion trapped inside a teardrop.
Get to know Ontario through
Pure good times.

(Pamela)

On these trips, following the tea ceremony, I encourage students to take mini-solos — not the multi-day fasting solo one might experience as a student on an Outward Bound course, but a solitude experience all the same. One might say it is risky to allow students unsupervised time to wander in the morning mist by canoe, but I say the rewards are worth the risk. Early in the canoe trip I repeatedly share a line of poetry from Australian poet Banjo Paterson (1981): "For the town folk have no time to grow, they have no time to waste." For many, it is a message to be in the present, to be part of that broadening experience that Erazim calls "the gift of solitude," (1984, p. 40) and Sigurd calls "creative silence" (1998, p. 33).

The thoughts of Erazim and Sigurd were abstract notions for me at one time. Now, after more than 30 years of guiding adventure experiences, I've seen too much of the associated emancipatory euphoria to chalk it up to the acquisition of new physical skills or group cohesion. The spiritual dimension cannot be ignored simply because it is more difficult to address and quantify. Again, student journals speak volumes about the gift of solitude.

Solo Walks and Solo-Sits

Once back in the city at school, we must curb the tendency for students (mostly urbanites) to think that nature is "out there," always a drive away. The city also offers moments for solo contemplation within nature. Even during a two-hour class we make time to head to a natural space, be it a city park or sports field. We may walk with some interpretive lessons and educational activities in hand, or we may just go for a hike. Along the way, I hand each student an envelope that contains a quote. I ask them to contemplate the quote while solo-sitting at a site of their own choosing.

Students reunite with a call. We do not debrief the solo-sit; rather, we point out that there are many opportunities to connect with nature in the city. We reject the insidious city-country dualism. Is such a simple hike and solo-sit showcasing a city's nature space worthy of a two-hour university class? You be the judge. Here are two student journal comments. The first is from a course journal entry, and the second from an unsolicited e-mail.

> *Found: one long-lost friend on Saturday, February 3, 2001, in Cootes Paradise. Under the canopy of the trees, Sharon and Nature were triumphantly reunited. The relationship needs minor repairs, but the strong bond is still intact. If my life reads like a newspaper, the above clipping would have summarized the front-page story. Inspired by my Outdoor Experiential Education class outing to Cootes Paradise, I returned the next day and made a miraculous discovery. In the woods that day I found something that lay hidden within me. I rediscovered my love for nature. Before this experience, my love for nature was hidden beneath a blanket of general malaise ... unable to pinpoint the cause of my dissatisfaction, my frustration grew. I felt spiritually disconnected. I felt lost, unsure of my place and purpose in the world. In the woods I experienced two strong yet opposing forces. I was drawn into a spiritual bond with nature and simultaneously was set free from my own self-doubt. Alone in nature, I felt like I had come home. In this home I found my place and my purpose.*
>
> (Sharon)

> *I have no real reason for writing, other than the fact that I really want to convey to you how much the eco-psychology class last week meant to me.... The last two months, I have been struggling with anxiety and insomnia.... That 10 minutes of time spent on the top of a hill, sitting on a fallen willow tree, I recognized that sense of connectedness with nature, the connection that I had forgotten because my brain was swimming in a pile of worries. That night as I lay in bed, no longer did thoughts pervade my every waking moment, I fell asleep. I had the most peaceful sleep that I have had since December. I was at peace with nature. I was at peace with myself. Thank you for opening my mind.*
>
> (Emily)

Solo Projects

Still later in the school term, my students are asked to complete individual projects. Several students have been drawn to an exploration of a newfound appreciation of solitude. One student (in the tradition of wilderness traveler Robert Perkins) filmed her three-day solo canoe trip. She had to negotiate this plan with me to insure her skill competency and cover the safety issues, and then with her parents to confirm the validity of what they viewed as an "unnecessary experience." Another student undertook a series of solo hikes on the Bruce Trail, a 700-kilometer hiking trail running through and beyond our city. Perhaps these were small steps but bold and important ones all the same.

In another course that runs the full teaching year, a student named John, jaded by years of doing term papers, contracted with me to spend one night of each school week camping solo in the woodlot surrounding our campus. He recorded the seasonal changes and his observations as a field naturalist would. His paper was his journal field notes. Ahh, the creative mind and creative silence at work. This was solitude by choice. It was simple, courageous, and often hard work. Truth be told, I could barely read John's handwriting, but that didn't matter. By April he was already familiar with solitude and its tensions with community, and was far from lonely in our Cootes Paradise Woods. He had, I think, experienced Cootes in the same way Oliver Morgan describes solitude. "Like the putting on of a worn but comfortable smoking jacket, or the welcoming of an old friend" (1986, p. 27). John's weekly solitude sessions had widened his native intelligence. Instead of waking every morning in a bed, in a room, in a building, he woke up with nature, with the blue sky and the green things, with frost and snow and streams of light beaming through the forest canopy.

The students who pursue such opportunities with solitude as a course requirement are moving beyond just another ho-hum assignment. These are Erazim's "perennial beginners." They have a quest, sometimes poorly articulated, that is deeply ingrained. As Erazim wrote of his perennial beginners, they are "taking the sense of lived experience in its primordial immediacy for their subject matters.... Their stance was one of wonder not of sophistication." (1984, p. xi). What are they after? What is their quest? Erazim answers:

> *We walk on asphalt, not on the good earth ... seldom do we have a chance to see virgin darkness, unmarred by electric lights, seldom can we recall the ageless rhythm of nature and of the moral law which our bodies and spirits yet echo beneath the heavy layers of forgetting.*
>
> (1984, p. x)

Perhaps some of these students remember the tea ceremony, short hikes and solo-sits, and some of the assigned readings. They are ready for more intensive solo experiences, and have made some conscious decisions about pursuing solitude. They are aware of an odd subversiveness in the act. These students are seeking a new way of knowing — learning from personal experience and personal perspectives.

Candles Around the Bay

On winter travel courses, all of our senses seem amplified. After we have traveled across a frozen lake on snowshoes, the emphasis on the first night of a five-day winter camping expedition is to acknowledge the social side of the trip with a sharing of a chocolate fondue in the comfort of a cabin. Once we have established ourselves socially, we must connect with our larger surroundings. We "bundle up" and exit the sanctity of the remote shoreline cabin for a single-file snowshoe hike across the lake. We travel, often through deep snow, about 20 minutes to the next bay. Matches and tea candles are distributed at the center of the bay, and then the students are asked to radiate from this center to the shoreline. There they find a place to settle for a quiet solo-sit. They light their candle, and soon observe a display of flickering lights around the shore. When people get cold, they return to the center for a hot chocolate. The solo time is often only 15 minutes or so, but the effect of this, perhaps their first solo time with the bush in winter, is to make the cold of our new winter surroundings welcoming, even friendly.

Later, while on our three-day camping trip, students are sent out for a solo winter hike. It is a layover day in our bush camp. People have settled into a routine of chores and camaraderie. There is now time for a solo wander. They leave camp for a few hours. Later, through journal entries, I learn a little about their experiences:

> I didn't realize the need for solo time until I was completely alone. While away
> from the group I collected a few boughs and set up a "Jamie chair." There I sat
> in the warm sun wondering who was watching me. Then I tried to recall and
> play with the ever-popular phrase [in 4D6 Outdoor Education Theory
> Course, that is], "I am watching you, are you watching yourself in me?"
> I sense a change in the group after the solo.
>
> (Fred)

> The cattails I knocked over swarmed me with their seeds and I carried them
> great distances, right to the end of the swamp and into the bush until it became
> too thick to continue and the path veered around and headed back toward
> camp. I stopped, looked around, took a deep breath — Nope! Not ready to turn
> around yet. I plopped myself down in the snow. The sun was behind the trees
> and a cool breeze brushed my warm cheeks. Then there was this feeling. I'm not
> even positive in my mind what it was. It was as if, for a moment, I understood

something; a certain knowing ran through my bones. That feeling, that very moment, all that was contained in that experience seemed so vitally important.

(Tracey)

Exit

In addition to learning about the gift of solitude and the valuable lesson of balance between solitude and community, there is so much potential for learning during these *introductions* to solo time. It is impossible for the teacher to be accountable for all this potential learning. In a curricular sense, the solo times are a small part of the overall classroom and canoe or snowshoe experiences, yet they are a critical component of working directly on what John Livingston called our "sensory deprivation" (2002, p. 51), and what Thomas Berry referred to as recognition that "the universe is a communion of subjects, not a collection of objects" (2002, p. 36).

Sigurd shares these sentiments:

In our cities the constant beat of strange and foreign wavelengths on our primal senses beats us into neuroticism, changes us from creatures who once knew the silence to fretful, uncertain beings immersed in a cacophony of noise which destroys sanity and equilibrium.

(1998, p. 131)

Erazim has equally strong words:

Is the person or is matter in motion the root metaphor of thought and practice.... Humans cannot conceive of the world as an absurd play of blind forces, yet retain the confidence of their own humanity.... Personalism in philosophy is the recovery of the primordial insight (and) the vision of a Kosmos.

(1984, pp. 125–127)

Be it sensory deprivation turned to reconciliation with nature, communion of subjects, working to recover primal senses against a backdrop of neuroticism, or acknowledgment of the primary thought and practice of the person, these authors speak with different languages but still share some of the ideas in this essay. Regardless of which language is spoken, these concerns and promises result from introduction of solo time into classroom field trips. I see these benefits in the emancipatory euphoria that students express in the moment and in their journal entries.

As our senses are nourished by the complexity of the more-than-human space/place we call nature, we are able to open our spirits and souls, exploring that vertical axis of knowledge that deepens and broadens our lives. In the process, we also expand our community. In our solo spots on the trail, we come to see the individuality and community in all things. Trees identified as "Oh yeah, Red Pines, I know them," can become what they are — individual trees. The track in the snow is that of a single otter, not all otters. There is a difference here. I think of these contacts as more genuine meetings. So many have written of taking the spiritual quest to negate ego and more genuinely meet "other." The nonhuman environment can offer sensory nourishment in acknowledging a rich complexity of which we are a part — not apart from.

I make no apologies for not plunging my students into more intense solo experiences. Not everyone has to go off on a month-long trip in the wilderness to know the wisdom of solitude. Perhaps our solo-seeking initiatives pale in comparison to what others do, but I choose to proceed with caution. The teacher must lead gently and nurture the student by small but not trivial opportunities for solo. We must remember that adventures can often become misadventures, and that is the case with solo travel. I will leave this essay with one great caveat that I first read in the early 1980s and since have kept close at hand.

> *Should some of my readers cherish the idea of traveling alone in the wilderness, I have three words of advice: "Don't Do It." It's stupid and hazardous. I know there will always be lonely trappers and prospectors, but probably they are unusual individuals. It's not worth it to go alone, just to find out that you are not that kind, that you are as vulnerable to loneliness as I was. I don't mean to imply that you would end up with ulcer. I'm probably just the type to get them, and the Churchill trip was the last drop in my cup. Actually I was lucky; your fate might be worse. And, what could be better than to paddle with friends and experience the river together?*
>
> (Pecher, 1978, p. 182).

Wait! Somehow it doesn't feel right to end on this note. I must return to Sigurd and Erazim for help. Erazim reminds me "I have not sought to prove a point, but to evoke and to share a vision" (1984, p. xiii). Sigurd tells me to treasure "those flashes of reality when the solo silence enters us" (1998, p. 134). I hope I can help students have and embrace such moments. Solos are a central strategy to this end.

Author's Note: I would like to thank John Maxted for letting me delve into his research files of readings concerning solos and outdoor education.

References

Berry, T. (2002). *In listening to the land: Conversations about nature, culture and eros.* Derrick Jensen (Ed.). San Francisco: Sierra Club Books.

Kohak, E. (1984). *The embers and the stars: A philosophical inquiry into the moral sense of nature.* Chicago: The University of Chicago Press.

Livingston, J. A. (2002). *In listening to the land: Conversations about nature, culture and eros.* In Derrick Jensen (Ed.). San Francisco: Sierra Club Books.

Morgan, O. J. (1986). Music for the dance: Some meanings of solitude. *Journal of Religion and Health, 25*(1), 18–27.

Olson, S. F. (1998). *Reflections from the North Country.* Minneapolis: University of Minnesota Press.

Olson, S. F. (1956). *The singing wilderness.* New York: Alfred A. Knopf.

Paterson, B. (1981). Clancy of the overflow. *The man from Snowy River and other verses.* Sydney, Australia: Angus and Robertson.

Pecher, K. (1978). *Lonely voyage: By kayak to adventure and discovery.* Saskatoon: Western Producer Prairie Books.

Shore, E. (1992). The soul of the community. *Parabola: The Magazine of Myth and Tradition, Solitude and Community, XVII*(1), 18–21.

Van Matre, S. (1974). *Acclimatizing: A personal and reflective approach to a natural relationship.* Martinsville, IN: American Camping Association.

CHAPTER 13

The Whisper of the Wilderness: Applying Personal Solo Learnings in Teaching Others

By Deborah Eads Greene

You want a place where you can be serene that will let you
contemplate and connect two consecutive thoughts, or that if need
be can stir you up as you were made to be stirred up, until you
blend with the wind and water and earth you almost forgot you
came from.... There must be room enough for time — where the
sun can calibrate the day, not the wristwatch, for days
and weeks of unordered time, time enough to forget the feeling
of pavement and to get the feel of the earth,
and what is natural and right.

(Porter, 2001)

A solo experience can provide a place for serenity, contemplation, and the time to get the feel of the earth, and its effects are both immediate and lasting. My first solo experience more than 30 years ago laid the foundation for who I am and what I do to this day. Regularly embarking on solo experiences provides me the insight and knowledge to effectively guide youth and adults through their own solo experiences.

This chapter will begin with reflections about pivotal solo experiences in my own life, what they have taught me, and how they have shaped the way I guide others through their solos. It will conclude with a discussion of solo's influence in academic settings.

The First Time

It was 1978. I was 19, and a sophomore majoring in natural science and secondary education at Towson University. At the time I had only a vague idea as to the direction my life was heading. Unknown to my consciousness, my first solo — as well as other adventures concocted by Craig Dobkin as part of the Outdoor Education program at Towson — would play a significant role in formulating my future teaching style and approach with students.

It took place at night in a wooded area on Towson University's campus in Baltimore, Maryland. I found myself hanging from a sturdy old oak tree in a handmade hammock that I had woven from a climbing rope. I was grateful our instructor had allowed us to hang our hammocks earlier in the day while there was still adequate daylight. We had also been encouraged to fill our bellies with a good meal before retiring to our airy cocoons in the setting sun.

In the light of day this had all sounded like a great adventure, but in the encroaching darkness, wrapped in a light sleeping bag of compressed down, I felt like a sardine hung out to freeze. A slight spring breeze had kicked up, and I found myself hanging from a swaying limb. Tethered with an extra piece of webbing and carabiners, I was secured to the tree in case my hibernacula gave way.

When later that night I felt the bodily urge of nature calling, I started doing calculations. *"Let's see … this should hit me in another few hours — about 2 a.m. if I'm calculating correctly."* As the only woman on the adventure, I lay there with my eyes wide open wondering how the guys were feeling at this point. I presumed they would just "hang out" of their hammocks when they felt the urge. Maybe, I thought, this was one of the reasons so few women were involved in adventure education.

Despite my idle speculation of bladders and the acrobatics involved in voiding water, I thrived that night. My imagination went wild. I saw myself precariously hanging on a 2,000-foot rock wall in Yosemite, high in the jungle canopy of Borneo, and spending hours in the big tree in front of the house where I grew up. I reflected on my life to that point, and wondered where I was heading. I set personal goals of achieving independence and self-reliance, sharing experiences like this with others, developing strong and lasting relationships, and running the mountain ridges of the world. Somehow, a career would figure into the equation. I realized I was there, in that tree, looking up at the stars on a spring evening because I chose to be. In a world of so much doing, this swinging cocoon gave me time for just being. I would not cheat, climb out, nor let my feet touch soil. I was in it for the challenge, and to show myself that I could do this simple task. As I basked in my aloneness, I was blissful. And I did not pee.

Soloing as an Adult

After expeditioning with a group of friends and fellow climbers on the slopes of Manaslu in Nepal, the Colorado Outward Bound School offered me a dream position: international instructor and course director in Nepal. So in 1994 and 1995, I led mountaineering courses in the Rowaling and Khumbu valleys of Nepal. Often, after dropping off students in Kathmandu, I quickly headed back to the hills by myself — for myself. Climbing remote high peaks alone always gave me a wonderful sense of freedom. In solo, I am totally independent — getting up when my body is rested, going at the pace I set, and letting weather and daylight dictate my decisions.

The Kingdom of Nepal is the roof of the world, and it is populated by some of the most genuine, caring, happy, compassionate people I have ever encountered. In places where I once expected only isolated trails leading to mystic peaks, I found people herding yaks, chatting on the streets in small villages, and farming at altitudes of 14,000–16,000 feet. There I learned to cherish the tenacity of the human spirit. Perhaps the magical peaks they inhabit give them the gift of inner peace.

Another reason I relish hiking and climbing solo in foreign lands is that the experience becomes more intense. The isolation of soloing enhances self-reliance. The farther people are removed from their native circles of comfort, the more extreme an experience can be. To make a decision alone with no English-speaking support makes the experience feel very intense, very real, and very rewarding. These experiences have taught me that I most often eek out life in arenas that most closely mirror my comfort zones, not in places where I feel threatened or out of control.

When I began traveling in Asia in the early 1980s, village people had not yet been exposed to American satellite television, and there were no roads that could support a bike, much less a motorized vehicle, throughout most of the Kingdom of Nepal. My backpack contained material items amounting to a lifetime of wages for the local residents. It took me a day's bus ride to reach the outermost parts of the Everest region and another three days of hiking along paths worn by centuries of Nepalese to reach higher elevations.

During one of my solo adventures above and beyond Namche Bazaar in the Khumbu Valley of Nepal, I stopped in Debouche Gonda, a village of a few houses and shops where I found a little book on the legends of yetis. Evenings sitting around cook tents and kitchen fires listening to Sherpas share their stories had piqued my interest in these mythic beings. More than once I had begged them to tell me about these sometimes-gentle beasts that had become living creatures in my mind. The little book became a constant reminder of the creatures that were thought to be so helpful to the Buddhist Lamas as they made their way over Trashi Labtsa, a steep mountain pass littered with rock and icefall. I read that yetis love to mimic human actions and are sometimes aggressive toward unwary humans but, as in most fables, their actions are often misinterpreted and ultimately benign to humans.

Alone in the mountains that evening, having left all other people behind among the lodges and teahouses, I was so isolated I could no longer see the smoke curling up from any of the villages. Camping at nearly 18,000 feet after a dinner of Ramen and yak cheese, I huddled in my bivy sac and eyed the peak I would climb the next day. Serenity washed over me as I savored this valley alone. High, safe, hydrated, and at peace, sleep came quickly. When I periodically peeked my head out of my bivy sac, I saw the thousands of stars that filled the night sky. In the blackness of the night, I must have looked like just another big boulder on the alpine landscape. At about 2 a.m., the gentle melody of bells in the distance woke me. I was too far away from any town or village for this tinkling of metal to be anything but yetis.

In yeti country, one is dealt an assorted hand of cards. If the yetis are friendly and trusting, all goes well. If they are females and feel threatened by a human female, they may capture or even kill her; if they are males, they may also choose to capture a human female to take her as a partner. This last thought spread a bit of terror through my being. I imagined, *"What if I am impregnated by a 9-foot tall yeti, and have to deliver a 19-pound yeti-human in a cave at high altitude, alone? Would it kill both of us?"* I wondered, *"What is the world record for one staying motionless in a sleeping bag without being detected by other beings?"* I had two choices: Either I could get out of my bag and relieve myself, or I could soak my bag in safety. To me, at that moment, the choices were real — and so were the yetis.

Eventually I had to act. I opted to take my chances with the yetis rather than wet my bag. I slithered out of my bivy on my stomach, too afraid to raise my body more than a few feet off the ground, took care of business, and then snaked my way back to the safety of my bag. I had slipped into the fabled world and back out again without being noticed. I was in a kingdom where the spiritual mountains flowed with energy. Lying in the darkness watching dawn slowly creep into the morning sky, I fully embraced a mystic time warp. Although I could not stay in that time-stands-still silence forever, that experience gave me a sense of how myths and legends are created. It also reinforced my belief in the power of the human mind and the influence of suggestion. We may have solo experiences at different points in our lives, but we are never in an emotionally objective place, because our subjective feelings always create context. Periodic solos give me time to see created emotional environments for what they are, because they offer the opportunity to sort out the fragments of my emotions and take possession of my realities, so that I can organize, prioritize, and derive meaning from my experiences.

The next morning, after crawling out of my bivy sack and taking time to appreciate the alpine environment, I threw on my pack and scrambled to the summit. Sunlight bathed me in a sea of calm as I stood alone on the summit of Pokalde at 5,745 meters, and shared the moment with a few weathered prayer flags left there by other climbers, I sent my prayers of peace, health, global acceptance, and understanding into the wind like a whisper in the wilderness, through the remaining fibers of those battered flags. They are part of Buddhist tradition, a way to carry an individual's prayers to heaven. I imagined that maybe there had been another solo traveler who had spent a few moments at this same spot taking in the 360-degree vista. I recorded the moment on film and then headed down to a lower, more oxygen-rich elevation.

As I clambered down from the summit, feeling simultaneously lightheaded and cautious, lighthearted and focused, I thought about why I sometimes choose to climb alone. I climb to focus my energy and attention on life. Climbing alone enables me to come to terms with some of my fears and expectations, and to think about where I am going in life. I often hear the question, "Why do we climb if there is no gold or other mineral to extract from the rocky crags, if there are no answers to benefit humankind, or if there is no wisdom to be gained?" I believe there is a lot of personal wisdom to be gained, if not of the physical world then of the psychological and spiritual worlds.

As I picked my way through iced-over boulders and crags, physical challenges helped me cross the emotional boundaries I had created for myself. I crept off a snowy pass, down chutes of snow and amid rotten rock pillars. When I reached the rock and talus covering the icy surface of the lateral glacial moraine, it gave me a less slippery surface to ascend, yet at the same time it impeded my progress. I wondered, *"How many road blocks, or moraines, do we encounter in life?"* There are always barricades that inhibit movement; how we choose to deal with these barriers makes us who we are.

Whenever I solo, the hardest part of the day is finding a reasonable place to rest my body. Long ago I gave up on finding great places, because my mind always created so many "what if" situations. Within the Sagarmatha (Everest) National Park in Nepal, individuals are not permitted to travel after dark because wild boars take over the landscape. I did not want to tempt boars of any sort, so upon reaching the far side of the glacier, I spotted what looked like an inviting cave. The problem was a relatively small glacial river that stood between me and my intended evening sanctuary. I balanced precariously on top of rocks that had iced over since the sun had left the valley. It was as if my feet belonged to another traveler — they went in one direction and the rest of me went in the other — down.

Wet, humbled, and ready to be nurtured, I stumbled back to the riverbank where I had started. Standing in the middle of the glacial froth, I looked upstream. I spotted a village I knew existed but had not been able to see from the pass. Yearning for human company, I hefted my pack without changing my wet clothes and headed toward a smoking chimney. I thought, *"Where there's smoke there must be fire, and where there's fire there must be hot tea."* Soon I found myself next to the door of a little house with rock-hewn walls and a slate roof. The family congregated by the kitchen hearth pulled me through the doorway. They sat me down and put a baby in my lap. I felt a joyful balance between being alone and self-sufficient and being welcomed into a family's home and being trusted enough to have a child handed to me.

I climbed several more peaks that autumn. I ran into a few Westerners here and there, but always attempted to find more back and side trails and stay away from the standard trekking routes. I love the solitude, the self-reliance, the getting *lost* with myself, the *solo* of it all! To travel solo is to give myself a gift.

Implementing Solo in Academic Settings

During the decades since that first fateful night in the oak tree, I have incorporated solo into public school settings, as well as into wilderness adventure programs around the world. Each group requires a unique and special framing for the experience that is determined by background, life experiences, and goals for the particular teaching moment. Always, however, I stress the key component of a successful solo: *to focus on the personal uniqueness of the moment.*

I believe there is a place for solo in everyone's life. The experience often results in some type of personal growth, although I don't believe most people enter solo with an attitude of "I'm going to learn something about myself as I do this." Self-discoveries result because we create time in our lives for them.

The quiet stillness of the morning or evening light that comes when sitting in a special place in solitude is a treasure. For the seasoned soloist, hiking, running, or romping in the mountains is also a perfect time to be alone with one's thoughts. It is important to be at peace in the setting, so that the stage is not an escape from one's mind but rather a door, facilitating one's reaching for her/his personal potential. Schools, parents, and activists can all open more doors, for themselves and all of us.

Solo does not always mean traveling halfway around the world and immersing oneself in some exotic land above the clouds. (However, I would certainly encourage anyone to seize any opportunity to experience foreign peaks or river systems.) What is important in our frenzied society is to be able to find a place of quiet peace and solace, and to be alone for significant periods. We must teach our children that time in solitude is not punishment but a gift. Solo time provides opportunities to reflect upon what is going on in the internal world. Without such spaces, life becomes a series of reflex reactions more than conscious choices. Children need such time too.

Sitting around dining room tables in countless homes across the country today, parents ask their kids, "How was your day at school?" In response the child typically answers, "Fine." The next question by the probing parent is a little tougher, "What did you do in school today?" By the time a child reaches middle school, these discussions are usually cut short by responses ranging from, "nothing" to "just talked with my friends." Helping adolescents break away from the notion that they are disempowered in school is critical. We must make their educational experience valuable, pertinent, and worthwhile in *their eyes*.

Guiding students to a reflective solo experience is a way of providing them with an experience of being simultaneously inquisitive and thoughtful. It empowers them by allowing time to formulate solutions to quandaries that arise. Solo experiences and public schools share common goals of developing critical, objective, reflective thinkers. If individuals are given the opportunity to develop skills to enhance their problem-solving capabilities, they will be better prepared to face challenges throughout life.

I have had the opportunity to incorporate solo experiences of various scopes in a number of school settings. The outcomes have always been beneficial. All too often, kids are hurried through the academic process without being given time to reflect on the world and situations surrounding them. Life can become an "information overload" of events. Solo gives students time alone, which tends to have a calming effect on most people, allowing them to focus. In addition, when journaling is incorporated into the solo experience, it gives students time to write and draw in a setting where the focus is on content, not grammar or diction. This allows them to develop their own style of putting thoughts onto paper, and it provides teachers a way of incorporating writing into academic areas outside of language arts classes.

Solo in the PASSAGES Program

In the 1980s, in progressive Colorado public middle schools, teachers were given a great deal of autonomy by the administration. A variety of programs had been implemented over the years to try to reach the diverse needs of students who, for one reason or another, were not obtaining the maximum benefit from their educational experience. In 1984, as a tenured teacher at Nederland Secondary School in Nederland, Colorado, I was granted permission to develop a program called PAS-SAGES. This was an optional alternative program created for seventh and eighth grade students who wanted something different from their educational experience. Students applying for PASSAGES were not necessarily problem students but individuals who were bored with the status quo and felt powerless to make any changes. Interested students were required to apply in writing by filling out a short questionnaire and needed parental support. Applicants were interviewed prior to the start of the semester, and 10 students were invited to participate in the program each semester. The program was self-contained, meaning PASSAGES students took all their academic classes as a group, so that coursework could be accomplished without affecting other programs in the school. Students accomplished an integrated social studies-language arts curriculum through a cultural journalism unit in which kids produced a magazine, *Cabin Voice*. Math was covered in running a fundraising "business" in school to finance the variety of experiences in which the kids were participating. Accounting was monitored by students, for students. Science was generally covered in the field.

As part of the PASSAGES program, students spent approximately 10 days in a wilderness setting, backpacking, completing a service project, and experientially studying canyon geology, astronomy, botany, archeology, hydrology, and ecology. Near the end of this wilderness component, students went on solo to reflect about the entire experience. They were guided to focus on the lessons they could take away. This reflective process was designed to assist these young people to take possession of their educational opportunities and glean from them what would be most beneficial. They had been provided with a unique opportunity to gain skills in asking for what they needed to help them succeed in school. After completing a semester in PAS-SAGES, students were reintegrated into the traditional classroom setting. Every student who participated in the PASSAGES program graduated from high school, many went to college, and there is even a Rhodes Scholar among the participants. The PASSAGES students who report in occasionally (they are now in their twenties and thirties!) still refer to PASSAGES as being the most fun and personally enriching academic experience of their lives.

Solo in Eagle Rock School

Following my time with PASSAGES, I was hired by the American Honda Education Corporation as an instructional specialist for Eagle Rock School and Professional Development Center in Estes Park, Colorado. Eagle Rock is a tuition-free year-round residential high school for students who don't find success, for whatever reason, in their home school. The American Honda Education Corporation hired a group of innovative educators to develop a program that would provide a place for such students to shine and promote change in the public school system on a national level. As in the PASSAGES program, students at Eagle Rock must go through an application and interview process, need an adult advocate, and must have the desire to make change in their own life.

Students drawn to Eagle Rock come from all walks of life. They range from honors students to those right off the streets and fresh out of treatment facilities. When you enter campus — 720 stunning acres in the Colorado Rocky Mountains — the student and staff diversity is immediately noticeable. Even so, there is a sense of unity: Everyone is at Eagle Rock to succeed, maybe for the first time in his or her life, and there is the impetus to create change.

Each trimester a new group of students (15–17 years old) is admitted. As part of the first trimester experience, every individual participates in a 25-day wilderness program. Students learn wilderness survival skills, environmental ethics, and safe wilderness travel techniques. They also have introductory rock and peak climbing experiences and a solo opportunity.

The solo is framed as an exercise to examine their direction in life and what brought them to Eagle Rock. Students are encouraged to scrutinize past behaviors and attitudes in school, and to make choices about their future educational career. Students are encouraged to reflect on what behaviors allow them to survive and thrive in a wilderness setting and to figure out which of those behaviors will be most beneficial to take back to the school community. Starting school in this manner puts students into a unique environment, where they must support and rely on people they don't know and with whom they have little or nothing in common. The wilderness experience as a whole gives them the opportunity to examine what has worked well for them in the past, to draw on their strengths, learn the power of group effort and, maybe most importantly, to reflect on what changes they need to make in their lives as they enter a community of learners who are there to create positive change in their lives. Students emerge from the experience feeling empowered and ready to start a new way of life. "The Wilderness Trip is like a whole new life; I was reborn in the woods," writes one student. "During my first trimester I learned to work in a group. I grew mentally in many incredible ways, and physically. I learned how to be away from my family and friends, and all of my old ways that I had grown way too comfortable with," explains another (Anonymous, n.d.).

Solo in Traditional Academic Settings

While these examples are of atypical teaching situations, it is possible to carry many of their philosophies and practices into public school settings. Admittedly, there are barriers to doing so, including curriculum mandates, limited physical space, time constraints, and some administrators' educational philosophies.

I believe, however, that teachers must allow students to engage in the reflective process. Students must know that their thoughts and concerns are valid and relevant. This can be achieved in regular classrooms in any content area. One way is by sharing a content-related yet thought-provoking passage or article with students who then go quietly ponder the significance of the shared reading. Teachers with a more imaginative or creative flare may use a cartoon that relates to a specific content area to get students thinking.

In a society where a child's only "rite of passage" is a driver's license, it takes the combined efforts of the community to provide youth with meaningful, thought-provoking opportunities that are not tied to the video player, DVD, or mechanized society. As teachers we must be innovative masters who stimulate students beyond what a machine can promote — a tough challenge. In my current role as a science teacher, I meet the challenge by taking an environmental perspective. I seek to blend cognitive understanding and emotional awareness of the natural world. I can easily incorporate environmental concerns and issues into my lesson plans that correlate with district, state, and federal standards. Actually teaching students to feel a holistic connection with all earthly things is more difficult. My interest in nature creates a passion to share my sense of wonder and fascination about the natural world with my students.

I believe that action without reflection is movement without meaning. After several trips outside to establish a comfort level and the giddy newness of tromping over the school grounds has passed, I have students select a personal *quiet spot*. Unlike traditional solo sites, the students are typically in sight of each other. After selecting their spots, students are encouraged to immerse themselves in the immediacy of their *kingdom*. I ask them to pay close attention to the selection of their spots. Taking territorial possession of them is encouraged. The students are told that the spot they select will be their quiet place for the entire year; it will be a place where they are to focus on their immediate environment, rather than on their classmates who may be as close as 15 feet away.

Early in the process of visiting their quiet spots, students are given specific directives for experiences that sometimes last as little as five minutes. Students begin by focusing on a particular plant of their choice in their space. They put a piece of flagging tape on the plant so that they are always able to find it throughout the year. Initially, students are asked to make observations of the plant. During their next visit, they are asked to draw a leaf or stem of the plant in detail. As the seasons progress, students are asked to observe changes, make more detailed observations, and examine the role of their plant in the larger ecosystem. As the year progresses, I give the students less structure, requiring only that they make journal entries while they sit in their quiet spot. Near the end of the school year, I provide students with longer blocks of time for solo.

Inside the classroom, journal entries are shared with the entire group by willing participants. Occasionally, this turns into an interdisciplinary activity with the language arts teacher. Student writing improves as their observation skills improve; they begin to reflect on the larger environment — including themselves. They begin to look at more global issues concerning themselves and others. They are able to tie other fields of science into ecology and then certain scientific concepts into their lives. I have found that with very little direction, only subtle suggestions during processing time, students learn how to examine their role on earth. Students often share these experiences with their parents. In turn, Native Alaskan parents have told me that their children are finally learning about the food plants their grandparents taught them to collect as kids.

Conclusion

As an educator, I am rewarded when students question larger issues. Middle school students are grappling with major developmental changes in both their minds and bodies. I can take advantage of their newly found sense of inquiry and blossoming awareness of the world around them. After coming back from solo time they ask questions such as: How does the aurora borealis work? What are the origins of the myths and legends surrounding the constellations in the night sky? Students begin questioning human and societal actions that lie behind the superfund toxic-waste sites poisoning the coastal environment. They come up with questions about mathematical string theory or the possibility of traveling in time by exceeding the speed of light that I can't even begin to answer. Kids are talking to their parents, parents are sharing with their kids, and generation gaps are bridged.

There is plenty of time for the plethora of labs that accompany our lectures on topics of physics, chemistry, biology, astronomy, geology, and genetics. If our students start to question the intricate nature of the world, they are defining their place in their unfolding educational experiences. I believe that if students are given the opportunity to self-discover relationships between organisms, seasons, and forces, their search for knowledge will lead them to an interest in scientific inquiry. Reflective solo time in the context of the classroom is critical to fostering natural curiosity.

Part of the process of discovery is searching internally for a sense of place. It can start with observing a small part of a plant of their choice at their quiet spots. It's amazing what can happen when students are encouraged to sit silently face-to-face with the life force growing throughout the year, changing with the seasons. After having her eyes opened to the fragile yet resilient bog ecosystem and listening to the perspectives of her peers, a student stated, "I don't understand how so many humans abuse the planet. I'm going to make a difference in how the earth is cared for."

If I could give my students one thing, it would be to encourage their innate awareness and sense of wonder about the world around them. This awareness, coupled with their "I can do it" attitude, facilitates their understanding and desire to help others in caring for spaceship Earth. By judiciously using time for solo and reflection in my curriculum, I attempt to temper the mountains of rote trivia that students must assimilate by introducing them to a powerful tool — solo experiences, the whispers of the wilderness.

My solo time in Nepal, climbing the peaks and valleys, will forever be a part of me. Now I am in Alaska, paddling the abyss of frigid arctic waters, and my goal is still to find answers for myself — about myself. In the classroom I've traded my bag of mountaineering tricks for an educator's bag of tricks, but the challenge is the same – learning how to best apply them.

References

Anonymous. (n.d.) Retrieved August 2005 from www.eaglerockschool.org/Wilderness.htm

Porter, E. (2001). *The color of wildness: A retrospective, 1936-1985.* Retrieved June 2004, from www.OutdoorEd.com/quotes

Russell, R. & Russell, T. (1967). *On the loose.* San Francisco: Sierra Club Books.

CHAPTER 14

Solo's Effect on Group Attitude

By William J. Quinn

*We are attracted by a deep forest or lake because it
gives the impression that there is some truth to discover,
some secret to abduct from the heart of the object.
It is the eternal seduction of the hidden.*
(Dufrenne, 1973, p. 398)

Most research and literature about the solo element of adventure programming focuses on solo's impact on the individual. While solo experiences are filled with opportunity for individual growth and learning, I believe its impact on the group attitude can be equally great.

I have participated in many solo experiences as a leader, independently and with the Outward Bound (OB) organization. I have participated in solo experiences during OB staff training, and subsequently led the activity as an assistant instructor and as a lead instructor. Time and again, I have found the activity to be an extremely positive and productive experience for students — and for myself.

Solo's Effect on the Psyche

Every group develops a unique *personality*, be it a sports team, a department within a business, or a collection of people on a guided wilderness adventure. In such groups, the whole is different than — and I would venture greater than — the sum of its parts. Anyone who leads adventure groups, teaches classes, or works with small groups in any capacity knows that each group possesses its own attitudinal and behavioral characteristics. Facilitators describe groups as being motivated, dysfunctional, energetic, enigmatic, full of conflict, and evolving, to mention just a few descriptors.

In the adventure courses I have led, there are always some people who are frightened by the prospect of solo and others who look forward to the alone time it provides. Whatever the perspective on solo, the anticipation it creates has an effect on individuals, and thus the group, from the moment it is proposed until long after the course is over.

Solo provides individuals the opportunity to break away from the intensity of group dynamics and the constant influence of participant attitudes and moods. This allows the individual to change his/her personal attitude and mood. As a result, the post-solo group personality is usually different than it was pre-solo. The effect of solo on a group's attitude often goes unnoticed for two reasons: (a) because the experience is debriefed near the end of most program sequences, and (b) pre-solo talks focus on the individual benefits the experience can have. Sometimes, however, the changes in the group are quite obvious, even if there are only hours remaining before the group disbands. Here is one story that illustrates how solo can affect group dynamics.

Solo's Effect in Practice

About 10 years ago I was instructing a standard class for the Voyager Outward Bound School in Ely, Minnesota, by myself. It was an eight-day canoe trip in the lakes of the Boundary Waters Canoe Area Wilderness. The group I was leading happened to be all male and ranged in age from 22 to 34. The class had not been advertised as an all-male trip or given any particular emphasis, as many Outward Bound programs are (e.g., Life Career Renewal, Outward Bound Directive, nor a Youth Leadership Program). This course was simply offered as an open enrollment experience for anyone who wanted to experience a standard Outward Bound class.

Day 1 was spent at the Outward Bound Voyager School base camp, orienting participants to Outward Bound procedures, getting to know one another, and learning a little bit about paddling. The following day we began our trek into the lake wilderness. For the next week, we paddled, portaged, and camped, but the real Outward Bound goals were meeting personal and group challenges, reaching inside oneself for courage and determination, and, of course, learning about the environment and using outdoor skills.

Solo was scheduled for Day 6, just before the final expedition segment and after five days of travel. Our solo location was Carefree Lake off the Kawishiwi River. Lakes in the Boundary Waters have colorful names, and "Carefree" is no exception. The irony in this case, however, was that the participants on this trip were definitely not carefree, and our route to the lake didn't lighten the mood any. Our beginning point was Little Grabbro Lake, which required an initial 250-rod portage from the vehicle drop-off. We had to cross 200 yards of knee-deep mud before we could dip a paddle — a difficult introduction. A few days later more mud had to be navigated between Bald Eagle Lake and Rock of Ages Lake. The travel was tough, but the attitude of the group was tougher.

As we traveled, two students, one 22 and the other 34, fixated on the upcoming requirements of solo. They were afraid of the possibility of bear attacks, being separated from the supportive framework of the group and the loneliness that a wilderness setting can create in people who live in suburban America. Their nervousness palpably escalated as the day for solo neared, with the younger fellow visibly working himself into a state of high anxiety. The nervous duo's energy around solo rubbed off on the others, creating an apprehensive unit.

During Outward Bound courses, the solo experience is designed for personal reflection as well as personal challenge. It stands in stark contrast to the rest of the adventure for a number of reasons: gear and resources are minimal, students are alone for the first time in days, weeks, or months, and the focus is on reflection and personal challenge. On an eight-day course the solo experience usually lasts 24 hours, while longer courses have correspondingly longer solo experiences that last up to three days.

The solo on this course was 24 hours long. It began mid-afternoon one day and concluded about the same time the following day. Students took the clothes they were wearing, rain gear, a bug tent, a whistle, a sleeping bag, and an optional cupful of granola. Students often refuse the granola and choose to fast. Students are asked not to go swimming, wander from their assigned site, or do anything that might result in injury. The whistle is a safety device used to summon instructors in the event of an emergency. Information on possible dangers in the area are always given; this group was aware that there had been two bear attacks in the Boundary Waters canoe area that summer. That fact definitely contributed to their apprehension level.

As we approached the spot where we had to leave the Kawashiwi and travel down a small tributary to Carefree Lake, the mood of the group changed from somber to almost hostile. The 22-year-old definitely did not want to solo, and he made that abundantly clear. The other fellow remained nervous but was relatively less vocal. The remaining four paddlers were apprehensive, more so because of the anxieties of their compatriots than anything else. Basically, the group as a whole would have been far happier to skip the whole thing. However canceling an activity because students are reluctant is not the Outward Bound way. The idea of *Challenge by Choice* has a far more limited application in this setting.

So by the time the small tributary off the Kawashiwi petered out and the route presented them with more mud to traverse, spirits were abysmal. When the tributary became non-existent, we left behind unneeded gear and waded through waist-deep mud and water for about 200 yards before clambering over a beaver dam and into a stagnant pond. The pond gave way to tall swampy grass for another quarter-mile before we finally made the shore of our destination. By the time we reached Carefree, it had been two-and-a-half hours since we left the Kawashiwi.

One at a time, students were escorted to their solo sites by canoe — they at the bow, me at the stern. Solo sites were located either on a small point of land jutting into the lake, a sandy bit of shoreline, or a higher promontory away from the water but easily accessible. Sites were strategically placed so that students could not see one another, and attempts were made to provide an acceptable amount of level ground for sleeping.

No other paddlers were there, and we all knew that no one else was likely to pass by. Students were not given a choice as to where they would be placed, but I purposely positioned the 22-year-old at a spot fairly close to my own campsite. This placement was done after four of the other students had already been placed so as to not make it obvious that he was being given any "special" treatment because of his initial fears. People's attitudes were interesting to watch as they gathered up their gear and exited the boat. Some were excited to get going, others exhibited signs of apprehension mixed with anticipation. Fear was present but not overwhelming, and no one balked when the actual time to embark arrived.

That night, no emergency whistles were blown, bug tents did their job, and the weather did not call for the use of the heavy Helly-Hansen rain suits. In fact, the weather was inspiringly beautiful. The solo that had begun with trepidation ended in elation, and our solo-ending banquet of pizza, cinnamon cake, Jell-O, peanut butter and jelly sandwiches, and tea was a resounding success. Students had previously agreed to make something for each other out of natural materials, and they all took the assignment seriously, producing beautiful objects to give as gifts. The presentation of these crafts during the feast was meaningful to all.

The debriefing of the solo experience was productive, poignant, and exciting. Many comments centered on the relief experienced when individuals realized they were indeed prepared for solo and that many personal misgivings were unfounded. One comment was, "I discovered that most of what I worry about never happens." We chatted for quite a while about that comment and how it applied to their everyday existence. Others spoke about the opportunity for reflection, and welcomed the switch from constant group living and subsequent pressures to the pleasure of spending some time alone. Our fearful 22-year-old was relieved, jubilant, and far more confident in himself. We left Carefree Lake in a rejuvenated frame of mind.

The return route through the grass, over the pond, slugging through the mud, and back to the Kawishiwi River took 45 minutes. The same men, the same equipment, the same supplies (less food), and the same route was negotiated in one-third the time. The only difference was the attitude of the individuals who made up our group, and this shift in mental attitude was created by the solo experience. Carefree Lake had earned its name! The solo, with its power to positively affect individuals, was the crucial turning point in this particular Outward Bound wilderness excursion.

Conclusion

The power of the individual solo experience on group attitude merits analysis by psychologists and sociologists. I am neither, but I am able to read a group and here are some concluding thoughts. First, I think that the anxiety and apprehension of two members of the group was most likely based on a fear of the unknown. Perhaps they were fearful of being alone. Perhaps they were fearful of bears and potential attacks. Perhaps they were fearful of failing the challenge of solo, the result of having doubts about their inner resources. In retrospect, I have wondered if I should have passed along more information to allay many of their individual terrors. I tried to do that, but perhaps our preparatory discussions could have been more effective. Information about the bear attacks probably should have been handled differently and protective measures outlined.

Before solo, the more steady members in the group had apprehensions of their own and held some realistic fears about foul weather, aloneness, boredom, and bears. The two anxious men likely elevated their concerns. When they arrived at their solo sites, everyone discovered that their fears were largely unfounded. Nature and solitude worked their magic — bringing relaxation — and inner peace to create a positive and fulfilling experience.

After the solo, with everyone feeling more positive, the *personality* of the group was transformed. Positive feelings about personal successes were predominant and righteousness about the whole group experience prevailed. Everyone rejoined the group with enthusiasm, was glad to leave the aloneness behind and was pumped-up for the return trip through swamp and mud. They had that "we can do anything" attitude that is one of the prime objectives of Outward Bound. Solo had done it again!

Reference

Dufrenne, M. (1973). *The phenomenology of aesthetic experience.* Evanston, IL: Northwestern University Press.

CHAPTER 15

Solo Experiences in the Summer Camp

By Faith Evans

Solitude is nearly a misnomer. To me, being alone
means togetherness — the re-coming-together of me and
nature, of me and being; the reuniting of me with all ...
whereby I see once again that the little things are little
and the big things are big.

(Prather, 1970)

Since 1921, Cheley Colorado Camps, in Estes Park, Colorado, has welcomed more than 50,000 young people from every state and more than a dozen countries, including many second, third, and now fourth generation Cheley campers. The mission, as originally stated in 1921 by founder Frank Cheley, is:

> *To inculcate in boys and girls that spirit of honesty, purity, unselfishness, love,*
> *alertness, determination, and courage which is the foundation for all that is big*
> *and fine in American life and character, and more than this, the Summer Camp*
> *aims to help boys and girls cultivate the ability to act spontaneously in the right.*

Acting spontaneously in the right? During nearly every moment of the waking day at Cheley campers have the opportunity to make spontaneous choices and to act or not act in the right. Campers choose activities on a *scope and sequence* basis, whereby learning experiences are arranged according to age, interest and ability. Throughout their camp experience feedback is available from peers and counselors, yet seldom is there time to think about the long-term implications of their choices — spontaneous or not.

As the program director at Cheley, I delight in adding new program components that cover a maximum of the needs and desires of campers, and meet the intent of the mission. Solos came to Cheley Colorado Camps in 1995. The Cheley staff decided that a solo program supported the camp mission by offering a place "where time slows down and people open up." Such uninterrupted time to daydream and wonder is a unique commodity in any residential camp. At Cheley, campers are taught to use solo time to reflect on the personal goals they set shortly after arriving at camp. Cheley staff also determined that a solo program could easily and inexpensively be implemented, would require a minimum of specialized training, and had no limitations based on gender, physical ability, or skill level. We were aware that there were both physical and psychological risks associated with solo programs, but we knew these could be managed with careful planning and preparation of the campers, and appropriate supervision by the counselors. We decided that campers 12 and older would be offered the choice to participate in a two-day, one-night solo experience on the camp property. The Cheley solo was designed to follow the spirit and intent of the Outward Bound version, tailored to the needs of a youthful summer camp population. Once implemented, the solo program became an instant and surprising favorite with campers, and there were soon waiting lists to participate in the opportunity.

When campers at Cheley take a risk and try a solo, they invite multiple opportunities to find out more about who they are. This paper outlines some of the key elements of the solo experience as it has evolved over several years in a camp setting.

Solo in Action

In order to minimize health and safety risks and maximize the opportunity for personal growth, solo experiences for young people must be well organized. Careful attention must be paid to all aspects of safety and to the facilitation abilities of the counseling staff. The following outline provides an example of how the concept of solo has been incorporated into the Cheley Colorado Camps. This outline is used to help the staff and the campers understand the nature of solo, and to prepare them for a positive experience.

Defining Solo for Campers

A solo is an experience:

...in which campers spend an allotted period of time

...in a designated, safe location in the wilderness

...alone and out of sight, but not earshot, of leaders and peers

...under non-intrusive but continual supervision by camp counselors.

Defining the Purpose of Solo for Campers

The purpose of the solo is:

...to be alone in the natural environment

...supervised and safe

...to think, reflect, observe, sing, draw, and write

...to rely on personal resources for food, shelter, and entertainment

...to rest and relax, away from daily routines, stresses and pressures

...and to afterward share insights gained, fears encountered, observations noted, challenges met, and plans created

...with others who have also had the *alone time* of solo

Four Basic Components of the Cheley Solo Program

Planning and Preparation by the Staff

Leaders will be required to do the following:

1. Plan the experience.
2. Select participants, brief them, and obtain their agreement to participate.
3. Implement the solo experience.
4. Debrief the solo experience.

Successfully facilitating the solo will require the leaders do the following:

1. Select a section of land and reconnoiter and map it.
2. Locate and inspect a site for the *leader camp* central to the area, where leaders will remain throughout the solo program, and mark it on the map.
3. Choose solo sites that ensure as much as possible that soloists will not see or hear other soloists and will be secluded from foot trails, vehicle traffic, and other distractions.
4. Name or number the solo sites and mark them on the map along with compass coordinates. (Previous campers may have already named the sites, or they can be named after the activity by the current soloists. Examples include Lone Pine Rock, Aspen Grove, and Front Range Hideaway.
5. Mark the solo sites carefully for other leaders who may use the area in the future.
6. Make a note cairn (post office) near each solo site. This entails: (a) creating a sturdy tripod of sticks and rocks positioned purposely; (b) marking the cairn with a colored cloth or bandana; (c) making sure cairns are far enough from the solo site so that the soloist does not see the coming and going of leaders.
7. Plan the activity itinerary and timetable for: (a) travel to the chosen area, including plans for vehicles; (b) walking the campers to their solo sites;

(c) preparing a campsite meal for campers after solo time; (d) collecting soloists and walking them to the leaders camp after the activity; (e) group debriefing of the experience; (f) return travel back to camp, including plans for vehicles.

Preparing the Participants

1. Frame the solo as an exercise as a personal challenge that requires:
   a. trust in inner resources and in counselors' supervision
   b. commitment to self, others, and counselors to not talk to others
   c. commitment to stay at the assigned solo site
2. Get verbal or written agreement to these commitments if possible.
3. Inform the participants what to bring, explaining that they are to take as little as possible. Counselors need to use their judgment depending on geographic location, time of year, weather, age of participants, and length of the solo. Items that will be needed include:
   a. sleeping bag and ground pad
   b. tarp for shelter
   c. 3 quarts of water
   d. warm clothes and rain gear
   e. food pack containing optional snacks, unless soloists choose to fast (apple, orange, bagels, peanuts, raisins, trail mix, drink powder)
   f. any necessary medical prescriptions
   g. emergency whistle
   h. notebook and pencils
   i. backpack or plastic bag to carry required equipment and supplies
4. Inform the participants what not to bring.
   a. matches, knife, flashlight, watch, camera, musical instruments
   b. soap, cosmetics, toilet paper, comb, toothbrush
   c. laptop, cell phone, Walkman or radio, battery-operated hand games
   d. compass, unless there is a planned activity to use it

On Solo Day: Provide a Framework for the Solo Experience

1. Agree with participants about the distance they may move from their assigned solo site (for example, 10 feet in any direction).

2. Agree with participants that they will not hike, climb trees, go for a swim, whittle, start a fire, or damage the environment.

3. Emphasize the commitment to solitude and silence; if a soloist feels that

s/he must talk to someone, s/he should walk to the leaders camp and not disturb a fellow soloist.

4. Emphasize keeping to the purpose of the solo by not intruding on the physical space and solitude of another. Contact, invited or not, will disrupt the strength and flow of the experience.

5. Leaders, not nearby soloists, should be contacted in time of emergency, depending on the type of accident, illness, or emotional trauma.

6. Option: Someone participating in a second solo experience could choose to be led to her/his solo site blindfolded. Emphasize that the point would not be to spend the time trying to figure out where they are, but to enter the experience with an open mind, being totally present and observant as if it were her/his first time on solo.

7. Pass out emergency whistles. Clearly outline what constitutes a *whistle emergency* and instruct participants regarding use of the whistle. Participants are to wear the whistle around their neck at all times, even when sleeping. In the case of emergency, sound out three blasts, pause, three more blasts, pause, three more blasts, and then listen for the sound of help coming — then repeat the procedure. Explain who responds to the whistle: Do only leaders respond to the whistle? Do all who hear respond to the whistle? Do others who hear notify the leaders? Or do you respond with a combination of options? Close by clearly re-stating safety considerations.

8. Pass out notebooks and pencils, which can be used to write notes to the post office cairns, and for journaling and drawing.

9. Carefully explain the use of the note cairns.
   a. Communication notes may be required or voluntary. Requirement acts as a safety net and compliance is important, because notes tell the leaders how the participant is doing and if there are pressing needs or questions.
   b. Other *minor* first-aid materials may be passed to leaders via the cairns.
   c. Tell the soloists the approximate hour of the day, maybe once in the morning and once in the afternoon, when notes will be picked up. Remember, campers have no watches.

10. Tell the soloists the approximate time when leaders will return to pick them up.
   a. Instruct them to try to be packed up and ready to leave.
   b. Instruct them to police the solo site and remove all signs that they were there, and to return it to nature by scattering any moved stones or sticks.

11. Give suggestions for optional activities for the soloist.

a. Write a *late letter* (a confidential letter, sealed in a self-addressed envelope to be mailed by the camp office for receipt six months later).

b. Make a gift from nature, following environmental guidelines, to give to another person in the group whose name can be previously drawn.

c. Suggest they find a symbolic totem from the solo site — a natural object such as a rock, a pine cone, a piece of wood — that represents a quality of the solo site or the solo experience.

d. Use their journal to write a poem, a thank-you letter, a song, a story, or a re-connection note.

e. Artwork is always a meaningful option.

f. Let soloists know they will have the opportunity to share writings, totems, or pictures with others during the post-solo debrief.

Staff Responsibilities on Solo Day

1. Organize the group for travel to the solo area.
2. Gather at the site of the leaders camp, and make sure all soloists know where it is.
3. Strategically select locations for individual campers.
   a. Consider who may need assistance, additional support, or a watchful eye.
   b. Separate those who might be tempted to break solo and visit each other.
   c. Assign outer limits to those who desire seclusion.
4. Escort campers to their solo sites.
   a. Have soloists gather their gear for movement to the solo site.
   b. Walk silently from the leaders' camp to the solo sites.
   c. Leaders may divide the group to conserve on time.
   d. Ideally, have the group wait silently at the note cairn while escorting each camper to her/his solo site.
5. Make sure soloists know:
   a. the location of their note cairn and procedures for using it; the location of the leaders' camp and conditions for return to it; the emergency whistle procedures
6. Take a final reading on the campers' emotional readiness for the solo.

Staff Activity During Solo Time

1. Act in a way that promotes solo and preserves its inclusion in the camp curriculum.
   a. Ideally, leaders will take a parallel solo. Although conversation and physical proximity with other leaders is necessary, it is important to keep as quiet as possible.
   b. Remember, in the quiet of nature, noise carries.

    c. The worst-case scenario is that leaders consider it social time or an opportunity to call friends on cell phones, or are otherwise unmindful of their responsibility to the campers.

    d. A unique consideration for staffing an overnight solo is that at least one of the leaders should be a light sleeper — or else they should take turns staying awake and on watch, as a camper might walk into the leaders' camp at any time.

    e. Leaders should be aware that any misstep may endanger the future of the solo program if it is not well established and widely understood. Parents are not generally as familiar with solo as a camp activity compared to the more traditional activities like swimming and hiking.

2. Periodically, leaders may want to quietly walk the area to assure all is well.

    a. Leaders should be aware that unintentional noises may cause undo emotional stress for campers

    b. If you do become visible or audible, don't make eye contact, and try to move quickly away.

3. Leaders should check the note cairns according to agreed timetable.

4. Only if there appears to be immediate need should leaders go to soloists, but remember that it's better to err on the side of caution.

5. During the final hours before camper pick-up, the leaders should prepare the meal to be enjoyed post-solo.

6. Pick up the soloists in the reverse order to which they were delivered to their solo sites.

    a. Leaders can divide the area in order conserve time.

    b. Proceed to the farthest solo site, and instruct the soloist to eye-check the site. Wait patiently, for some soloists may have completely lost track of time (that's a good thing). When the camper is ready, walk away together in silence.

    c. Plan enough time for the pick-up, for hurrying may completely undo the rest and relaxation that occurred during solo.

    d. Leave all site markers and note cairns intact for the next group — unless no other group is likely to follow, in which case dismantle all markers and cairns.

    e. Remember, the solo experience is not over when the group arrives back at the leaders camp.

7. It is then time for the meal.

    a. Soloists will be hungry.

    b. Light and fresh food is preferable to a heavy or overly sweet intake.

    c. Set a slow pace of eating to prevent upset stomachs that can result from haste and gorging.

Post-Solo Debriefing

This is the time when insights gained during the solo experience can become clear. The following are guidelines for conducting a post-solo debriefing.

1. Sit together (a circle is inclusive).
2. Let the returning soloists talk.
    a. Spontaneous talk is certainly okay in the beginning.
    b. Encourage them to talk one at a time and listen to each other.
    c. Return later to topics that warrant more discussion.
3. As the debriefing unfolds, leaders may wish to ask some of the following suggested questions.
    a. How are you doing?
    b. What was the hardest part of solo?
    c. Are you glad it's over? Why?
    d. Do you wish it could have been longer? Why?
    e. What, if anything, was easy? Or easier than you thought it would be?
    f. Were there any surprises? What?
    g. What did you miss most during your solo?
    h. Are there things or people in your life that you take for granted?
    i. What will you remember most about your solo?
    j. What will you tell others about your solo?
    k. What do you want to take with you and apply to your life?
    l. How are you different now from when you began your solo?
    m. What was your experience of being hungry?
    n. What did you do instead of eat?
    o. What would you do differently if you participated in another solo?
    p. Would you like to solo again? Why? Why not?
    q. Did anyone *break* solo?
    r. Did you learn anything from not following the guidelines? What?
    s. How do others feel about breaking solo?
    t. If you broke solo and visited another camper, was the decision mutual?
4. Leaders may wish to incorporate some of these activities into the debriefing.
    a. Invite sharing of journal notes, poems, pictures.
    b. Invite sharing of personal totems and their meaning.
    c. Exchange gifts made at the solo site.
    d. At some point it may be appropriate for leaders to share an experience, a story, an insight.
    e. Songs could be part of a debrief and closing ceremony, if there are camp songs that everyone knows.

     f. Share inspirational readings about solo, nature, solitude, and self-discovery.

     g. The group could make symbolic friendship crafts — a monkey's fist to be worn, a sand candle, a friendship bracelet, or other memento.

After the Solo

1. Be aware that for some campers moving back to the "full speed ahead" camp environment may be challenging after the quiet time of solo.

2. Other campers will be curious about what happened and will ask a lot of questions. Assure soloists that it is quite permissible to not share anything they don't wish to, and encourage them to tell those who express interest to experience solo firsthand.

3. Be prepared for exaggerated stories and high drama as the days go on. Tall tales of bad weather, wild animals, or other anxiety-producing incidents will grow; for instance, spiders can became monsters and coyote calls became wild hyena cries! Let campers have fun with their stories, but help them maintain a realistic perspective.

Camper Reflections About Solo

    The Cheley Colorado Camps solos have become very popular with the campers. Here are a handful of paraphrased responses youthful soloists have shared during their debriefs:

> *I like all my friends and all ... and at first I missed someone to talk to. And then I got hungry, but after I ate, I just liked watching the ants and it was okay. I fed them my bagel crumbs and watched where they took them.*

> *I was tired when I came on the solo, but now I feel like not so tired. I took a lot of deep breaths and fell asleep in the day. I've never done that before. My room at home has to be really dark for me to sleep!*

> *The time went soooo fast. I just looked up and you were there to pick me up. I didn't want to leave my place. It was all mine and I could smell the leaves and the ground.*

> *I ate all my food as soon as I got there and then wished I had saved some. I don't like raisins but I liked them in the woods. I knew I would make it and if I didn't I could blow my whistle, and so I drank my water slower.*

I made my tarp into a cozy tent. I forgot the knots we learned but just tied a bunch of them and it worked. I put all my stuff inside my tent. Then I sat outside it until the sun went down and it started to get dark. I saw some dark clouds and wanted it to rain so I could get inside my cozy tent and stay dry. It didn't rain. It felt peaceful. I could hear the mosquitoes flying.

I thought about my family and cried a little while, but then I wrote a letter to them and felt better. I thanked my folks for sending me here. They work hard.

I didn't like being alone. I am glad I did solo but would not sign up again. I kept thinking scary thoughts about the Texas Chain Saw Murders, but nothing bad happened.

I wrote this poem about shadows and the sun. I wrote another one about a butterfly that sat on my knee. I won't read them because I liked the writing when everything was quiet.

I watched the clouds and drew pictures in my journal of what they looked like in my imagination. I got dizzy at first, looking up, but then I named the pictures and had fun making up silly names.

I kept wondering what my friends were doing at first. Then when the frogs started chirping I listened to them and went to sleep. I woke up with cold feet and put my socks on and listened to more frogs and went back to sleep. They were LOUD!

I made a new friend. A chipmunk visited me and so I shared some of my food with him. I watched him for a long, long time. His tail kept swishing and I think he was trying to tell me things. Once when I was almost asleep, he ran over me in my sleeping bag. I named him Brownie and I would like to go back and visit him at my place.

Summary

The solo experience can be creatively redesigned and adapted for the summer camp. Experiences valued by adults may be equally valuable for youth, but activities for younger soloists should be modified to fit their psychological and physical states of readiness. Campers unfamiliar with the concept of spending time alone in nature can be introduced to a *mini-solo* that has been modified from the traditional solo experience offered for older participants.

Programming solo activities for youth in the summer camp requires that leaders do more planning, preparation, and close supervising than is the case with adults. This paper outlines many of the details that must be attended to, but it certainly is not all-inclusive. Each camp program must carefully create and organize solo programming for the particular population it serves. There must be attention to the needs and requirements of both the staff and the students. Caring camp staff can insure physical safety and a meaningful structure for time alone in nature.

For young soloists, there must be careful attention to pre-solo organization and briefing, close supervision and support during solo, and meaningful focus on the post-solo debriefing. Solo experiences, even with the staff within earshot of a whistle call, may serve as an initial step on the journey toward longer and more rigorous solo experiences. For youth, a mini-solo can trigger a lifetime appreciation of time alone in nature and reflection.

Reference

Prather, H. (1970). *Notes to myself*. Moab, Utah: Real People Press.

CHAPTER 16

Exercises and Activities to Prepare for the Solo Experience

By Thomas E. Smith

Focusing is a body-centered process of self-awareness and emotional healing. It's as simple as noticing how you feel — and then having a conversation with your feelings in which you do most of the listening....
Focusing is a process of honoring the wisdom that you have inside you, becoming aware of the subtle level of knowing that speaks to you through your body.

(Cornell, 1996)

The solo can be a growing and learning experience in its own right, and an opportunity for meaningful introspection and reflection on other life experiences. When a person is taught some skills to use during the solo experience, however, it can be even more effective.

Most programs offering solo experiences include pre-solo instruction designed to teach basic skills for establishing and maintaining physical comfort, such as fire and shelter building, toilet use, and first aid. Pre-solo instruction that teaches the student how to establish psychological comfort and how to use the time in solitude should also be provided. The fact is many people do not know how to be alone. They find solitude frightening, boring, or unproductive. We should never send students on solo without teaching them some basic skills and attitudes to use during the experience to reduce stress, enhance comfort, overcome boredom, stimulate nature discovery, and achieve other personal and program goals. Many formats or frameworks for the solo experience require special behaviors that can be learned and practiced prior to the actual solo.

This paper suggests some exercises that can be of value in preparing students for solo experiences. Many of these can be offered in small groups before solo and some require individual practice during solitude. Like solo itself, most of the suggested activities are valuable during solo and for future use.

Breathing

Restricted breathing is related to overall body tension. Participants should be able to overcome anxiety and tension while in solitude and to achieve a state of relaxation that can enhance reflection. Basic breathing exercises can accomplish this. In less than an hour of pre-solo time, facilitators can provide useful tips and teach a few basic exercises. Introducing tips on proper breathing early in a challenge education sequence makes the most sense. That way, breathing for relaxation can be practiced as the group participates in other activities. I have found it useful to attend to proper breathing as the group settles down for a debriefing session. I simply suggest that everyone close their eyes, take a few deep breaths, relax, *and come to this place*, as they circle for sharing thoughts and feelings.

Deep Breathing

Deep breathing involves inhaling through the nostrils, taking in as much oxygen as possible, and then exhaling slowly and completely through both the nose and mouth. It is helpful to think about the breathing process while doing this. I often suggest focusing thoughts or expressing vocalizations in sync with the inhaling-exhaling process; for example, *re ... lax, calm ... down, full ... empty,* or *sunrise ... sunset*. Visualizations can also be helpful, such as projecting an image of the lungs expanding and contracting. Deep breathing also involves the stomach and diaphragm. While more complex deep breathing exercises can help one attain total body relaxation, for adventure program applications the following activities are quite sufficient. (Do a keyword search for *deep breathing* on the Internet for more information.)

> **Activity: Deep Breathing**
> Sit in a comfortable position. Slowly allow tension to flow out of your body. Breathe deeply and rhythmically. Your chest and abdomen should move together as you inhale and exhale. Direct your attention to a particular image (a stream, a quiet landscape). You can also concentrate on your own rhythmic breathing or a favorite word or phrase that you can say out loud or silently to yourself.

Natural, uninhibited breathing is the goal. After a few deep breaths and the associated relaxed feelings, the individual should be breathing quite naturally. Holding the breath for as long as possible before exhaling is often practiced as part of deep breathing instruction. The instructions are to inhale, hold the breath while counting silently, and then exhale — then repeat and increase the count for holding the breath in. Some argue that these breath retention exercises may create body stress instead of relaxation, and thus recommend it only when working with advanced yoga techniques. My recommendation would be the teaching of natural breathing rhythms (for example, breathe in, hold for 3–4 counts, and then breathe out). Hyperventilation, which is often associated with stress, involves short choppy breaths in and out. As a way to demonstrate optimal breathing patterns, it can be helpful to have participants take choppy breaths so they can better understand the more desirable rhythms of natural breathing.

Walking-Breathing

This technique can bring the rhythms of natural breathing into harmony with the rhythms of the walk. Slowly breathe in for a count of three steps (1–2–3), hold the breath during the next two steps (4–5), and then slowly exhale to the count of three steps (6–7–8). After the rhythms are mastered, the person need not focus on counting breaths or steps, the body will simply move along naturally and in balance with the breathing. Walking-breathing can become a good habit. The combination of counting steps and counting breaths adds up to a way of moving in space in a balanced way. Gary Snyder said it clearly: "Walking is the great adventure, the first meditation, a practice of heartiness and soul primary to humankind. Walking is the exact balance between spirit and humility" (1990, p. 34).

> **Activity: Walking-Breathing**
> Stand erect, exhale, then start walking. Take three steps while inhaling, hold the breath in for two steps, exhale for three steps. The breathing should be done in one continuous flow: Do not inhale in short breaths.... If you feel three steps are too long for you, count two steps and hold for one. If, on the contrary, three steps are not enough, take four or five steps as you inhale and again as you exhale. The secret is to balance the walking and breathing, and keep it rhythmical. You can do this activity any time while walking.

Centering

Being centered is a state of relaxation, balance, and psychological grounding. It is a state in which the body is so relaxed that one is hardly aware of it. In a state of being centered, individuals can become aware of a spot — a ball of concentrated energy — deep inside themselves. Being centered readies the individual for meditation and reflection, or for forthcoming decision-making and problem-solving. Outdoor adventure leaders should spend some pre-solo time teaching participants to *relax, take a deep breath, and come to center*. One can learn to center in standing, sitting, or reclining positions. In the standing position, centering is closely associated with the parallel concept of psychological grounding. When teaching tai chi, the masters start with lessons on centering in a standing position and becoming firmly grounded.

Centering was suggested as an educational tool about 30 years ago in *The Centering Book*, which provides many simple activities for learning to center (Hendricks & Wills, 1975). *The Second Centering Book* offered more activities for children, parents, and teachers (Hendricks & Roberts, 1977). (Do a keyword search for *centering* on the Internet for more information).

Activity: Centering

Sit comfortably in a chair with eyes closed. Empty your mind, intend to do nothing but be present, having your total attention extroverted. You don't think being there or anything like that, you just relax and do nothing. Notice the space you are in and the sounds about you. If thoughts are going through your mind, let them die out and get back to just being there. Don't force yourself to not think, simply relax into a quiet space of just being there. The same goes for physical reactions you may have. If you twitch or yawn, just notice that and get your attention to just being there. You should be able to get to the point of doing this for a couple of hours, sitting relaxed without doing anything other than being alert. When you succeed in doing that, time disappears and you can sit relaxed for any amount of time with your attention centered.

I wrote a personalized instructional narrative for gravitational centering in my first book (Smith, 1980), and many readers have commented on its value. The complete instructions for that 35-40 minute exercise, and the full narrative for it is presented in Appendix III. The exercise begins with the following words:

> *Listen...*
> *There is a Center to our Universe.*
> *There is a Center to our Body.*
> *The Center of our Body is the Center of our Universe.*
> *The energies of the Universe, in their continuous flow*
> *through timespace pass through the Center.*
> *The gravitational, seasonal, and stellar energies of our*
> *world transfer and recharge at our Center.*
> *Within each of us — to be known best when we find*
> *balance and harmony with the gravitational and*
> *Universal forces — lies our Centerpoint of peace,*
> *balance, and energy.*
> *Let us come to Center.*

Through the years, I have facilitated centering exercises as a precursor to climbing and rappelling, ropes and teams courses, caving experiences, and conducting personal growth adventure sequences. An exercise I learned when studying with Native American Sioux elders can be of great help in introducing the concept of centering to participants. It is an activity that quickly helps them understand the relaxation and mental emptiness one seeks in being at center.

Activity: Starstretch

Lie on your back, feet apart about 10–15 inches. You are a star. Simultaneously lift all five points of the star (arms, legs, and head) off the ground about 6 inches. Hold that position until you feel your stomach muscles tense. Hold that tension for a few moments and then let out a big breath as you drop all five points of the star back to the ground. This is not a test of endurance. You should hold the position only until the solar plexus tension builds, and then collapse back to the ground. As you do this stretch and release, become aware of the feeling of emptiness that comes at the moment you release all the tension. Try to identify the spot where the stomach tension builds and releases; that is your center — that is where you need to go when you want to become centered. Practice the Starstretch a few times, and come to recognize your center. (Smith & Quinn, 2004, p. 64)

Stretching

People going on solo experiences would benefit from a few basic stretches to bring relaxation, tension-reduction, awareness, and energy. There is stretching with the primary goal of readying the muscles for physical activity, and there is stretching that also readies the mind for forthcoming experiences. Simple hatha yoga exercises can be taught to participants readying for solo, as can some of the basic movements of tai chi. The Tao's message about balancing yin and yang forces speaks to bringing the body and mind into harmony, and bringing mental and physical energies together.

Many students tend to dislike exercises that resemble physical education calisthenics, but I have found that introducing stretches adapted from the teachings of indigenous land-based peoples can pique their interest. One of my favorites is The Raccoon and the Eagle.

Activity: The Raccoon and the Eagle

Begin on your hands and knees, palms down on the Earth, fingers spread apart to feel the soil. Slowly slide your hands forward through the grass, and angle them toward each other. As your hands come together, lean forward and place your forehead on them. Feel the texture of the Earth with your fingertips, and breathe deeply and inhale the aromas of the soil. Hold your breath while slowly rising up, dragging your hands across the soil and up your own body. Then, letting the breath out slowly, tip your head back and stretch your arms upward. Take another deep breath from the Sky, and let it out slowly as you return your hands across your body and to the Earth. Lean forward and breathe of the Earth again, and then stretch it to the Sky. Repeat the whole process 3–4 times, a deep breath from the Earth, and then a deep breath from the Sky, while stretching with isomorphic tension. (Smith & Quinn, 2004, p. 64)

Stretches not only tone the muscles but stimulate the mind. When facilitating basic stretching exercises, leaders can add stimulating thoughts about the goodness and nurturance of Mother Earth, and about the energy and wisdom that is available from Sun and Sky. For example: When I facilitate The Raccoon and the Eagle, I note that raccoons are of the Earth, and they know the darkness of the night sky, and many little things of the environment. They are wisdom-keepers who know the importance of little things. Eagles are of the Sky, they know the wonders of the sunrise, and the vastness of landscapes. They are wisdom-keepers who know the importance of big things.

Another exercise that stimulates both body and mind is Sunshine Facewash.

Activity: Sunshine Facewash

With eyes closed, turn your face to the Sun. Feel the warmth on your skin. Hold both hands palms outward, with fingers pointing toward each other. Overlap the hands slightly, and perform rolling, rotating motions that alternately shadow your face and then let the Sun shine through. You will be able to feel the shadow and coolness, then the light and the warmth of the Sun. You will get an awareness of brightness and darkness. It can be stimulating to roll your hands rapidly, creating a flickering effect. When your arms are tired, lower them to your sides. Then use your hands to massage your face for a few minutes. The Maori of New Zealand have a saying, "Turn your face to the Sun and your troubles will fall behind you." (Smith & Quinn, 2004, p. 66)

Focusing

Focusing refers to a group of mind-body practices first developed by psychologist Eugene Gendlin (1981). It is not thinking, and it is not feelings; it is a process of simply paying attention to your feelings.

> *Focusing is a body-centered process of self-awareness and emotional healing.*
> *It's as simple as noticing how you feel — and then having a conversation*
> *with your feelings in which you do most of the listening.... Focusing is a*
> *process of honoring the wisdom that you have inside you, becoming aware of*
> *the subtle level of knowing that speaks to you through your body.*
>
> (Cornell, 1996)

Focusing involves an introspective attention to one's body sensations and emotions, especially those that rise to the top when one relaxes and lets them come. These *felt senses* are the body's way of responding to the world. If humankind did not have language, we would move through the world relying on what we sensed about the environment and various situations, just like other animals do. The problem is that our words often cut us off from the wisdom of those sensations. Paradoxically, our words also can guide us to tapping into that wisdom. To focus on feelings and let them flow, individuals need to know their emotional variations.

Identification of feelings is a learned skill. For young children, leaders often start with the mad-sad-glad-scared *feeling square*, which has the four words, or four caricatured faces, in the four quadrants of a poster board. Children are asked to point out the quadrant that best matches the way they are feeling, or to discuss the nature of the various emotional states. When we ask children to identify what they are feeling, we are giving them a skill that will be helpful for focusing.

Participants in experiential programs can profit from activities that involve cultivating and expanding their personal language of feelings. I carry a pack of 3" x 5" cards with feeling adjectives printed on them (for example, angry, frustrated, jealous, confused, warm, challenged, hurt, trusting, sad, bitter, playful). The cards can be laid out in front of the group, and instructions can vary from "Find a card that describes how are you feeling right now," to "Select the word that best describes how you have been feeling recently." The cards can be dealt out, and the recipients are asked to talk about their personal understandings of that feeling, or tell about the last time they had those feelings and associated emotions. Exercises that can expand the language of emotions are beneficial for group processing sessions and can be helpful as participants learn the skills of focusing.

Since focusing began as a simple aid for people in psychotherapy more than 30 years ago, it has been elaborated upon and applied to many other areas, including personal growth, creative expression, leadership development, environmental awareness and spirituality. (Do a keyword search for *focusing* on the Internet for more information). Through the years, the system has become more complex, and can take considerable time to learn. Still, there are some basic activities that can be offered to participants prior to their solo experiences to help them focus. As participants practice focusing on the language of their body and the language of their emotions, they will improve the process of translating bodily states to consciousness. Sharpening this skill can prove of great value when they are on solo.

Activity: Focusing
Start by relaxing, breathing, and centering. Turn your consciousness to what your body is telling you at this moment. Ask yourself: How do I feel? What is bothering me most, right now? Wait for your body to give you a message — a word, a feeling, an image, a memory. If nothing comes, just wait. When something does come, attend to that feeling or image and just let it be. Notice how it feels in your body, but don't try to figure it out with your head. Your body will tell you when it has spent enough time focusing on this feeling, and then you can let your awareness move back to the outside. (Campbell & McMahon, 1987, p. 17)

Sensory Awareness

The experience of solo can be enhanced if the individual pays careful attention to the full range of sensory inputs. Participants often have to overcome their tendency to think about the world instead of simply experiencing it sensually. Students should be encouraged to see, taste, smell, hear, and touch all the things of their environment. There is a theory and practice called *acquiring sensory awareness*, which originated with the work of two educators, Elsa Grindler and Heinrich Jacoby, in Germany in the 1920s. (See www.jacobygrindler.ch/gindler.html). One of their students, Charlotte Selver, brought their ideas to America and became influential in the development of humanistic psychology and the Human Potential Movement. She influenced Fritz Perls and Alan Watts, among others (Brooks, 1986). Perls and his students of Gestalt therapy made sensory awareness a cornerstone of their practice and developed many exercises to steer clients to the full range of their sensory experience (Stevens, 1973). (Do a keyword search for *sensory awareness* on the Internet for more information).

Professionals who identify with the notions of sensory awareness argue that its techniques can help people find balance between cognitive, emotive, and experiential modes of existence. Sensory awareness exercises can cleanse and revitalize all the senses, enabling the individual to know the world (him/herself included) more completely.

Sensory awareness activities can be facilitated in classrooms before outdoor programs begin, or in the early stages of the challenge/adventure program prior to soloing.

Activity: Special Friend

In a small group setting, have everyone take one item from a pile of similar objects — (e.g., leaves, apples, popsicle sticks, pencils). Have them examine their choice very carefully. Look at it. Touch it. Smell it. Listen to it. What is unique about this new special friend? Then place all the objects in the centered pile again and mix them up. Have students return to the pile and find their special friend. You can repeat the exercise to demonstrate improvement in sensory awareness. You can have the students pair off and tell each other about the characteristics of their special friend, and then see if they can find each other's selection in the pile.

Activity: Feeling the Box

Cut a small hand-sized hole in the top of a cardboard box, and fill it with a variety of small objects (e.g., a key, a die, a pinecone, a super-ball, an eraser, a whistle, a rubber worm, a small bottle, a cracker). The contents of a touch box are only limited by the imagination of the person who packs it! Blindfold the student, and then have him/her reach a hand into the box to touch or pick up an object. Without taking the object out of the box to look at, can they identify it? You can have each student touch only one object, and once it is identified it is removed from the box; or you can have each student touch and identify as many of the objects as possible.

Activity: Hearing the Box

Stash a number of objects that make sounds, or can be used to make sounds, in a cardboard box. The contents of a soundbox are only limited by the imagination of the person who packs it! Have students put heads down or blindfolds on and then try to identify the unseen sounds you create (e.g., shake the keys, rattle the pills, bounce the ball, crinkle the cellophane).

Nature Awareness

The goals of nature awareness activities are similar to those of sensory awareness activities in that they rely on opening all sensory pathways. Guy Murchie (1978), identified more than 30 *senses*, and Michael Cohen (1989) added more than 20 more. Here are some of the wonderful examples from their lists: sense of color, sense of gravity, sense of physical place, sense of season, sense of temperature, sense of time, sense of weather changes, sense of movement, sense of direction, and sense of spiritual presence.

In nature awareness activities, participants focus on the special connections between self and the rest of the world. For most it may be a process of "reconnecting with nature" (Cohen, 1997), or learning how to "reawaken your connection with nature" (Swan, 1992). Discovering the interdependency of humankind and nature may be important for the biological, psychological, and spiritual well-being of people — and for the health and destiny of the earth (Van Matre, 1972; Cohen, 1997; Swan, 1992; Rozak, et al., 1995; Duncan, 2004).

Environmental awareness and sensitivity are the primary goals of some solo experiences and become a part of most every solitude experience in nature. Participants can be introduced to nature awareness activities prior to the solo and will find them valuable when in solitude. Traditional small group activities such as Blind Walk (leading a blindfolded person on a walk so they can touch, feel, and hear things of their environment), and Square-Foot of Earth (the individual carefully examines everything he/she can find in a small section of the earth, touching, digging, smelling, describing in a journal, or drawing pictures), are examples of nature awareness activities.

Activity: Hug a Tree

Spend time with a tree. Touch it. Hug it. Look at it. Smell it. Lean against it. Lay down on the ground and look up at it. Talk to it. Listen to it. Maybe you can carefully climb into the branches. Sit under your tree. "If you were to sit under an oak tree for an entire day, you would have enough information to write an entire book."

(Burroughs, 2001)

Activity: Special Place

Find a special place in nature and spend time there. Let it be a place that calls you. Take a note pad and pencil if you like. Write feelings, ideas, poetry. Be aware of the movements in nature — winds through the trees, spiders climbing, bees flying, waves lapping, etc. What attracts you? What seems to call you? Reflect on the experience.

(Shaw, 2004)

Activity: Nature Communion

Become something in nature. Sit in front of a rock, tree, or lake. Feel the air on you, notice your weight and your height or depth. Notice how the world looks from your perspective.... Being something in nature immediately takes your mind away from your worries and puts you in the present moment. It plunges you into another reality; it wakes up your senses and your curiosity. It's the most intense relationship — like walking a mile in my shoes.

(Baetz, 1997)

Activity: Wildlife Focus

Locate an animal and observe its movements carefully. You will need to sit as motionless as possible, and you may benefit from binoculars. Make a list of the body movements that are repeated during the observations. Move your body the way the animal does. When you rejoin your group, mimic the movement of that animal and see if others can guess what animal you are.

(Knapp, 1988)

One time-proven tool to take on a solo experience is a magnifying lens. People enjoy looking at the little things of nature close up. If participants are introduced to the joys of a hand lens prior to spending time in solitude, chances are good they will use the lens when they do. Even if the goals of the solo experience are for psychological growth, careful inspection of some of the earth's little things can make a contribution. In fact, the magnifying glass may stimulate the person to look deeply at self, self in relationship to environment, and the spiritual connectedness of all things.

The book *Adventures With a Hand Lens* (Headstrom, 1976) has always been on the top shelf of my bookcase. When I adventure out, a magnifying glass is always in my pack. There is such wonder in close examination of a little beetle or the petals of a flower. One can find wisdom in the veins of a leaf , the wings of a butterfly, and the belly of a caterpillar. I have facilitated groups of 20-25 people crawling through the woods or along a riverbank with a hand lens. People find things to excite them and call others over to see. John Muir said, "Only by going alone, in silence, without baggage, can one truly get into the heart of the wilderness" (Muir & Gifford, 1996). I think I would ask him for permission to take along my hand lens.

Labyrinths vs. Mazes

A labyrinth is a symbol of wholeness. It combines the plane of a circle with a weaving but purposeful path. People have walked the paths of labyrinths since ancient times, around and around, toward the inside and back again to the outside. The walk is a metaphor for life's journey to our center and back to the outer world again. The way in can be the way out. Walking a labyrinth is a mini-pilgrimage to your inner self. The walk teaches about the connectedness of *the wilderness beyond* and *the wilderness within*.

Labyrinths can be painted on floors, constructed from marble or slate patterning, grown with hedges, or printed on a fold-out plastic sheet. They can even be drawn on a lapboard for tracing with one's finger. Many think labyrinths are mazes, but they are not. Mazes have cul-de-sacs and blind alleys. They are a puzzle with twists, dead ends, and misleading pathways. Mazes must be solved in order to exit, so they challenge the choice-making skills of the individual (or group). The only choices with the labyrinth are to enter and walk a slow winding trail that leads you to the center and back out. In a maze, your mind is active in exploring, remembering and problem-solving; in the labyrinth your mind is passive, prayerful, and receptive to the insights of the moment.

In spite of these differences, walking the symbolic journey of either a labyrinth or a maze can be seen as metaphors for the solo experience. Having participants spend some time working with labyrinths or mazes before an actual solo experience can enable them to get more out of the time in solitude. (Do a keyword search for *labyrinths* on the Internet for more information).

Journaling

Journaling, as a means of reflection and to record notes and questions on observations and experiences for later reflection, is often part of the solo experience. For some participants, however, the whole process of journaling turns out to be difficult and discouraging.

If participants have good language skills, blank pages may sometimes be filled with wonderful thoughts and insights by the end of their solo experience, but for many novices this is an improbable result. Participants sometimes report frustration over being forced to write in their journals, because they are unclear on where to begin or what to write about. "It appears that student journals fail to live up to their potential in helping to facilitate reflection" (Dyment & O'Connell, 2003).

My personal preference is to use structured journals, which provide sentence stems to complete, stimulus words and thoughts to ponder, instructions to draw pictures, and language of feelings check-off lists.

I often prepare a special journal for the adventure sequence, with preparatory attention to the activities that will unfold during the journey, so that the pages of the journal provide cues to processing the unfolding events.

Activity: Journal Structure

(1) Focus on the present — observing, exploring, making connections with the environment — staying in the now. (2) Focus on the recent past — experiences you have had and things you have learned. What was most enjoyable, and what was most difficult? (3) Focus on the future — what would you do differently if you started this whole adventure over again? How might your recent learning have impact on your tomorrow? (4) A fourth approach is to balance your thoughts and feelings about the present, past, and future, or to clear your mind of thoughts and feelings and just be. Let your thoughts flow, and write them down.

(Cliff Knapp, personal communication, 2004)

Providing suggestions for how to write also can be helpful:

Keep it simple. Even if what you want to write about your thoughts and feelings seems complicated, be brief and concise. Write quickly, allowing the words to freefall from your subconscious. Keep writing, no matter what. Don't erase or cross out any words. Use your journal for sketching as well as writing.

(Blue Lantern, 2004)

Perhaps the key word is practice. Experiential education programs often focus on the group briefing and debriefing processes, and do not provide much opportunity for the individual to practice reflection in solitude and writing in a journal prior to the solo experience. If participants are not prepared, they may open the journal and stare at it without knowing how to use it. It is worthwhile to forego some group discussion time in favor of introducing solitude journaling.

Recent research suggests that we might have more success with open-ended journals if we offer some basic instruction on journaling first (Dyment & O'Connell, 2004). Perhaps we would have more success with structured journals for the solo experience if we provided some sample page worksheets and used them for reflecting on pre-solo activities.

Conclusion

Appropriate development of attitudes and skills before a solo can make the experience more meaningful for the participant. Pre-solo activities ready participants for solitude and can give them skills that will be useful when they are alone. Facilitators should consider pre-solo activities in which participants can learn basic procedures for relaxation, breathing, centering, stretching, focusing, and sensory and nature awareness. Experiences with labyrinths and structured journals also are useful for participants when they are in solitude. There are many other possibilities (e.g., teaching them about reading the night sky; giving some overview to the trees, plants, insects, birds, and other critters they might see in the area where they are going to solo). Although we often teach participants the necessities of camping comfort and safety, we sometimes neglect to teach them ways to make their solo experiences more relaxing and growth producing.

References

Baetz, R. (1997). *Wild communion.* Center City, MN: Hazelden Publishing & Educational Services.

Blue Lantern. (2004). *Creative Journaling.* Retrieved January 2004, from www.bluelantern.org/journaling.html

Brooks, C. (1986). *Sensory awareness: Rediscovery of experiencing through the workshops of Charlotte Selver.* New York: Felix Morrow.

Burroughs, J. (2001). *Time and change: The complete works of John Burroughs.* New York: Fredonia Books.

Campbell, P. & McMahon, E. (1997). *Bio-spirituality: Focusing as a way to grow.* Chicago: Loyola University Press.

Cohen, M. (1989). *A field guide to connecting with nature.* Eugene, OR: World Peace University Press.

Cohen, M. J. (1997). *Reconnecting with nature: Finding wellness through restoring your bond with the earth (2nd ed.).* Minneapolis, MN: EcoPress.

Cornell, A. (1996). *The power of focusing: A practical guide to emotional self-healing.* New York: New Harbinger.

Cornell, J. (1987). *Listening to nature.* Nevada City, CA: Dawn Press.

Duncan, G. (2004). *The psychological benefits of wilderness.* Retrieved January 2004, from www.ecopsychology.athabascan.ca/duncan.html

Dyment, J. & O'Connell, T. (2003). Journal writing in experiential education: Possibilities, problems, and recommendations. *ERIC Digest, September, 2003.* Charleston, WV: Eric Clearinghouse on Rural Education and Small Schools.

Gendlin, E. (1981). *Focusing (2nd ed.).* New York: Bantam Books.

Headstrom, R. (1976). *Adventures with a hand lens.* Mineola, NY: Dover Publications.

Hendricks, G. & Wills, J. (1975). *The centering book.* Upper Saddle River, NJ: Prentice Hall.

Hendricks, G. & Roberts, T. (1977). *The second centering book.* Upper Saddle River, NJ: Prentice Hall.

Knapp, C. (1988). *Creating humane climates outdoors: A people skills primer.* Charleston, WV: ERIC Clearinghouse on Rural Education and Small Schools.

Muir, J. & Gifford, T. (1996). *John Muir: His life and letters and other writings.* Seattle, WA: Mountaineers Books.

Murchie, G. (1978). *The seven mysteries of life.* Boston: Houghton Mifflin.

Roszak, T., Gomes, M., & Kanner, A. (1995). *Ecopsychology: Restoring the earth, healing the mind.* Berkeley, CA: University of California Press.

Shaw, S. (2004). *Connecting to nature's spirit.* Retrieved February 2004, from www.ecopsychology.org/gatherings.html

Smith, T. (1980). *Wilderness beyond.... Wilderness within....* McHenry, IL: McHenry Press.

Smith, T. & Quinn, W. (1998). *The challenge of Native American traditions.* Cazenovia, WI: Raccoon Institute.

Snyder, G. (1990). *The practice of the wild.* Denver, CO: North Point Press.

Stevens, J. (1973). *Awareness: Exploring, experimenting, experiencing.* New York: Bantam Books.

Swan, J. (1992). *Nature as teacher and healer: How to reawaken your connection with nature.* New York: Villard Books.

Van Matre, S. (1972). *Acclimatization.* Martinsville, IN: American Camping Association.

PART IV

Personal Perspectives

CHAPTER 17

Sauntering: A Soul-Journey in the Woods With Thoreau as My Guide*

By Tom Owen-Towle

I went to the woods because I wished to live deliberately, to front only the essential facts of life, and see if I could not learn what it had to teach, and not, when I came to die, discover that I had not lived.

(Thoreau, 1970, p. 88)

In 1845, at the age of 28, Henry David Thoreau went to the woods at Walden Pond, just two miles outside his home in Concord, Massachusetts, "to front only the essential facts of life." In the final decade of the 20th century, at the age of 48, I left my metropolitan haven to face certain fundamentals of my existence: stillness, silence, darkness, nature, gods, demons, and angels. I chose a mountainous area because I trusted wilderness would drive me to depths unfrequented in the bustle of normal city life. The woods could *educate* — literally *draw forth* — my soul in ways consequential for the second half of my life. I would enjoy, as Thoreau depicted in his Walden retreat, "my own sun and moon and stars, and a little world all to myself."

With a month of sabbatical to spend, I might have been tempted to study in an academic setting at the feet of illustrious theologians and poets. Fortunately, I knew better. What I needed, at this point in my midlife quest, was not more formal education, however stimulating, but a radical change of pace and scenery, far from seductive centers of ambition, where I could take spiritual stock, emptying myself of professional pressures and social obligations. I required sacred space and unscheduled time to search my soul, behold nature, and invite the transcendent pursuits sorely neglected in my all-too-hectic existence as a parish minister.

I recalled reading a magazine article about the Dorland Mountain Arts Colony, a wilderness habitat in the Temecula Valley, an hour or so northeast of our San Diego home. Dorland provides a pristine, untrammeled Southern California refuge situated on the western boundary of the Palomar mountain range, bountiful with local wildlife, and punctuated by winding trails through chaparral and tree-dotted canyons. It is a working retreat for musicians, artists, and writers.

Dorland furnishes six residents with private, Spartan-like cottages, but its main gift is uninterrupted time to deepen the spirit while enhancing one's craft. Nestled in the woods, without electricity and other amenities of urban life, Dorland would prove ideal for sauntering — burrowing inwardly into soul and gazing outwardly amid nature. Having applied for temporary residency, I was accepted for the month of February and I seized the opportunity.

My journey to Dorland furnished fascinating comparisons and contrasts with Thoreau's trek to Walden. His mid-19th century pilgrimage, which has transformed millions of renowned and ordinary lives ever since, also influenced my modest sabbatical. Thoreau, while not my guru, remains one of my pivotal spiritual guides. Thoreau retired for two years, two months, and two days into the Walden Pond surroundings. I lived near Ticanu Pond (Indian for *water of everlasting youth*) for one month.

Thoreau was a New Englander, and I a Californian — my children being fourth-generation natives. We performed our respective soul-work on opposite coasts. Thoreau built his own 10-foot-square cabin; I rented a larger cottage for $5 per day. He and I both departed to the woods to write, but Thoreau logged ample time working the land, while I spent the bulk of my days and nights tilling fallow, inner terrain.

Thoreau regularly entertained friends, like Ralph Waldo Emerson, and crammed as many as 25 to 30 people inside his cabin at any given time. Much to my delight, we were disallowed visitors from the "outside world," and our sole communication with fellow Dorlandians was a communal message board. Most days I greeted only animals.

Neither Walden nor Dorland are menacing wilderness areas to be braved by rugged pioneers. Neither of us was Daniel Boone. Our journeys were symbolic adventures more than sustained ways of life. Thoreau called Walden an "experiment" and his visits with nature and soul "excursions" — apt descriptions for my trek as well. At Dorland I remained an urbanite enjoying a rustic change of pace. My soulful Sabbath traversed, Buddha-like, the middle path between ascetic deprivation and self-indulgence — "half civilized," as Thoreau observed.

Although we both took to the woods to regain spiritual equilibrium, Thoreau and I were hardly idle or passive. What with considerable walking and faithful writing, neither of us would qualify as a wastrel. In fact, it was a constant struggle to keep my legs and mind from too much activity. I tried, in my sojourn in the woods, to be disciplined, "to live deliberately" as Thoreau would say, without being driven. I wanted to entertain the serendipitous stream of this wondrous yet foreign realm.

Finally, Thoreau penned: "My purpose in going to Walden Pond was not to live cheaply nor to live dearly there, but to transact some private business with the fewest obstacles." My Dorland hermitage was likewise spent in transacting my own private business, that is, paying homage to the commodious cavities of my soul. I ponder an old Quaker greeting, "How is it with thy spirit?" The truth is that we hard-driving types don't slow down enough to answer that question. The mature, abundant existence is marked by the capacity to probe directly both the far-flung cosmos and one's spacious inner universe. This is what Thoreau meant in his summons for humanity to "explore thyself." *Explore* is the correct term for soul-work, since it denotes a vigorous and thorough, yet open-ended search. Thoreau beckoned us to *explore* — not merely *know* or *trust* — thyself. The difference is striking. Explorers keep traveling beyond acquired wisdom and self-confidence. Equally at home amid discoveries and mysteries, true pilgrims journey ever onward, their quest unfinished even at death. Note the two faces of *thyself*: we are exhorted to explore the natural realm firsthand and to farm our own souls as well.

Sometimes these twin explorations — looking around and looking within — are overlapping pursuits. Naturalist John Muir confirmed this in his musing: "I only went out for a walk, and finally concluded to stay out till sundown for going *out*, I found, was really going *in*" (1938, p. 439). Our soul may awaken precisely while we are tracking the woods, and interior investigation may thicken our ties with animals and trees, firmament and turf. In any case, both explorations are toilsome, sometimes unseasonably harsh. Bristling with thorns, beauty is strenuously achieved while exploring thyself. Both quests are inexhaustible as well, since more soul and nature always remain to be fathomed.

So I left for the Dorland Mountain Arts Colony with eagerness and trepidation. My wife Carolyn drove with me to the colony refuge, toured the premises awhile, and then returned to San Diego. I felt deposited like a fledgling Boy Scout at base camp. But I came prepared. I was equipped with thermal underwear (even Southern California's Februaries are chilly), alarm clock (although I ended up paying scant heed to either clock or watch), two flashlights, Calamine lotion, binoculars, and gloves with open fingers so I could write while shivering, and tweezers for splinter or tick removal. I also brought along my Native American *talking stick* and Tibetan *singing bowl* as meditative catalysts. I left my guitar, radio, and typewriter at home, trusting the mellifluous sounds of nature to be sufficient provision.

I wasn't without niggling anxieties. I was worried about prowling animals, keeping warm, and the failure of any and all kerosene-operated pieces of equipment in my cottage. Thankfully, Dorland supplied a site manager to rescue mechanical dumbbells like me. I had another fear. I had to guard against sabotaging my appointments with nature and soul by curling up with books next to a blazing fire. So I brought little to read and, armed with firm resolve, I avoided intellectual enticements until darkness prevailed. The bulk of my waking hours was spent honoring Thoreau's wilderness imperative: "Read not the *Times*. Read the Eternities."

But my most absorbing consternation had to do with what I would find — or worse yet *not* find — during this earnest exploration inside my being. Perhaps I would become utterly bored, or discover my interior castle barren; worse yet, it might be filled to the brim with unpleasant beasties. I was about to find out.

It has proven comforting to know that countless pilgrims throughout human history made similar treks into the woods — soul journeys, if you will. Jesus launched his ministry, at the age of 30, by entering the wilderness to encounter existential temptations. The third stage of the Hindu's life is the invitation to be a *forest dweller*. Nonetheless, all soul-journeys ventured by us earthlings — whether short or long (the Japanese sage Kam-No Chomei spent 30 years in his hut), whether relatively dangerous or safe — are admirable. Such pilgrimages are both emblematic and real. Humans make these journeys because we must; our souls wither without them. They expand our horizons and often transmute the very course of our tomorrows.

Thoreau at 28 and I at 48 made our respective trips at crossroads in our evolution. When you consider that at the turn of the 20th century, life expectancy was 47 (in fact, Thoreau died at 44) and today it is 77, Thoreau and I both were navigating midlife quests. There comes a critical juncture in our lives when we know indubitably that we have crossed over from the morning to the afternoon, to use Carl Jung's apt metaphor.

In the morning of life we conventionally develop outreach skills, we go forth to make good in the world, get educated, partnered, rear children, and care for older family members. But, as Jung relates, "whoever carries over into the afternoon the aims of the morning must pay for it with damage to the soul."

In the second half of life, or the afternoon, we hanker to search within, to know life more deeply, to inquire rather than acquire, to summarize our singular destinies, to locate sacred spaces for solitude and serenity, to enter the woods, figuratively or literally. That is what Jung unabashedly called "the religious outlook." All patients whom he saw in the second half of their lives were suffering from what he considered malaises of the soul.

In the afternoon of our human journeys, we cease looking for outside mentors, and realize that we, ourselves, are such. We slow down, take stock, behold trees and stars, make peace with our souls, and pare our life down to essentials. To use Thoreau's suggestive word for walking, we *saunter*.

At Dorland my existence was spare, revolving around these constants: Owen-Towle, Thoreau, and Ticanu Pond. Whether venturing a few miles outside the village, meandering across the globe, or simply sitting in a quiet corner in the attic, our adventures must be custom made. Two elements are universally necessary: the willingness to gaze deep, deep within, and the openness to behold the boundless luminosity of the universe with keen eyes.

I Thrive Best on Solitude

After our late afternoon arrival, Dorland's coordinating fellow, Jane Culp, a visual artist, spends the better part of an hour stating the rules and teaching me how to keep my electricity-free cabin reasonably warm and adequately aglow with woodstove and lanterns. She gave Carolyn and me a tour of the refuge, pointing out the hiking trails, the spring-fed Ticanu Pond, the communal garden, and the Dorland library, and then wishes me a blessed solitude. Carolyn, sensitive to my mounting anxiety and the impending dark, embraces me lovingly, steers me back into my dank headquarters, and drives home. Thoreau may have thrived on solitude; at this point, I would settle for survival.

When the darkness slowly fills the valley, I turn on all available lanterns, cozy up next to the fire and dive into Annie Dillard's *The Writing Life;* I thirst for the kind of inspiration she has delivered during the past two decades. I don't progress beyond this melancholy passage: "When I came home in the middle of the night I was tired; I longed for a tolerant giant, a person as big as a house, to hold me and rock me."

Annie's plight is similar to mine; only the locales differed. She is retreating in Cape Cod; I on the opposite shore, in the Southern California mountains. Our yearnings, however, are identical. It is no later than 7 p.m., yet I hanker for soothing comfort in the worst way, in the shape of a person smaller than myself, "to hold me and rock me." Carolyn is her name. By 8 p.m. or so, it hits me that conjugal visits clearly will be off limits at Dorland during the month of February. I read a bit longer, down some orange slice candies (a love gift Carolyn secretly nestled in my pack), put on warm socks, don my thermal underwear and nightshirt, and then, after turning out the lanterns and testing my penlight, I climb deep down under a mound of covers and sleep fitfully for 10 hours.

At 6:30 a.m., the darkness has lifted. Five semi-wild cats are making a ruckus outside my cabin, Orchard House. I am unable to hide out any longer. Clambering in slow motion, I join the noisy throng, and the six of us head out together on the trail to Far Spring.

Explore the Private Sea

Dorland is rustic acreage basically uncorrupted by civilization. It furnishes a perfect setting for *exploring the private sea* of my soul. Privacy is a rare treasure indeed, and once we modern folks possess some, we tend to ignore it, squander it, or race to fill it up. Being apart from observation or company, secluded, free from unauthorized intrusions is a far cry from life today. We seldom stop talking and producing long enough to find out what we truly believe and cherish. As Dag Hammarskjold lamented: "Too tired for company, we seek a solitude we are too tired to fill."

Being *private* is a state distinct from being *personal*. Americans are trained to be cordial and gregarious. We grow close to others, often with ease and alacrity. We are personal, yet few of us have a working acquaintanceship with our solitariness. My hunch is we are scared of what we might uncover. So we are safely "personal" with others to avoid being intimately "private" with ourselves. The truth remains: Unless we begin to cultivate our private sides, our personalities shrivel from malnutrition. We must learn to pay serious, ongoing attention to our privacy without becoming isolates, navigating an ennobling sea in quest of spiritual fulfillment.

Alone Does Not Mean Lonely

If you ask yourself when was the last time you were totally alone, solitary as a jaybird perched in an empty tree, you would probably be hard pressed to say. Even if you live alone, you are visited continually by phone calls, TV personalities, neighbors, colleagues, mail carriers, sales people and more. Take a head count of all the human contact you've made — wanted or unwanted — during the past 24 hours and you will be startled.

As short as one month is (and February is the shortest), it could seem an eternity to one as uninitiated as I in the mysteries of solitude. Oscar Wilde, the Irish writer, confessed he could never become a Socialist because he liked to keep his evenings free. Most of us in the "helping" professions are people addicts. We clergy are notorious offenders, working into the wee hours of most nights, unscrambling problems of the universe or people. We cringe at being left alone, untouched, under appreciated, unproductive; so we, unlike Wilde, book our evenings solid in order to avoid hours of lonesomeness.

When there are worthwhile things to accomplish in the vineyards of the Lord, and human beings to serve or save, solitude can seem an unnecessary luxury, perhaps a waste of time. Nevertheless, a spiritual pilgrim as astute as Blaise Pascal chides us in *Pensees* that "All of our misfortunes spring from the single cause that we are unable to stay quietly in one room."

Needless to say, Dorland is doing its damnedest to turn me *outside in*. Inexorably, I am acclimating to my aloneness, becoming more at home in my inner residence, finding moments of solitude gradually less terrifying. I am recognizing that being *alone* is not equal with being *lonely* and that, on the contrary, the former abets my every effort to diminish the latter. The truth is that human creatures are restless when racing compulsively from pillar to post; only when we drink leisurely from the wellsprings of solitude do we bring impressive, durable resources to either our vocations or companions.

Tempted to Cheat

In Woody Allen's movie *Annie Hall*, the protagonist says: "I was thrown out of New York University for cheating on a metaphysics exam. The professor caught me looking deeply into the soul of the student seated next to me." At Dorland, even in my braver moments, I am sorely tempted to stare into everyone else's soul but my own: Annie Dillard's, Loren Eiseley's, Alice Walker's, Wendell Berry's, or Denise Levertov's; any one of the other Dorland artists ensconced in their own private business; even the rowdy cats meowing on my roof.

If I were desperate enough, I could bury myself in my car, turn the radio on, and bask in the decibels of American civilization. But Dorland is a driving taskmaster, and so is Thoreau's relentless admonition to "explore thyself," to "explore the private." Nonetheless, I cheat a little, because I plaster the walls and floors of my cabin with written imperatives from other solitary questers, all promoting the interior hunt. Their wisdom emboldens this reluctant adventurer:

> *Without great solitude, no serious work is possible.*
>
> (Pablo Picasso)

> *Solitude is employing the richness of self. Loneliness is facing the poverty of self.*
>
> (May Sarton)

> *Nobody can counsel and help you, nobody. There is only one single way.*
> *Go into yourself.*
>
> (Rainer Maria Rilke)

> *Never am I less alone than when I am by myself; never am I more active than when I am doing nothing.*
>
> (Cato)

> *And now, the best of all, is to be alone, to possess one's soul in silence.*
>
> (D. H. Lawrence)

Dorland, oh Dorland, keep insisting that I look long and lovingly into my chest, to see what my soul doth wear!

A Simple and Sincere Account

It has been a venerable male proclivity to write abstractly rather than confessionally. Theology is the most grievous culprit, being a discipline dominated, until recent times, by men who have flourished in pulpits six feet above contradiction, majoring in esoteric ruminations and lofty edicts. Thoreau pulls us crashing back to earth, to "simple and sincere accounts" of what is happening in our very own lives. "Explore thyself," he exhorts, "explore thyself," and then report your learnings.

A Sufi fable tells of a seeker of enlightenment who sets out on a pilgrimage to a distant destination. Not finding wisdom at the end of her journey, she disappointedly returns home and, lo and behold, discovers that the treasure so ardently sought elsewhere lies within her own abode, more specifically, in her own soul. Maybe that's why Thoreau seldom traveled far from home, holding that truth dwelt wherever he did. "It is not worth the while to go round the world to count the cats in Zanzibar," he announced, being disenthralled with straying from either Concord or his soul.

Thoreau proposed that, once life's dust settles, the only odyssey worth relating is our own. Our human mission is no more complicated that transmitting our stories in simple and sincere fashion. If we were all brave enough to do that, humanity would be the beneficiary of a splendid treasure trove. As Lao Tse noted: "Understanding others is wisdom; understanding yourself is enlightenment."

Consequently, the core of my Dorland experience consists in reading nature and my soul rather than devouring outsiders, however tantalizing and delectable. "Explore thyself" and uncover wellsprings of illimitable refreshment.

A Few Moments

We can rationalize our way into avoidance of solitude, claiming that if we are unable to retreat for a year, a month, or even a weekend, we might as well spurn the practice altogether. But the length of our forays into aloneness is not at stake; seizing "a few moments" alone, daily, can keep our souls sufficiently awake and fit.

The Christian Scripture provides one of the most compelling examples of the power of regularly making time for just a few moments alone. Emphasis is placed on the start of Jesus' ministry (40 days in the wilderness) and its close (a lonely vigil in the garden), but the fact is that the Nazarene prophet took mini-sabbaths throughout his life. The New Testament recounts Jesus withdrawing from life's tumult on a regular basis: "And when he had sent the multitude away, Jesus went up into a mountain apart to pray; and when the evening was come, he was there alone." (Matthew 14:23).

Solitude is not so much a cup to replenish as a stream to experience. Solitude is a state that may be visited whether we are energetic or bushed, ready to give birth or prepared to enter one's final night. But four rules apply: One, because we are always too busy, we must pluck opportunities to be alone; two, there is seldom the wrong time to explore solitude; three, we need "to lean into solitude" (Denise Levertov's image) rather than skirt lazily on its edge; and four, a few moments is enough to refresh our souls.

"Three Chairs"

I had three chairs in my house; one for solitude, two for friendship, three for society.
                                                                (Thoreau)

My trip to Dorland was an excursion to be not merely alone, but meaningfully alone, to stay in intimate alignment with myself without drifting off into my "monkey mind" (the picturesque Zen Buddhist phrase for mental clutter), hiding from the illuminations and blemishes of my soul. Despite frequent visitors and periodic trips home for his mother's home cooking, Thoreau was a loner. He could honestly report: "I never found the companion that was so companionable as solitude." He was never as comfortable with society — its dictates and resources — as he was with nature and his own company. Emerson accurately conferred on his associate "the bachelor of thought and nature." Bachelor in both senses of the term: diploma recipient and unmarried man.

My quandary differs from Thoreau's. Feeling more at home in society, I have less need for visitors during my retreat than he did. At Ticanu Pond I entertain nobody. I shun people. When one of the cats recently scooted into my cabin, I chased it out. Only the rats race around Orchard House, day and night, and that's because I can't get rid of them.

I retreated to Dorland for one overarching reason: to befriend my solitariness, so that when I leave the woods I might relish holier moments apart and alone. An ironic bonus follows. Being secluded for a month from social tumult and fury brings me closer not only to myself but to others as well, in a healthy, less symbiotic way. My controlling instincts are fading, as sense of perspective is gained, and the well of affection for those nearest and dearest to me is refilled.

So, at Orchard House, I occupy my three chairs differently than Thoreau did. One is for meditation, sitting still. Two is for writing. Three is for night reading. I remain absolutely critical, at this delicate juncture in my spiritual blossoming, that "my soul hath elbow room" (William Shakespeare) and that I be "the Soul that has a Guest" (Emily Dickinson). I share a soulful of company in this small cottage. My chairs are amply filled by me, myself, and I.

"Fitted for a Higher Society"

In my solitude I have woven for myself a silken web or chrysalis, and nymph-like, shall ere long burst a more perfect creature, fitted for a higher society.
                                                                (Thoreau)

When I leave my Dorland sanctuary and return to the rigors of valley existence, my fervent prayer is that the inner solitude I attain in the woods will be re-created during my work day, in the corners of my home, on the road, while at play — wherever I live, move, and have my being. May my spiritual repose be a moveable feast.

The purpose of retreating is to cultivate the soul, then return renewed, "fitted for a higher society," prepared to participate afresh in the creation of a lovelier, loftier commonweal.

"Some Essentials"

Dorland and Thoreau have forced me to prune, then prune some more, my essentials to a nourishing few — essentials sturdy yet elastic enough to transport my soul far, far into tomorrows beyond counting.

First, I choose to experience some beauty, inner and outer, every day — so if I should suddenly die, it would be enough.

Second, as Thoreau urges, "I must live above all in the present." This means I plan for the future, I remember my past, but I dwell only in the present.

Third, Thoreau penned in another journal entry, "You must walk so gently as to hear the finest sounds, the faculties being in repose. Your mind must not perspire." One of Dorland's chief lessons has been to slow down, sit still, sleep, saunter — don't sweat life, large or small stuff, so much. I am practicing the fundamental "four dignities" recommended by the Chinese: "Standing, lying, sitting, and walking."

Finally, the measuring rod of any sojourn into the woods, such as Thoreau's, is whether its lessons are embodied during one's homestretch. Thoreau left Walden Pond after 26 months, but the remaining 14 years of his short life exhibit the same ferocious devotion to simplicity, journal writing, and excursions into soul and nature that he had initiated at Walden Pond. He even continued his pattern of committing mornings to writing, afternoons to observing nature, and evenings to books and company.

I will have more difficulty than Thoreau in replicating Dorland back home in San Diego, but my soul-journey, if of enduring worth, will modify appreciably the focus and pace of my remaining years. I am dedicated to lengthening my experiments at Ticanu Pond in being inwardly rich and outwardly simple.

I believe in keeping imaginary mountains operative in my daily dreaming and in holding Dorland's real forest indelibly printed in my spirit's vision. I will need all the mountains and woods at my disposal for life's homestretch.

So, here's my journal, replete with holes and smudges, revised over a five-year period, a "simple and sincere account" of my sauntering in the woods with Thoreau.

*This chapter has been excerpted from *Sauntering: A Soul Journey in the Woods with Thoreau as My Guide*, written by Tom Owen-Towle and published by Bald Eagle Mountain Press (1996).

References

Cramer, Jeffrey S. (Ed.). (2004). *Walden: A fully annotated edition.* New Haven: Yale University Press.

Wolfe, L. M. (Ed.). (1938, 1979). *John of the mountains: The unpublished journals of John Muir.* Madison: University of Wisconsin Press.

CHAPTER 18

Two Letters From Solo

By Elias Amidon

Why do I do this? … I do this for some reason that remains
half-hidden from me, that keeps surprising me.
I do it to burn up the dross that collects in my soul.
I do it to burn up my forgetfulness and sloppy ways of living.
I do it to remember simple gratitude.

(Amidon, 2005, p. 240)

A Letter to My Father*
Death Valley, California
March 5, 1994

Dear Pop,

I write this from Death Valley in one of the most remote places I've ever been, on the fourth day of a solo fast. I feel quite weak, but peaceful. It is so quiet here. Time is nearly still — as still as my breathing. I have very few things with me – a sleeping bag, a tarp, some clothes. There are no distractions.

I think of the luxuriant green of your surroundings, the wind through a million leaves. I hope the hibiscus we planted survived after the cows got at them. I love the image of you chasing them off with a slingshot!

Here the valley and mountains are bare — just scattered creosote bushes on an undulating expanse of rock and sand. As my friend Meredith says, you sit on Grandmother's bones out here.

My little camp rests between two smooth hills that rise up on either side of me like breasts — I'm in the bosom of the earth. As I look up from this page, I see for miles across Death Valley to the Last Chance Mountains. This area is full of portentous names....

Why do I do this? Certainly not because it's fun (it isn't), though tomorrow, when I hike out of here, will be wonderful and joyous. The thought of a piece of good bread, or a strawberry! No, I do this for some reason that remains half-hidden from me, that keeps surprising me. I do it to burn up the dross that collects in my soul. I do it to burn up my forgetfulness and sloppy ways of living. I do it to remember simple gratitude. The ordeal of going without food or companionship or things to do is a surprisingly hard teacher — and an honest one.

I've been praying a lot out here. "Praying!?" I hear you say. I can imagine the idea of prayer may strike your Unitarian soul as superstitious or sentimental. And it's true, superstition and sentimentality are demons in the spiritual heart — I do my best to keep vigilant. Out here in this Big Quiet I rise in the first light before dawn and climb to the top of one of these hills, from where I can see for miles and miles. I do the same at sunset. And there I sing my prayers for a long time as the sun slowly rises or sets. I pray for the well-being of everybody and everything I can think of. I pray that your days will be many and filled with love, that your heart will be open and your mind free and your body strong. Simple things. I pray that all those who suffer will find peace and be comforted, that all those with vicious intent will be blessed with mercy, that all the hands about to commit violence toward another will be stayed. I pray for all my loved ones and family and friends. I pray that my life will be an offering to grace the beauty of the world.

And to whom do I pray? Who listens? No one. The God I pray to is unknown to me. I know that any conception I have of God is not God. Of course I address this unknown God with many names: *Oh Gracious One! Oh Spirit of All! Oh Earth beneath my feet! Oh Loving Sun! Oh Moon and Mountain and Water of Life! Oh Generous Heart that beats through the world in ways known and unknown! Oh Great Mystery! and many more....*

These names of the Nameless open up the ground I stand on and the air I breathe and the light we all share, and suddenly Everything is Listening! Rock, lizard, crow, cloud — everything listens! I feel as if I partake in the Great Kindness of the universe — my prayers melt me into that.

Do you remember what Einstein asked, what he called the most fundamental question: "Is the universe benign?" I agree that the question is fundamental, but the answer is easy. To me the universe is so obviously "good" — though ruthless and indifferent at the same time. I believe that what we have emerged from, and what we will return to, is the indescribable essence of Blessing. This is not to say that I can turn away from or trivialize the world's suffering — whoever does that trivializes themselves — but even in the face of suffering, even in the midst of my own, a kind of Unfathomable Tenderness holds us, an Unbounded Grace — although these words — *Tenderness* and *Grace* — are only distant approximations of what is.

How did such an old humanist/atheist like you spawn such a wide-eyed pantheist like me? Actually, I suspect beneath the exterior you're a wide-eyed pantheist yourself. Maybe come Judgment Day we all will be.

I came upon the remains of a wild burro down in the wash the other day. Mostly bones — she had been picked pretty clean. Her skull was grinning, as all skulls do. What's the joke I wonder? Somebody once told me that at the very moment of our death we wake up laughing. That little burro did.

Just before I started this letter I was sitting here gazing out at the Quiet and you came to my mind. I thought of your 82 years and that very likely, though not for sure, you will die before me, and suddenly I was filled with a great pang of missing you. I haven't written anything since I've been out here — it's too distracting — but that pang made me get out my pen and paper.

The idea of a world without you in it makes me lonely, though who knows, you might be dead even as I write this, or I might as you read this. We live mostly in an illusion of our own projection. And maybe that is the magic of prayer and its power: It calls us to dive deep into what matters most to us, to find it, acknowledge it, and bring it up into the air. That's why singing my prayers aloud in my sing-song chanting way up on this hill with no one listening fills me with such love and gratefulness. An illusion of my own projection, which becomes truth. Like existence itself bursting out of emptiness, we mimic that incomprehensible act in our own little ways.

But what do you think? Is there a purpose or a meaning to all of this, or is it senseless? I wonder if the answer might be neither, or someplace between meaning and meaninglessness. It's like that beautiful painting you did years ago of a hand lifted up and open to the cosmos — all we have is the gesture. Meaning falls away, and meaninglessness falls away, in the beauty and thoroughness of each momentary gesture. And that's how I believe in prayer — it's a gesture, an offering flung up into the wind and blown away, an act of creation, with no grasping for the results. "So be it," I sing, "Oh bless them and heal them and love them and make the way open before them in beauty! So be it!" And then? Only the Quiet remains, taking the prayers within it like invisible seeds, and I am left not quite who I was, no different from anything else, though so very me.

My subjectivity loses its edges out here. I remember reading somewhere that Jacob Boehme said, "Whatever the self describes, describes the self." And so this projection, this gesture of prayer, describes us. It is a chance to unfold ourselves through what matters most to us — like great music and art and dance and poetry. But then, all of our gestures carry this potential of prayer within them — a handshake, a kiss, making a meal, making love, wishing each other good morning, good night, have a nice day, be well! Prayers to the heart we share, and the Silence that holds us so tenderly. And yet, for all this high-minded talk of prayer, it's really not so special — in fact, it's quite ordinary. It's simply what we give. Prayer is what we give. We give thanks, we give love, we give support, we give respect, we give solace, we give compassion. Prayer is our gift back.

Well, maybe that's not always true — there are the prayers I sing for myself and those are gifts to myself.... "Oh Dear Heart, bless me with strength and responsiveness, free me from self-pity, teach me graciousness when I am self-centered, make my life an offering...." But look, there it is again, the gifting. We seek to rise above our heaviness and self-preoccupation. Why? To give and live more authentically, to love each other beyond conditions.

That's why I come out here, and why I guide others to come, because in some mysterious ways it completes the circle, allowing me to touch without distraction all that I care for and value, and to offer my life to that.

Of course it's also uncomfortable, and boring, and lonely — the wind blows incessantly or it rains for days or you can't keep your mind off food — but in the end you know it is the ordeal itself that transforms you. Strange, isn't it? Tomorrow, when I'm finally back in the world of towns and traffic, I'm going to find a strawberry and eat it slowly — and may I never again forget the blessing of that taste!

Well, I hope all this talk of prayer hasn't put you off. The demon of sentimentality lives off words — so often when we try to express the Ineffable it turns into pap. That's why I love singing my prayers all alone out here — the words matter so much less than the spirit they carry. Writing them down like this is much more treacherous. Perhaps a higher way would be to learn how to pray without words. Can we do that?

In the end I think prayer simply calls from us our deepest sincerity about what we love. When it does that, it escapes superstition and sentimentality and heals our isolation. In this spirit I pray your days will be gentle and fulfilling and your nights full of peace.... But now the wind is up, blowing sand in my face, telling me Enough Words! So may the Silence bless you.

Love,
Elias

* Reprinted from: Adams, C. (Ed.). (2002). *The Soul Unearthed: Celebrating Wildness and Spiritual Renewal Through Nature.* Boulder, CO: Sentient Publications. (pp. 55–58).

Letter From the Road, No. 22
Hell Roaring Canyon, Utah
Late September 2003

At the moment, Rabia and I are waiting in the silence near a remote canyon in the Great Basin Desert of southeastern Utah. We are waiting for a small group of people we have guided out here to return from their three days of solitude and fasting. This is Day 2.

Each of these people has found for themselves a "power spot," a place they are particularly drawn to out amid the red-rock cliffs and the gnarled juniper trees, a place in which to hold their fast, pray, consider their life's purpose and direction, and listen to the silence. Once each day they go to a prearranged circle of stones and place a stone inside the circle to signal they are all right. Otherwise they have no contact with anyone. No one even knows exactly where their site is, although we have a general idea in case of emergency. Their aloneness is sacred.

Imagine what it's like to be out there. There are no distractions, nothing to do. Your eyes follow a solitary hawk turning in a thermal, and then it disappears beyond a ridge. You feel the soft movement of air on your face. You shift into the shade of a piñon pine. You wait. Sand runs through your fingers. You watch your thinking mind thinking, and it becomes uninteresting. You feel old like the cliffs, and the story of your entire life becomes present to you, its great loves and little failures, its hopes, its first dreams.

Sometimes you might cry, remembering some wound of your life. If you decide you want to be finished with it, you might pick up a little stone and whisper into it this thing, this wound, until the stone signifies the entire sad affair. Then with great determination, you dig a hole with your hands and bury it, or pitch it into the abyss of the canyon. You make little rituals like this.

Sometime you might imagine this day is the end of your life, the last one of all your days. As evening comes, you say some prayers or whatever you need to do to state your intention and make the moment sincere. Then you close your eyes and wait to see who comes to say goodbye to you since these are your last hours. Maybe your children come. Maybe your grandmother comes, even though she's been dead for many years. Maybe someone comes who has caused you pain, or to whom you have caused pain. You sit with each person, one by one, listening to what they have to say and responding in whatever way you wish to make things good between you. In this way you clean up your life.

When night comes it makes you humble. You see the universe. There are no city lights, and with the moon absent, as it is at this time, the blackness is complete. Thousands upon thousands of stars are scattered across the heavens. It is utterly silent.

As you lay on the earth looking up you feel as if you are falling outward into endlessness. You can hear your own breathing and the beating of your heart. You might choose to hold a vigil on one of your nights of solitude, staying awake until sunrise. It's a hard thing to do, to stay awake that long, asking for guidance or healing or simply giving thanks for your life. The stars slowly wheel in their great arc and you all but disappear.

When the dawn comes it comes with the slowest grace, a pale lightening in the east, then lavender-coral-rose-gold and the faintest blue-white of the approaching sun. Finally the sun pierces the horizon's edge with a diamond light that is unbearable but so comforting, like a companion who loves us without speaking.

When the sun warms up the rocks you might go to a place where the tan entrada stone spreads out, an ancient sedimentary layer that is smooth and curved like skin. You might take off your clothes to be as naked as it is, and lay with your belly against it. Things are simpler, and the stone teaches you about that. You remember your origins.

Often you are hungry, but even if you were offered food you would turn it away, not wanting to abandon the clarity fasting gives your body. "There's a hidden sweetness in the stomach's emptiness," writes Rumi. "We are lutes, no more, no less. If the soundbox is stuffed full of anything, no music. If the brain and the belly are burning clean with fasting, every moment a new song comes out of the fire."

When the final dawn comes on the fourth morning you pack your few things, scatter any ceremonial stones or altars you have made, brush out your footprints as best you can, and return to base camp and your life among people. You are glad to be back, glad to eat, glad to look forward to a hot shower, but the time spent out there "alone with the Alone," as an early Christian mystic described it, will never leave you. In fact, it will keep working inside you, patiently returning you to your primal perspective and revealing the strength that is naturally yours. It is, to quote Rumi again, "free medicine for everybody!" The strength and gratitude you feel becomes a source you can draw from to give away to others — free medicine. And that's the whole point. "You go out in order to come back," as our late great teacher, Steven Foster, said, "to bring a gift for your people."

So here we sit, waiting for our brothers and sisters to come back. We pray for their safety and that they will be able to receive what is revealed to them. They are doing a hard thing and need whatever help our little prayers might bring. They are doing it for all of us.

Blessings,
Elias

CHAPTER 19

Visiting Dreamland

By David Sobel

When you go to sleep at night, you go into dreamland.
And when I go to sleep, I go into dreamland too.
And even though I will be very far away in Canada, all
the streams flow together to connect all the parts of
dreamland. When you go into dreamland, find a stream
and follow it. And when I go into dreamland, I'll find
a stream and follow it, and we will meet
where the streams flow together.

(Sobel, 2005, p. 250)

Can you think back to your first solo experience? Wandering off into the woods at the edge of your yard, turning around and not being able to see your house. Feeling that surge of panic and tears. Or, you're in the supermarket and you look up and realize the hand you just grabbed does not belong to one of your parents. "Where's my Mommy!?" you wail, and she quickly appears around the corner, fresh from her quick jaunt to the pet food aisle. Maybe it was the first day of kindergarten. You've just hung up your sweatshirt and taken your place in the circle on the rug and your red-haired teacher seems really nice and smiley. But when you turn around you see your mother waving and sliding quietly out the door. You thought she was going to be there for the whole morning! The feeling of "She's leaving" sweeps over you like a bad dream, and you try not to cry even though you feel abandoned. It's a long three hours.

These first memories of being separated from your parents, especially from your mom, are the early prototypes of the solo experience. Gather recollections of earliest childhood memories, and they are often queasy memories of aloneness — having to stay in the hospital overnight by yourself, first sleepovers, grandparents coming to stay at the house while parents are away. This is where the emotional foundation of dealing with aloneness is laid. It can be done coldly, without care for the emotional life of the child, or it can be done thoughtfully, with an eye toward developing the inner resourcefulness of the child. But what's the developmentally appropriate approach to dealing with missing mom in early childhood? The solution has to draw on the richness of the imaginative life in young children. And the goal needs to be constructing a delicate bridge from loneliness to connection. If children are taught early on to cope with feelings of loneliness, they are given a tool they can use throughout life.

My children's first encounter with solo came one summer, when my daughter was almost five years old and my son was two and a half. It's mid-August, and we have returned home from a family vacation in Maine with friends. In a few days, my wife Wendy is leaving for 11 days on a women's canoe trip in Ontario. I am anticipating being a single parent for this period with mixed excitement and trepidation. She will not be reachable by phone most of that time and has never been gone for more than two nights at a stretch. The children are feeling kind of shaky. They are used to spending big chunks of time with me alone, but they sense that this is quite different. It's an emotional challenge for everyone. As her departure approaches, the children become increasingly fragile. "Don't go canoeing, Mommy. Don't go!" they plead and sob.

Wendy leaves in the evening and that first night is unsettled. Tara cries herself to sleep and has a fitful night. Eli wakes up frequently. We all start the next day feeling lonely and like motherless children. I am not prepared for how melancholic I feel. I am a bit daunted by the sense that I have to hold all the emotional pieces together for both children. While Eli seems fairly cheery during the day, Tara is having a harder time. Before lunchtime she dissolves into a puddle of tears. "I miss Mommy. I want Mommy to come home!" It takes a while for her "to get all the crying out," as she would say.

That afternoon, realizing I need to do something to raise our spirits, I devise a plan. During this phase of fatherhood, I was committed to a particular form of storytelling. I liked starting stories from the serendipitous particulars of the time, place, and people of the moment. When my children would say, *"Tell us a story, Daddy,"* it was a challenge to make one up on the spot, with little preparation. The story began in the present and gradually took on its own shape and form. It's like the path that diverges from the road through the woods. The road is level and predictable, wide and comfortable. The path rejoins the road not far ahead, but between here and there it seeks elevation, it narrows and twists through an unexpected forest. As you diverge along the story path you can still see the main road, but it gradually disappears from view. The story explores new terrain, discovers talking animals in the woods, but then the road appears through the mist of the forest. The landscape looks familiar again and soon you're back with the road comfortably secure beneath your feet. My children are always entranced with these story explorations, and I have come to see them as one of the crucial elements of childhood and parenthood.

I take both children out to the hammock to be close. We bring a couple of pillows and a blanket. We settle into the dappled shade under the apple trees; I put an arm around each of them and I tell a story, mostly for Tara's benefit.

꙳   ꙳   ꙳

Once there was a little girl whose mother was going away for a long trip. The little girl was staying home with her brother and her father. They were planning lots of special things, but the little girl was afraid that she was going to miss her mother terribly. Before her mother left, the little girl cried and cried. "Please don't go away, Mommy. I'm going to miss you."

The day before she left, the mother sat down with the little girl. She said:

I know you're going to miss me, and I am going to miss you too. We'll both feel sad. But I have an idea. When you go to sleep at night, you go into dreamland. And when I go to sleep, I go into dreamland too. And even though I will be very far away in Canada, all the streams flow together to connect all the parts of dreamland. When you go into dreamland, find a stream and follow it. And when I go into dreamland, I'll find a stream and follow it, and we will meet where the streams flow together. We'll stay together in dreamland for a while and then we'll hug each other goodbye and follow the streams back to our own beds.

That night the girl went to sleep and went into dreamland, and when she got there she found a beautiful, crystal clear stream. It rippled gently and flowed through a mossy forest. She walked and walked until she came to a place where another stream joined and together they flowed over gently sloping smooth rocks to form little carved pools. She looked into the bottom of one of the pools and found some sparkling, polished stones. She reached in to pick them up and just then noticed her mother's reflection in the surface of the pool. She looked up, and there was her mother standing next to her! They collected stones, waded in the cool water and lay down in the moss next to the stream. Then it was time to go. They gave each other big hugs and kisses, and the little girl walked along the stream back to her bed and her mother returned the other way.

When she woke up the next morning, she felt happy because she had visited her mother in dreamland.

꙳   ꙳   ꙳

I pause for a moment to make it clear that the story is finished. "So Tara, maybe *you* can try to visit Mommy tonight, like the little girl in the story." She looks both intrigued and unsure about this idea but willing to try. I put her to bed that night, reminding her about the story, and she nods her head in acknowledgment. I ask her at breakfast if she visited Mommy during the night, and she immediately provides the following description.

> *I was in dreamland, I followed the stream and I met Mommy and we swam in the pools. She went back to where she was and I went with her. The only part of land was a beach and there was water everywhere. She found a place where someone had been digging, and we found a box with necklaces and pearls. In it I get to keep them, but I can't tell anyone or my wishes won't come true. I stayed with her a little while and then I came back home.*

I nod acceptingly and tell her I'm pleased she got to visit Mommy, but internally I am giddily amazed that it actually worked. Then a thought crosses my mind: Perhaps, in an effort to take care of me, she's just making up a quick story on the spot. But I am struck by her tone of voice and the straight-ahead way she describes her dream. It sounds similar to her tone on previous occasions when she has shared dreams. Later that day she says, "I don't miss Mommy so much because I feel like I'm part of her and I'm sort of her heart." The next two mornings, she describes the following encounters.

> *I met Mommy in dreamland, and there were pools and waterfalls. And you know what? The pools were made not just from water but also with diamonds. Mommy and I took off our clothes and slid from one pool down the waterfall to another pool and then down another waterfall and another waterfall.*

> *I met Mommy in dreamland. We swam through a pool and through a cool flickering stream and it flowed all the way to Africa and we danced all night. We saw lions and giraffes and I got to ride a giraffe, a baby one. And I rode baby horses and I got a beautiful hat with roses around it. And then we went back to our places.*

By this point, I am becoming a believer. The changing quality of the events in dreamland that she reports from day to day suggests that she is really having these dreams. Wendy has talked about a trip to Africa when Tara is 13 years old, so it makes sense that this would emerge in the dream. Riding on giraffes and hats with roses, however, are not anything I have ever heard them talk about and these feel like genuine dream images. This same day I overhear Tara talking to Jodi, the baby sitter. She says, "I miss my Mommy, but I know I can visit her in dreamland at nighttime." She says this unaware that I can hear her. The dreamland experiences seem to be serving as the emotional bridge for which I had hoped.

Two more days pass before I ask about dreamland again. She's been having crying spells each day and her mood seems to be deteriorating. She seems as melancholic and sad as the first night. When I ask her if she visited dreamland last night, she says, "I went to dreamland to visit Mommy but she wasn't there and I miss her." She starts to cry. That evening, I am putting her to bed and the sobs begin again. I lose my patience and raise my voice.

> David: *Tara, I'm tired of this! Mommy's gone and we all feel sad but we have to get used to it. Look, she'll be back in about four days. That's not very long. Now stop crying.*
> Tara: *Daddy, stop yelling at me! Sadness is like the stripes on my dress. The stripes go in and out. The blue stripes come out and the white stripes go in. The sadness comes inside me and goes outside, back and forth. Now don't you see?*

I feel put in my place and remind myself of the importance of riding with the ebb and flow of the appropriate sadness she describes.

The next day Eli is taking a nap and I take Tara back out to the hammock. I have another story to tell.

స్ట్రా   స్ట్రా   స్ట్రా

Once there was a little girl whose mother was going away on a canoe trip. The girl was sad that her mother was going away, and so her mother sat down and told her that they could visit each other in dreamland every night. ("Daddy, you already told me this story," Tara interrupts. "Just wait a minute," I chide and continue.) The little girl visited her mother in dreamland, and they had wonderful times together finding treasures and sliding down waterfalls and dancing in Africa. Then, one night, the little girl went to dreamland and walked along the stream and her mother didn't come. She waited and waited and still her mother didn't come. She walked back along the stream, returned to her bed, and when she woke up the next day she was very sad.

The next night when the girl went to sleep, she didn't bother to go to dreamland because she didn't want to feel sadder. That night her mother walked along the stream and waited and waited at the pools, but the little girl never came. The mother went back to where she was sleeping and was upset. She was concerned that something was the matter with the little girl.

The mother talked to all her friends about how upset she was. She wanted to meet the little girl in dreamland again, but she wasn't sure how to make it happen. The mother couldn't call on the phone, so she decided to try to talk right into the father's mind and tell him to tell a story to the little girl encouraging her to visit dreamland again.

ॐ   ॐ   ॐ

As I finish, Tara's face looks surprised, bemused and puzzled. Then the realization dawns on her:

Tara: *You mean this is the story you were supposed to tell?*
David: *Yes.*
Tara: *I can hear them whispering to me in my mind right now. "Come to see Mommy in dreamland tonight, Tara. Come to see Mommy."*

Tara leans over and whispers this last comment in my ear to demonstrate what she is hearing. We decide they are trying two different ways to communicate with us to make sure she gets the message. The next morning I inquire about her dreams and she reports quite cheerily.

I walked along the stream and met Mommy and we came back to the house and there was the strangest thing. You weren't here. We looked all around and we walked down to the frog pond and you were there with Eli. You were fishing for frogs. You put bugs on and then rolled the line in. (With her hands, she gestures putting bugs on hooks and reeling in line.) Then we all came home and Mommy went back. We were all awake during this part; it wasn't a dream.

Later that day Tara is busy playing with her favorite stuffed animal, a white rabbit called Bun-Bun. I listen from afar as she suggests to Bun-Bun they play that she is going away on a canoe trip and Bun-Bun has to stay home.

Bun-Bun: *Don't go, Tara, don't go. I'll miss you.*
Tara: *It's okay. Just remember that when you go to sleep you can visit me in dreamland. Just walk along the stream and I'll meet you.*

For the next two days before Wendy returns, Tara is cheery and high-spirited. She had hit a low point about halfway through, correlating with the times when she wasn't going to dreamland. After the second story, things became progressively more upbeat. When Wendy returns, Tara refers to the times they met each other, presuming that Wendy had the same experience, but there's no apparent need or inclination for her to confirm this.

Tara's last comment in the final dream account is an interesting one. "We were all awake during this part, it wasn't a dream." She has said this kind of thing many times before. "Peter Pan came and took me away to Neverland last night. I really flew. It wasn't a dream." When I ask her, "If I came up to your room while you were in Neverland, would I see you in bed?" She shakes her head "no" quite definitively.

The point is that the dream experience feels as real and is sensed with the same texture as waking experience. And she feels no logical need to confirm or test out her perception. She doesn't ask me whether Eli and I went fishing for frogs. It happened, she wasn't dreaming, she saw it; it just is. And, regardless of the objectivity of the experience, dreamland did create a tangible presence, a keepsake memory of Wendy for Tara that she could hold on to while Wendy was gone.

Tara's experiences in dreamland are, I think, a simple example of the possibilities of "lucid dreaming" in childhood. Lucid dreaming occurs when we take our conscious volitional thinking into our dream life. Many of us have had the experience of getting to a place in a dream where things get uncomfortable and we say, "This is my dream, and I don't want it to go in this direction." Or sometimes we will ourselves to wake up at this point. Some people are even more fortunate and can stay vividly conscious while in the dream, bringing a quality of refreshing exhilaration to the dream experience that is distinctly different from the fuzzy, monochrome quality of conventional dream life. Similarly, a few people are skilled enough to decide what they want to dream before going to sleep, and that's the starting point of their dreams. But for must of us, it's catch as catch can.

Tara's access to dreamland each night, her finding of the stream, suggests some volitional control over her dream content. Somehow she was able to hold on to the suggestion from waking life and bring it into her sleep. Once she found the stream and followed it, the fluid, unexpected quality of dream imagery took over. As the dream started to wane, she seemed to be reporting that she returned home, another conscious or volitional act.

Lucid dreaming doesn't happen for most of us because the pathways between dreaming and waking consciousness have become overgrown. We can't find the way anymore, and moreover we don't have the time. In early childhood, when the worlds are still merged, children can go in and out, like the blue and white stripes on Tara's dress, like sadness. After an impromptu story in the bathtub one night, Tara volunteered a wonderful description of just how the process works in her mind. She said, "When you started to tell the story, I saw pictures in my head, and then when you kept on, I went into dreamland as you told the rest of the story and watched it happen." Clearly, the dream and story experience are woven together in Tara's experience.

Solo experiences later in life, in adolescence and adulthood, often take the individual back into dreamland. The solo experience, in creating isolation, immersion in wildness, deprivation of food, is intended to open the doors of perception, to allow the seeking of a vision. Dream life and waking life have become split and isolated from each other in most of our lives. The solo offers the opportunity to bring them back together. By taking advantage of the easy access back and forth between dream life and waking life in early childhood, it's possible to lay down pathways that won't be completely overgrown by the vines of time. And through showing Tara that she could visit her mom in her dreams, I gave her a tool for finding solace when she's alone.

Tara's going to be 18 soon. She's in her last semester of high school. Last weekend she took her first solo road trip in her slightly scuffed '97 Subaru Outback Sport to visit her boyfriend in college. I was anxious about her driving by herself for six hours on roads she's never been on to a place she'd never been. She was leaving after work at 6 p.m., not getting there till about midnight. I was nervous but knew it was important to let her go. She came back energized, as much for the experience of meeting the solo challenge as from seeing her boyfriend.

As a transition between high school and college, she's heading off to Costa Rica to do a teaching internship at The Cloudforest School in Monteverde from January through May. She'll live with a local family, get plunged into Spanish (which she barely knows), and be on her own, far away. She's nervous and thrilled. Me too. But for the past five years she's had this image of living in a small, dusty village in the Latin American highlands. Though she will be among people while on her adventure, there will be times when being far from all she knows well will leave her feeling very alone. But I know her inner fortitude and ability to weave her dreams into everyday life will see her through any loneliness she may feel. She learned early on how to navigate solitude and to reap its benefits. The solo experience, and the benefits we reap from it, can be experienced early and can take new developmental forms throughout life. I'm looking forward to listening to her new stories — and I plan to visit her in Dreamland while she's gone.

CHAPTER 20

The Silence That Isn't Really Silent

By Chris Heeter

Coyote knows we do not matter.
He knows rocks care nothing for those who wander
through them; yet he also knows that those same
individuals who care for the rocks will find openings —
large openings — that become passageways into the
unseen world, where music is heard through doves' wings
and wisdom is gleaned from the tails of lizards.

(Williams, 2002, p. 25)

*I*t never occurred to me to go alone. I've guided women's trips for more than 20 years, and never thought much about a solo trip. It crossed my mind periodically, but I always told myself it was the shared experience of nature that I love — the opportunity to teach, learn, connect and enjoy the natural world with others. Coyote, known as the trickster to many Native peoples, is also with me when I go into the wilderness, so I am never completely alone. When I finally did go on a trip without other two-leggeds, however, it changed my life. Here is my story.

One of my mentors told me I couldn't get my own wilderness needs met while guiding others. I have taken that message to heart over the years, making time for personal trips in and among the "work" trips, but somehow the notion of a solo trip never made it to the top of the list. Guiding is work. It is *great* work, but it's not a vacation by any means. Our experience of nature is vastly different when we are "on" as opposed to simply being present to the moment. As wilderness professionals, we need to keep our passion alive. We need to continually reinforce our connection to the natural world, and re-kindle our sense of wonder from time to time by being in nature without the responsibility of guiding a group.

In the fall I often travel to Utah to relax for a week, get reacquainted with the canyons, and do a small trip with my partner before my guiding begins. When she was unable to go early and join me, my first thought was that I would have to change my schedule. Fortunately, I have good friends who suggested it might be time for me to meet the canyons on my own.

Though I guide primarily in the Northwoods, my second love is the desert. I look forward to the times when we guide groups on river trips in the canyon — among the red rocks, the sand, the mud, the heat, and the echoes. I feel a deep connection to those canyons, and gratefully receive their geological and spiritual wisdom. So, that autumn I decided to paddle the canyon river alone. Nothing has moved me as deeply or given me a greater understanding of why I do what I do than that week I spent in the canyons — alone.

As it happened, I had scheduled a focus group for my business just days before I left on my solo trip. The aim of the meeting was to help me clarify marketing ideas for the professional speaking part of my business. When the group learned of my forthcoming solo adventure, they suggested I continue to work on my presentations and marketing while I was out there. They suggested I speak out loud to the canyons to claim my voice, to clarify my message, and to move my professional speaking to the next level.

When I set out for Utah, driving for two-and-a-half days and pulling the canoe trailer, I was excited and nervous — and I had some fears. I was concerned that I would be bored and paddle the route too quickly — I don't sit still well. I imagined finishing the route in two days and being stuck at the take-out waiting for my shuttle. As a woman traveling alone, I was concerned about my safety and predator two-leggeds I might encounter on the river. I was also concerned about how alone I would feel when the shuttle first pulled away, leaving me on the river's edge with my canoe and my gear. And I was concerned about the nights; how long they would seem — and how many dangers I would invent in the darkness.

To my relief, the start of my trip was uneventful. The shuttle pulled away, and I set about packing gear into my canoe. I was immediately struck by the silence that isn't really silent. It was my first experience of extended time in the canyons with no human sounds other than my own. There was none of the talking, packing, splashing, laughing, and nervous energy of a group at the start of a trip. Indeed, there were plenty of sounds to hear — river sounds, canyon wrens, and raven's wings echoing their flight along the canyon walls. But it still felt like silence in the absence of human sound.

Not far down river, I came upon a group of canoeists. Rather than pass them, I decided to stay back, to read a little from a naturalist book as I floated along. As I drifted, with no clients or friends on which to focus, my mind shifted to the wonders of the magnificent canyon. I have never considered myself much of a naturalist. I have a bad memory for isolated facts, am easily frustrated by field guidebooks — and I don't sit still well! Being out there alone, however, the natural world opened up to me in new ways. I was fascinated by my surroundings, eagerly experiencing them, reading about them, and coming up with continuous questions and thoughts. Maybe the reason I don't consider myself the naturalist type is because I get easily distracted by the needs of others and human interactions. Maybe time alone is the very best way to engage and learn about our earthly surroundings.

As time went by, good things happened. My ability to sit still improved, and my relationship with my beloved canyons deepened. I was amazed by the amount of noise other groups on the river produced, and grateful for the peaceful solitude when they paddled on. I was aware that most of the time I am far more like that other group — talking, laughing and singing their way along forest trails and down rivers. My groups are respectful, but our impact in terms of sound is unavoidable.

My worries about the first night evaporated as I went through the routines of setting up camp and cooking dinner. There was so much to look at and listen to, I forgot to feel lonely. The first night in my tent, I heard many sounds nearby. There were visitors walking about my campsite, and I could hear their little feet scamper about and a great deal of chewing. I laid quietly in my sleeping bag and listened. They were just "critter sounds," not scary, just fun and interesting.

The next morning, I perused the tracks left during the night. Kit fox, coyote, beaver, and heron had all paid a visit. As the rays of the morning sun filled the canyon, I heard more chewing, and saw a beaver just 30 yards away munching on her breakfast. I'm not sure how long I sat and watched. I finally got hungry and the beaver and I had breakfast together; she didn't seem to be bothered by my presence, and I certainly was not bothered by hers.

As I paddled that day, I was reluctant to speak out loud, as my focus group had suggested. I just didn't want to make any more sound than was necessary. Even the sound of the canoe going through the water echoes in these canyons. That seemed like enough. I spent the day absorbed in my surroundings, noticing how different I was when left to my own devices.

That night, I had a dream that the canyons were telling me to *"get on with it"* in terms of doing some work on my speaking career while out on this trip. I packed up my canoe, thinking hard about my speaking topics and what I really want listeners to take from my message. Just then, my watch squeaked and popped and made other strange noises. Then it died. At first I was concerned; I had a shuttle pick-up at noon in three days. How would I know what time it was? How would I know how fast I was traveling? The panic only lasted a minute, and then I found myself laughing out loud as I realized the colossal joke Coyote had played. One of the primary messages in the speeches I give is about setting aside time, being present, and paying attention. The watch incident? It was just a little nudge from Coyote, the wise trickster. I began paying closer attention. And decided it was time to *get on with it*.

I noticed something about myself, and suspect it is true of others who solo as well. As I traveled alone, I was shedding layers — layers of guardedness and uniformity that I carry around in town. While group trips into the wilderness free me from many habits and inhibitions, traveling solo peeled away even more layers. On my own, I was free to believe in and embrace the relationship I was building with the canyons, without explaining, belittling, or defending it in front of others. There is a freedom in eliminating the worry of what others might think. And there is a vulnerability in being alone in wilderness that makes me open to possibilities and connections that are otherwise easily dismissed or ignored in the company of other two-leggeds — even close friends.

As the layers fell away, I realized how much I was thoroughly enjoying the whole experience of being alone for an extended period of time. By Day 3, I had stopped the obligatory "hellos" to the other parties on the river. A nod seemed quite adequate. And on Day 4, while leaning against a sand bank, soaking up the shade and sounds of the canyon, I felt no need to open my eyes or acknowledge the couple that hiked past me up the wash. The peace I was feeling mattered more than an interruption and a near meaningless hello to strangers.

I also found I could set aside my rules for setting up camp. The first evening I had been much like I was on any trip, taking care of chores, setting up the tent, trying to have the cooking and dishes done before sundown. Each night, the reason for such procedures became less clear as I realized it was just me, and I have always enjoyed being out in the dark. On the fourth night, I arrived at my sand campsite at dusk, and cooked and ate in the dark. I didn't even put up my tent; I slept under the stars and full moon, and knew that after this experience, I would encourage my groups to be outside more in the darkness.

On that last night, I burned a braid of sweet grass that I had carried for years and never used. This ritual helped me claim my voice and my place among those I respect in the field of professional speaking. I would definitely *not* have done that with other people around. Rituals, images, and symbols often help me make sense of my life. Early in the trip, I began making a coyote track on my arm out of mud each morning and letting it dry like a canyon tattoo. I brought a little tub of mud home with me after the trip, and I still make my mud paw print on my arm when I need to feel the wisdom, the strength, and the peace of those canyons when they feel far away. It helps me bring back my solo trip, and reminds me of all I loved and learned on that adventure.

The last morning, after I played the canyons a *thank you and goodbye* song on my Native flute, I took some time to think about an upcoming guiding trip. I thought about each member of the group, and asked the canyons to help me guide them well. I imagined them packing and getting ready for their adventure. I imagined them arriving here in this magical place and feeling blessed for the privilege of being here. I imagined the laughter and camaraderie that often takes place on my trips. And I imagined the spontaneous silence that also takes place, in which the whole group gets quiet, without any prompting. I told myself to watch for those moments, and encourage more of them as we traveled the canyon.

My solo trip ended, and by then I was surprised to discover I could have been out on my own for much longer. I had discovered my naturalist side — the fascination and curiosity that blossomed as I let myself learn more about this place. I realized many of my fears were unwarranted — loneliness and external threats were concerns that were not actualized. I learned a lot about the joy of *sitting still*. I found I could sit quietly for a long time and not need to fill my time with books or other distractions. I made some strides in my speaking career, too, as I came to know that the strength and wisdom of the canyons would be there with me when I am speaking. I learned to look for Coyote's lessons more often as I follow the trails of my life. I shed many layers of burdensome thought and habit I had constructed through the years. I found new awareness of who I really am, not only in town but in the wilderness as well. I learned, in yet another way, that I can set aside some of the rules and follow my inner wisdom. And I prepared myself for my next group far more mindfully than for most other trips. It was no surprise that the following week's trip was wonderful, with much laughter, appreciation, and transformation among the participants — and even some periodic silence!

I would not have had this experience without the practiced nudge of a few good friends. I knew I had the skills but was uncertain how I would like the experience. I knew the canyons were a powerful and intense place. I had decided to push myself, to go solo despite the fears, and enter into the power and vulnerability of the red rock canyon.

As leaders, it's important to push ourselves into periodic solos, so we remember the newness and fears our participants experience. It is important to renew ourselves and our relationship with the places we travel. And it is important to feel vulnerable at times in wilderness, not always in complete control and responsible for many people. When we guide in wilderness, we go there for the group, not for ourselves. When we solo in wilderness, we offer ourselves to places we love — to learn, to connect, to grow, to appreciate.

Guiding wilderness trips is an incredible privilege to be undertaken with respect, humility, and humor. Whether we are providing a solo experience for group members, or embarking on a solo journey ourselves, solitude has the potential to be a life-changing experience — and for me, one that I hope to explore in many ways.

In the future, when you paddle the waterways, you may see me. I will be part of that group of women you see on the water — smiling, laughing, telling stories. But I may also be that woman you see paddling on her own — the soloist who will give you a nod as you pass by, relishing the silence that isn't really silent.

Reference

Williams, T. T. (2002). *Red: Passion and patience in the desert*. New York: Vintage.

CHAPTER 21

Hanbleceya: To Cry in the Prayer of Vision Seeking

By Clifford E. Knapp

*A vision has been described as "when you see
something with your inner eyes, that means
with all your soul and spirit." In the dream or the vision,
the individual experiences all that happens
in the vision as if he/she were awake.*

(Beck, Walters, & Francisco, 2001, p. 97)

Vision quests are not unique to Native American cultures. Cultures and religions throughout the world have long practiced unique versions of the tradition for various purposes. This paper, however, will focus on my experience with the Lakota vision quest called *Hanbleceya*.

Translated into English, the Lakota word means to cry (sing and pray) in the prayer of vision seeking; this also defines the purpose of this ancient rite. It's a ritual that involves being alone outdoors for a period of one to four days and fasting in a prayerful and humble way. Sometimes a vision or direction in life is sought, but the seeker might also wish to connect with the universe, make a personal sacrifice, and pray for individuals and the good of the community. Traditional Lakota believe the universe is divided into 16 parts and contains all of creation. The Hanbleceya provides an opportunity for individuals to spiritually connect with these elements of the universe.

This paper describes my preparations for a 24-hour Hanbleceya and records some of my impressions before, during and after the solitude experience. Along with these thoughts and feelings about the impact of my vision quest, I also provide some background information to expand the reader's knowledge about this important spiritual practice.

The details of the vision quest ritual vary with the teachings of the tribe. I have discovered that there are many "right" ways of performing rituals in "Indian Country." The "rightness" of the ritual depends upon what the leader was taught and by whom, and the expectations and preparations of the participant. Knowing this has made me less critical when I see different ways of doing a Native ceremony. The importance of any ceremony hinges on the underlying beliefs and *good heart* or intentions of the people who conduct and participate in the ritual. The attitude of the vision seeker is critical. If the purpose for doing a Hanbleceya is for self-centered reasons, such as to inflate personal egos, or gain attention or bragging rights about surviving an ordeal, then the deeper purposes of the ritual are missed.

Choosing good teachers for this ceremony was very important to me. I wanted to learn about the Hanbleceya from people who were taught by traditional peoples. I wanted to experience a time-tested ritual hundreds of years old. I wanted to participate in a way that was as close to historically correct as possible. I wanted to respect my teachers and feel comfortable with them on a personal level.

Two mentors instructed me on the tradition and practice of Hanbleceya. The first was a wise and learned man who was the fourth keeper of Sitting Bull's pipe. He was of Cherokee heritage and had been adopted by the Lakota People. It was he who versed me in the tradition of the ritual. My second mentor guided me through the preparation period leading up to the actual ceremony and through the Hanbleceya itself. He was a person I had known for about 10 years. When I first met him, I knew there was something special about him, although I couldn't pinpoint exactly what it was. Lakota elders taught him, and he follows a traditional medicine path. I was confident he would guide me through the authentic steps of the vision quest and help me make sense of my experience.

In modern times both males and females can participate in a vision quest when they reach an age of understanding about the purpose of the ritual. In many Native cultures boys use this coming-of-age ceremony to be recognized as a man by the community. According to Black Elk, an Oglala Sioux holy man, a woman could seek a vision in the same way as a man, but little has been recorded in history about this (DeMallie & Parks, 1987). The authentic ritual of the vision quest is not to be taken lightly. It is a serious, prayerful experience that should be sought only after a person has adequately prepared, both intellectually and spiritually. Here is part of my Hanbleceya story.

> *I am a White man following the Red Road and considered an elder by my Native friends. I've been on this spiritual path for more than 10 years now and have a passion for learning about indigenous life ways all over the world. I don't understand all my reasons for pursuing this road with such intensity but realize that matters of spirit can transcend cognitive understandings. Some questions in life can only be answered by listening to my inner self or soul. I know that one of my motivations to walk the Red Road was to fill a spiritual void. This path provides the direction I needed to feel more connected to myself and others and the earth.*

In 1993 I organized a weekend educational conference to help educators learn more about Native American cultures. To accomplish this, I gathered a group of knowledgeable people to serve as resource leaders. My first mentor for this project was the fourth keeper of Sitting Bull's pipe. He had extensive experience as an anthropologist, activist, museum director and appraiser, and teacher. He provided the firm support I needed to bolster my confidence and expand my knowledge of Native cultures. He provided enough assistance to enable me to successfully coordinate the conference for several years.

Through that educational conference, I made many Native American friends and gained access to a network that led to my participation in various rituals and ceremonies. First, I experienced the purification or sweat lodge ceremony (inipi), then a pipe ceremony (channupa), followed by a naming ceremony. Later, I participated in an Ojibwe restoring-the-mourner ceremony a year after my son died. Later still, I was invited to attend a sun dance as a supporter, a person who helps the dancers. As time passed and my confidence and knowledge grew, I felt ready to carry a personal prayer pipe. My second mentor told me that the best way was to make one myself, and instructed me in how to do so. I made my prayer pipe from a piece of pipe stone (catlinite) given by a friend and a white ash pipe stem gifted by another friend. Only after I felt that all the physical and spiritual pieces were in place could I take the next step of asking to be led in a vision quest.

According to the written directions my first mentor had given me, the Hanbleceya puts a person in touch with other parts of the universe. It allows humans to directly discover their allies — the stones, insects, birds, mammals, wind, sun, moon, and other parts of creation. It provides the basic experiences to better understand the Lakota expression *Mitakuye Oyasin* — we are all related. Those who prepare for a traditional Native American vision quest must think about the importance of prayer in their lives. The Hanbleceya provides the opportunity to be humble before the Creator and be open to new learning.

The next step was to ask my Hanbleceya leader for his guidance. It was then that I turned to a second mentor. In the Lakota tradition and in many others too, a tobacco offering accompanies such a request for help. If the tobacco is accepted, the preparations continue. Customarily, no money is paid to traditional medicine people for conducting ceremonies, but their expenses should be covered, as well as providing other necessities such as the stones for the purification lodges, hardwood for the fires, and food for a feast that follows.

Other rituals prepare the seeker. In the Lakota tradition vision seekers make many prayer ties of different colors attached to a continuous line of cotton cord. A prayer tie (*Canli wapahta*) consists of a pinch of tobacco tied into a piece of colored cloth. Each tie is made with a prayer directed to the spirits of the universe. The symbolism of the colors is important. In the Lakota tradition followed by my teachers, the black represents the west, the red the north, the yellow the east, and the white the south. In addition to the small prayer ties, six differently colored flags, each tied to a stick, were prepared to mark the four directions and each side of the altar where my pipe rested. A blessed pipe, tamper, smoking material, shell or clay bowl, sage, wooden matches and a leather cloth to wrap the pipe and accessories were also taken. These items were gathered beforehand and should be used respectfully. No other items such as reading or writing materials or other modern technologies were allowed because ancient vision seekers didn't have them. Putting words or other technologies between the vision seeker and the natural world would tend to distort the senses and change the experience.

> *When the time came, I was unsure about when to begin the vision quest. I didn't know if my teacher would take me out just before dark or early in the morning. He said that I could choose, but he recommended going out in the morning. On a previous visit, I had chosen my site for the Hanbleceya. I walked a field until I found the right spot. I had the help of a tufted titmouse (a small gray, crested bird). The bird darted out of a bush, perched on a branch, and I thought I heard it call, "Here it is, here it is, here it is." I knew without a doubt that my animal guide was telling me where to go. The night before going, I ate a meal with my teacher and friends who were supporting me. They agreed to help me prepare the area and the feast that followed my fast. After dinner I offered my filled pipe to my teacher to confirm his acceptance of the role of guide. I was uneasy with the procedure because I didn't want to make a mistake in doing the ritual as I was entering into new territory. This vision quest was certainly a stretch into a new world. I wanted to participate in the ritual in a way that was as true to Lakota tradition as possible. That night I slept fitfully and arose the next morning with feelings of reverence and anticipation.*
>
> *Before the inipi I was taught how to make a special fire to heat the stones (Grandfathers) for the purification rite. When the stones were cherry red, I placed my pipe on the altar and entered the lodge with my teacher. It was a*

time of prayer to prepare me for my adventure alone. He asked me again if I intended to follow through with the ritual. Of course, I said "Yes." I had prepared too long to change my mind. I tingled with mixed feelings of joy and fear. I had read the preparation sheet carefully and reviewed many other stories of vision quests, but this time it was happening to me and it was real. After the inipi, I crawled from the lodge and picked up my pipe before being led to the site. The long string of prayer ties was placed in a circle about 10 feet across. The four directional sticks and flags were placed according to the compass directions and the pipe altar was flanked with the green flag and the blue flag. My teacher gave me some final instructions. He said that if a bear, snake, or other animal threatened me, I should point the pipe stem toward it and tell it to go away. I wondered why he hadn't told me that before? Maybe this vision quest had some built-in risks I hadn't considered. He also told me to hold the pipe as much as possible and to pray during my time alone. His parting advice was to offer tobacco to the biting insects in hopes that they would give me some peace. He also told me how to ask for help if the sun's rays became unbearable.

According to my first mentor, it is important to honor the seven directions in prayer. Yankton Sioux elder, Joseph Rock Boy, Teton Sioux holy man, Frank Fools Crow, Western Sioux medicine man, Lame Deer, and other Native Americans taught him over many years. Several weeks before he died, he explained some Lakota beliefs to me: Because most traditional Lakota believe that the natural way of moving is in a clockwise direction, the way the sun circles the earth, the different directions are honored in a certain sequence. The West is prayed to first because it is the direction of both life and death. Rain comes from the dark thunderclouds that often approach from that direction in the Northern hemisphere. The rain gives life to growing things and the powerful lightning and thunder beings originate there. The focus for prayer in the West is strength and perseverance and its color is black. The North is honored next. The Red Road or spiritual path of life begins in the North. Its color is red. Human blood is red no matter what race a person belongs to. The North is the direction from which the souls or spirits come when babies are born. Prayers to the North are offered for health, wellness, and curing. The next direction to be honored is the East. The color is yellow like the sun that rises there. My mentor said that he believed the sun teaches the plants to grow. Prayers for knowledge, wisdom, and understanding are offered to the East. Prayers for the South offer thanks to the Creator for the blessings of those who have *walked on* or died. The color of the South is white.

My mentor believed that as we travel the Red Road our bodies gradually turn into a soul. At birth the soul divides into four parts: Niya, the breath of life, goes into your mouth and enters your heart, mind, and lungs. Towan, located at the top of your head, goes ahead of you and is your guide for life. Nagi surrounds you and serves as you protector. Chekpa, meaning twin, can be found in an animal totem that serves as a teacher or guardian. Nagi and Chekpa stay behind before a person begins to walk the Red Road. Towan and Niya travel with the person along life's spiritual journey from North to South.

The Lakota believe that if a person deviates from that good road, bad things will happen. When people pray, they should ask the Creator to put the straying person back on the Red Road. The South is the end of life on earth and the beginning of the spirit journey along the Holy Road or the Milky Way in the sky. The dense clusters of stars are believed to be small campfires along this holy road. The order of honoring the next two directions sometimes varies. My mentor chose to honor the direction of Mother Earth next. The color of this direction is green. Prayers are offered for the plants we eat, the medicines we gather to heal us and conduct ceremonies, and for the plants that feed the animals. The sixth direction is located above us. Its color is blue like the sky. Grandfather sky is the power that operates in the universe. A seventh direction, the center, is also honored. When people are born, they are given the privilege of establishing the center of life. Where they put down a stone or smoke a pipe in prayer, they establish the center of the universe. Many believe that the color of the center is whatever you want it to be and sometimes comes to you in a vision.

I was alone without other humans for 24 hours, but I didn't feel lonely because I had many other visitors. When I selected my grassy site, I noticed two cherry trees that would offer me partial shade. As the sun slowly arched across the sky, I discovered that they would not shade me for very long. I had not prepared my pale skin for the sun's onslaught. As the day progressed, I became hotter and redder. Although dressed only in swim trunks, I sweated freely as the temperature rose. At first, I brushed away the flies and wasps that landed on me. After a while, I realized that to do that for the next 24 hours would distract me from my main task of prayer and opening myself to the experience. I decided to let the flies and wasps drink my perspiration and in turn they fanned and cooled me with their wings. We worked out an arrangement that benefited us all.

Because I was an elder, I was allowed to have two blankets. During the day, I sat on one of them and held the other over my head to protect me from the piercing sun. When I tried to disregard the heat, my thoughts turned to food and water. My stomach groaned for food and my mouth begged for water. At home, I rarely thought about food or water until minutes before eating or drinking. Here I knew that neither food nor water was allowed until the next day. Gradually, the desire for food subsided, but my mouth felt as though it had been stuffed with cotton. I was learning that water was more difficult to do without than food.

Because my teacher had advised me to use as much of my time as possible for prayer, I began to pray. As I write this, I find it hard to believe how I've changed in that regard over the years. For most of my life, prayer was something that religious people did and I didn't feel very religious. Later in life I wanted to develop the spiritual part of me that I had ignored in the past. As I learned more, I gradually created a philosophy of prayer. I needed to understand why I prayed and, most importantly, to whom I was praying. Through my network of Native American friends, I had slowly grown to understand and value prayer. I saw prayer not only as asking for things I didn't have, but as a way to think positively about the needs of others and to connect with my inner self. I found that by concentrating on special people in my life, I could think about how I could help them and about their needs.

Praying to the Creator of Great Mystery was very new to me. I had long abandoned the image of God as a bearded white man sitting on a throne in heaven. Through my ritual experiences with Native Americans I formed the concept of the Creator as a mysterious and powerful force that accounted for the origins of the world and the time before and after my life on earth. The mystery also accounted for how the world and its travelers worked in miraculous and intricate ways. The Creator became an intricate set of laws that operated a nature and human science. The Creator became a source of strength and inspiration and a way to connect with my deeper spiritual self.

As the day unfolded, I came to a better understanding of my place in the universe. I was more connected with the sun, moon, winds, plants, animals, mountains, and streams. I felt the sun sweep overhead, sometimes too slowly for my comfort. I felt the cooling winds on my sweating body and thanked them for the relief. I felt that the plants and animals were related. I knew the stream, a short distance away, could cool me, but I would have to wait until later for its blessings. The web of life became more than a shallow phrase with only surface meanings. I felt that I really understood what it meant to be a part of the larger community of other beings. In the distance I saw what appeared to be a bunch of leaves moving against the background of other stationary leaves. These leaves moved like a pair of jaws chewing, or was I seeing the jaws of a plant spirit? I never could explain why one small patch of leaves moved and all the others were still. Was this a spiritual creature that was trying to teach me something about my place in the universe? I also saw a patch of red amid some leaves in the distance. That red color would appear and disappear throughout the day — another unexplainable event.

As night fell, the bats appeared and swirled around me. They devoured insects in a graceful, acrobatic sky dance. Then suddenly they disappeared and the moon, stars, and planets took center stage in this evening performance. As the night advanced, I watched the moon slowly move across the sky along the path of the sun and the stars gradually circle the North Star or disappear below the horizon. I dozed on and off until the sun replaced the lights of night. As the sun rose, a hummingbird hovered nearby as if to say "good morning," before racing away. Later, a great blue heron and turkey vulture flew directly overhead to remind me that a new day had arrived. Have you ever heard the sound of vulture wings slicing the sky? These winged ones were the dominant visitors throughout my vision quest. What did that mean?

As the sun rose higher, I was growing impatient and annoyed that my teacher didn't come for me to end my quest. I was sunburned, hot, tired, thirsty, and hungry, but feeling satisfied with my accomplishment. It was finally time to return to the purification lodge for the last step in the vision quest ritual. After what seemed like hours, he finally arrived. I had learned another lesson in trust and patience from the solo. The purification lodge was a time for more prayer, and after what seemed like an eternity I was offered water in a buffalo horn cup. Never had water tasted so sweet. I had a chance to share my thoughts and feelings about the experience and to ask questions about what I didn't understand. We talked for a while and then the ceremony ended with a feast celebrated with my friends. My first vision quest had ended, but I immediately looked forward to my next one the following year. I was ready for another challenge and time of peace, prayer, and reflection.

My vision quest followed the Lakota tradition as taught to me by my chosen teachers. The ritual was composed of specific steps that began long before and lasted long after the actual event. My main purpose was to reflect on my life and open myself to messages and lessons from the universe. Visions do not always arrive with clarity or during the actual vision quest. Sometimes they don't arrive at all. My insights came through prayer and contemplation about my place in nature and human nature. My understanding of words such as harmony, balance, respect, reverence, interrelationships, human needs, and the web of life were deepened in a spiritual way. No longer did I doubt my intimate connection to the universe. I benefited in other ways too. Following traditional Native teachings allowed me a glimpse into the past of the Lakota nation. I gained confidence about my ability to endure physical and emotional difficulties in life. I am better able to appreciate the values of solitude. I know I can sacrifice for spiritual reasons and meet my basic human needs for warmth, food, and water. I now appreciate the comforts and conveniences of home more and know I can survive with fewer. I also discovered an important paradox: I realized how blessed I am to have the luxury of depriving myself of modern civilization's luxuries.

Not everyone can take the time necessary to prepare and participate in a vision quest like this. Not everyone can find the good teachers I did. My senses and spirit have been opened to direct experience with nature's sacred web, away from modern distractions. Vision quests can take many forms, but mine gave me a special message about my life focus on teaching, ecology, and the importance of understanding my community. That was my vision of the future and the hope for the survival and quality life for all.

References

Beck, P. V., Walters, A. L. & Francisco, N. (2001). *The sacred: Ways of knowledge, sources of life.* Tsaile, AZ: Dine College.

Demallie, R. J., & Parks, D. R. (Eds.). (1987). *Sioux Indian religion: Tradition and innovation.* Norman: University of Oklahoma Press.

CHAPTER 22

Solitude for Growth and Healing: 10 Memories

By Thomas E. Smith

It is easy in the world to live after the world's opinion,
it is easy in solitude to live after your own;
but the great man is he who, in the midst of the world,
keeps with perfect sweetness the independence of solitude.

(Emerson, 1929, p. 623)

Solitude has always been an important part of my world. It has helped me grow, and it has helped me heal. People often ask about the origin of the name I was given, and accepted, while studying with Native American elders. It is *Raccoon*. When I first opened my heart to Native wisdom, I was a husband and father of three, living and working in suburbia. A few years and two more children later, my Native friends thought I should take a name. They noted that while I lived and worked in an often unhealthy and misguided society, I still had the heart of the wild; I was still deeply connected to Mother Earth. "Like a Raccoon," one of my friends suggested, "you'd rather be in the forest, but since the white man has turned the woods into housing developments and concrete malls, you have adapted." "You have balanced a walk on both the Red Road and the White Road," said another. One of the elders listened, and then approved, "Yea, he's really just an Indian who eats out of the white man's garbage can." The name fit. I could survive in suburbia as long as there was time to go to the wild. I could walk the streets of the city but still keep my natural heart in place. I could do that because I often had opportunities to spend time in the wilderness. I needed that wildness for maintaining health and for healing when I hurt. I needed to balance time with the crowd with time alone. I had learned that many years before, and I have many memories that illustrate how solitude has healed and taught me.

My father died when I was 6 years old. For the next two years, while my mother went off to establish herself in a teaching career, I lived with an aunt and uncle. My mother came to visit me almost every weekend, but on Sunday afternoon, as she packed up to leave, my heart always filled with sadness. The final goodbyes were just too painful, so I learned to avoid them. About an hour before she would leave, I would escape to the nearby park and climb up a tree by the riverbank. I would sit there quietly, watching the currents of the river, listening to the breeze flapping the leaves, and attending to the flow of my own thoughts and feelings. It was a time of reflection in solitude. I discovered that the wondrous complexity and mystery of nature enabled me to set aside sad feelings of separation and disconnection, and replace them with feelings of warmth, joy, curiosity, and independence. I did not realize it then, but the cradling branches of that tree were taking the place of my mother's arms; that wonderful maple tree was my first therapist, my first experience with the healing powers of nature. Conservationist Alison Rush explains what was happening to me in psychodynamic terms:

> *The natural environment is experienced as a nurturing matrix, close to and perhaps identical with the Klienian 'good breast.' The boundaries of the ego are relaxed, and we have a sense of 'taking in' the richness and beauty of our surroundings. Precisely because the environment is not human (does not judge us or place any demands on us), it also acts as an unresisting receptacle into which we can project unwanted feelings or parts of ourselves — and so 'takes us in.' This powerfully relieves our anxieties and confers a sense of release and liberation.*
>
> (1997, p. 4)

At about the age of 8, having rejoined my mother, I often played with friends, climbing the tall, slender, poplar trees that lined the nearby golf course. We used to sway from side to side in those flexible trees until they almost touched the ground. It was high adventure! It was Csikszentmihalyi's "flow" (1990). It was, for a boy of 8, a "peak experience" (Maslow, 1968). I remember that when my friends went home for dinner, I would stay behind just to sit in the treetops. I liked being alone. As Isabel Colegate noted, "It is in solitude that the self meets itself" (Colegate, 2002, p. xiv). In solitude I discovered myself, I talked to myself, I questioned myself, and I listened to myself. I would sway the tree a little to feel the air from the outside world, and then would look inside myself for thoughts and dreams.

During the summer of my 10th year, my loving uncle took me on a 42-day canoe trip in the Canadian wilderness. We drove to the end of the Gunflint Trail in the Upper Peninsula of Michigan, and then paddled north into Canada. It was a remarkable adventure. Although we were almost always together, there were many times when we were both silent — just listening to the peaceful sounds of the paddles in the water, the crackling of the wood in the fire, or the rumbling of distant thunder. We were together in that grand *wilderness beyond*, but each of us was also on a solo journey to our own personal *wilderness within*. I liked it when my uncle took out his pocket lens, and we kneeled together over a little flower or a crawling bug. In retrospect, I was experiencing an intimate and complex relationship with nature and human nature. It was that feeling of "oneness" that Kaplan and Talbot (1983) concluded was one of the benefits of wilderness experience. It was what Ruth Baetz calls "wild communion" (Baetz, 1997). My uncle enjoyed solitude, too; sometimes in the evening he would paddle his canoe away from the campsite to explore what was around the next bend of the wilderness shoreline. I would sit by the campfire, sometimes a little frightened by the distant howl of wolves, but more often quite relaxed as I listened to the calling loons and explored what was around the next bend of my wilderness within.

When I was 16 years old, my uncle arranged for me to take flying lessons. He had always wanted to fly, but his wife had frowned on it. When he confronted her with the idea that it would be good for me to learn to fly, she finally relented, and we both took flying lessons. After many hours of instruction, it was time for that intense, unforgettable experience of a first *solo flight*. It is an experience that can only be fully understood by others who have had it. Flying alone, high in the sky, especially when I cut the engines and just glided through the clouds, brought moments of intense awareness of self and earth. I was aware, maybe for the first time, of a spiritual presence in earth and air, a *Great Spirit* that was overseer of all that is. When my airplane left the runway, I was symbolically and literally disconnected from the earth and moving in a unique wilderness. Many have suggested that greater spiritual awareness is an important benefit of wilderness experiences. Indeed, my solo flights had a spiritual quality.

My uncle died when I was 18 years old, and I dealt with my grief by heading for our beloved Boundary Waters. I solo journeyed into the wilderness. I paddled out across Farm Lake, walked the long portage trail to the Kawishiwee River, and then paddled to a small island where we had camped together a few years earlier. As soon as my canoe touched the shoreline rocks, I exploded with emotions of grief, sadness, and anger. It was dark, and the stars were out in their dancing brilliance, when I thought about a gift my uncle had given me many years before. It was a book that his father had given to him, *The Collected Works of Ralph Waldo Emerson*. He had book-marked Emerson's essay on nature. I remember that at the time I could not understand some of the words, nor the complexity of some of the thoughts, but I have grown to appreciate what was written. Emerson wrote:

The lover of nature is he whose inward and outward senses are truly adjusted to each other. His intercourse with heaven and earth becomes part of his daily food. In the presence of nature a wild delight runs through the man, in spite of his sorrows.

(Emerson, 1929, p. 2)

I spent three days in solitude, in the comforting arms of Mother Nature, and I healed. Delight came into my consciousness despite my sorrows. Once again, the wilderness was my therapist, my healer.

Three years later, as a Marine at the front lines of the Korean War, I was ordered to take time alone — in the darkness, with all my anxiety and fear — in listening *outposts* and trench line *fighting holes*. I recall those long hours, looking up at the stars and trying to tune out the artillery shells that exploded on nearby hillsides and the rat-a-tat of machine gun fire that loomed even closer. I remember trying to sort out the sounds of possible enemy patrols, but in such dark and fear-filled moments my mind jumped from focus on the outside to focus on the inside. I remember looking up at the Big Dipper and tracing the line to the Little Dipper and the North Star. I remember thinking how that distant star looked the same as it did on a clear night back in Wisconsin, and those thoughts comforted me. I visited home in my mind, and sat beside Madison's Monona Bay. I remember being snapped back to the reality of the night by sounds from out in *no man's land* in front of my position. Then, when those sounds passed, I turned again to the inside, reflecting on the puke and ugliness of war, death, and dying, and my wishes for peace, love, and home.

In the early 1960s, I spent two summers studying with Native American elders in the Pipestone area of southwestern Minnesota. There I experienced my first *inipi* (a sweat lodge purification ceremony of the Lakota Sioux) and went on my first two-day *Vision Quest*, involving fasting and solo time in the wilderness. Being alone with nature was not a new experience, but framing it in Native American cosmology and the traditions of the First People made it very significant. I had no surreal vision, but I journaled thoughts about the connection between *the wilderness beyond* and *the wilderness within*, which was to become the inspiration and mantra for my professional career.

In 1977, when the not-for-profit human services organization I had founded four years earlier was going under, I took a week-long solo camping trip. Like one of my heroes, Don Quixote, I had been knocked off my white horse by the political forces around me. I needed time for healing, and time to find new visions of appropriate personal and professional directions. I canoed one afternoon down the Wisconsin River, as I had done 20 years earlier with a friend. I rolled out my tarp on a sandbar to create a barrier between me and the sand fleas and watched a lightning storm in the south. I thought about another of my heroes, Zorba the Greek, and how he danced along a beach in spite of the catastrophic collapse of the log shoot they had been building for months. So I got up and danced, I danced along the soft sand, with the distant thunder accompanying me. I felt so alive, like that little boy swaying in the trees, and my thoughts came together, my choices began to be clearer. Solitude had done it again — healed me, stirred my growth, and energized me to get on with my life. That dance in the sand would stir in me the energy to refine on a collection of my early papers and publish my first book, *Wilderness Beyond....Wilderness Within....* (*1980*).

Throughout the 1980s, I found time for solitude at my homestead in southwestern Wisconsin. During the first few weeks of ownership of that 35-acre wonderland, as I hiked and then skied about the property, I came into a relationship with a very special 100-year-old hard rock maple tree. We talked and decided that it would be quite appropriate to build a grand tree house cabin in her branches. I agreed to construct a year-round cabin, complete with woodstove, but the building would be with cables and turnbuckles — she did not want to be punctured by nails! Anyway, the tree house I built became the office for the Raccoon Institute, but it was also a special place for solitude and the accompanying reflection. I often worked there alone, always in touch with the earth around me, and the squirrels and opossums who shared the tree. Sometimes I would take my sleeping bag to the top of the ridge or into the woods for a night under the stars, but the best sleeping place was always there in the tree house. If I wanted solitude, she would be quiet, and if I wanted conversation, she was there to pass on her wonderful wisdom. Sometimes, sitting on the attached deck, I would watch satellites travel across the sky, and I would think back to times when things were not so complex; but my friend, my counselor, my tree, being twice my age, would chuckle and tell me, "You ain't seen nothing yet."

One day about 20 years ago while sitting alone in my tree house, I got to thinking about the importance of special places and penned this little poem:

My Special Place

I have a very special place, that I like to call my own,
I like to go there sometimes, when I want to be alone.
You know the kind of place I mean, for quiet and for rest.
When things get hectic and confused, I like to go there best.

I like to sit, and take deep breaths, and let my eyes rove 'round,
I check the sky, I smell the air, I reach and touch the ground.
Sometimes I stay there quite a while, sometimes for not so long,
There's never rush, I take the time, I need to feel strong.

Whenever I leave that special place, I'm better than before,
I've thought things out, I'm all calmed down, but there is even more.
I take away some special thoughts, I seem to find new light,
Things that seemed so wrong before now tend to seem more right.

I'd take you there, if I could, so you could find some peace,
So you could watch your troubles pass, and have your heartaches cease.
But then again, it probably would not work for you,
My special place is just for one, two would never do.

I guess that you will have to find your very own special place,
You'll know it when you find it, for it's like no other space.
If you just sit down, take deep breath, and turn your worries off,
You'll find your place, with clean fresh air, and ground so very soft.

It may be near a pond shore, it may be by a tree,
When you find it you will know, that is the place to be.
I hope that your place does for you what my place does for me,
I hope you find some quiet peace, and inside harmony.

10 Last summer, after the fifth of my six children, a daughter, aged 38 and mother of three, lost her battle with cancer, I turned once again to the healing powers of the wilderness solo. I hiked the trail of a nearby nature preserve, through restored Wisconsin Prairie, and across the marsh to the lookout tower. I looked at the sky, the cattails, the swamp grasses, and the wood ducks circling the pond in the distance. I watched a Sandhill Crane swoop down to perch on the branch of a shrub that was not strong enough to hold her. She flapped a few yards and tried to land on another too weak to hold her. I thought she might give up and fly over the marsh to the woods, but she kept on trying. Finally she was able to balance precariously atop a shrub. She seemed happy enough with her accomplishment, but after a few minutes she took off to meet the next challenge. Like many lessons of the wilderness, the message was not that clear at that moment in time. As I looked out over the beauty and grandeur of that *wilderness beyond*, and was sorting out the pain and the disorder of my *wilderness within*, I wondered why she was so fixed on the process and did not seem to enjoy the goal nearly as much. Wisdom of the elders, in the form of my older sister, was to come the next day at the memorial service. I had shared with friends for some months that there was never-ending pain in my heart, because "you're not supposed to outlive your children." I said that to my sister as we hugged, and she nodded, saying softly, "No, you're not supposed to." Then she stepped back, looked me square in the eye, and boldly announced, "But I'm sure gonna try like hell." The lesson from the Sandhill Crane which I was able to interpret only in retrospect, had to do with healing.

Conclusion

Going on wilderness solos, moving to the outside and then to the inside, has served me well. I think it can serve those in experiential education and counseling well too.

Experiential education leaders should think more about, read more about, and do more about, the many varieties of solo. As professionals we should think more about our goals of solitude experiences for others, and we should give thought to the process of preparing them for the experience. Solitude can teach about self, others, environment, The Other, the self-other interdependency, the self-environment interdependency, and the self-other-environment-Other-ONENESS. My personal being and becoming has been often inspired, enriched, directed, and healed by experiences of solitude.

References

Baetz, R. (1997). *Wild communion: Experiencing peace with nature.* Minneapolis, MN: Hazelden Press.

Colegate, I. (2002). *A pelican in the wilderness.* Washington, D.C.: Counterpoint Press.

Csikszentmihalyi, M. (1990). *Flow: The psychology of optimal experience.* New York: Harper & Row.

Emerson, R. W. (1929). *The complete writings of Ralph Waldo Emerson.* New York: William Wise and Company.

Kaplan, S. & Talbot, J. F. (1983). Psychological benefits of a wilderness experience. In I. Altman, & J. F. Wohlwill, (Eds.), *Behavior and the natural environment.* New York: Plenum Publishing.

Maslow, A. (1968). *Toward a psychology of being.* New York: John Wiley & Sons.

Miles, J. C. (1987). Wilderness as a healing place. *Journal of Experiential Education, 10*(3), 4–10.

Rush, A. (1997). A presence that disturbs. In Scott Taylor's *Research in Ecopsychology.* Retrieved July 2004, from http://www.c-zone.net/taylors/#G

Smith, T. (1980). *Wilderness beyond.... Wilderness within....* McHenry, IL: McHenry Press.

APPENDIX I

Editors' Dialogue

Tom: As we complete the book, I am left with more questions than answers. I think some of these questions are important for leaders of solo experiences to contemplate. Let's start it off with this one: **Can the solo experience be facilitated without the outdoors?**

Cliff: Solos can be beneficial in any type of environment, and different environments, no doubt, have different impacts on the participants. **Maybe another way to ask this question is to inquire about how the solo setting influences the solo taker.** If there is any truth in the idea that the outdoors can provide metaphors for life's lessons, then it is obvious that fewer messages will be translated in most indoor settings. **That makes me wonder what a person might learn by soloing in a greenhouse or an indoor enclosure such as a zoo?**

Tom: I tend to interpret the solo experience as one of going to the inside, to *the wilderness within*. That puts less emphasis on location, because one can benefit wherever one finds solitude. This idea helps me understand the potential of solo experiences of varying duration. Personally, I prefer the outdoor setting — there is something special about having the beauty, the mystery, and the nurturance of the natural world surrounding me. Of course, I realize that the outdoors can bring discomforts such as rain, cold, snow, wind, and other forces. But still, it is that wonderful *wilderness beyond* that stimulates my journey to the *wilderness within*. It doesn't have to be remote wild nature; it can be a riverbank, a forest preserve, a park, or, yes, a greenhouse.

Cliff: The impact of the outdoors on a solo can be great — and not always positive either. I have vivid memories from my *Hanbleceya*. I remember when the sun beat down on my pale skin and my thirst mounted. I remember trying to rest on the hard ground as the temperatures plummeted at night. Thinking more positively, I can recall many pleasures of soloing outdoors and being inspired by the beauty and surprises I observed. Nothing can compare to seeing a great blue heron spear a fish, witnessing a multi-colored sunrise or sunset, finding shapes in the clouds or leaf patterns, or having a hummingbird hover within inches of you. Perhaps the ideal setting for a solo depends on the person, the purpose, and the environmental conditions.

Tom: This makes me remember a lesson learned years ago. I was having difficulty with a youth from the city who had behavior problems. He just wouldn't cooperate with anything the group was doing at the outdoor center. Finally I took him aside to sit under a tree to find out what was going on. As we talked, he explained, "You just don't understand.... I just don't feel comfortable when I haven't got concrete under my feet." I doubt that a solo in the wilderness would have been appropriate for that boy at that time. **This memory makes me wonder if it is possible to find special places at the ends of alleys, on rooftops, in vacant lots, or under concrete viaducts for urban solos?** I wonder if anyone has explored this idea?

Cliff: Certainly a person who is eco-phobic would prefer the comforts of a shelter and might not gain much from any outdoor setting. I've had some wonderful solo retreats to a cabin when I was writing a book or article. My preference for traditional solitude experiences is the outdoors because of my interest in re-creating indigenous vision quests. I never heard of a Native person doing a solo in a shelter, but maybe it has happened.

Tom: Still, Native wisdom speaks of listening to the spirits of the forests, the animals, and the winds — so there were probably times when the individual native was alone communicating with the outside and the inside. The Lakota's rites-of-passage vision quest of four or more days was probably a more meaningful solo journey for the Native youth — but I suspect there were many shorter solo experiences both before and after the sacred quest for a vision, which leads me to another question: **How long should solos last to be most effective? Shouldn't duration be considered in relation to the goals involved?**

Cliff: Yes, it should. As leaders, we should think about providing more than one kind of opportunity to solo. I think solo takers should be able to choose the length of their retreat. Some people would have a difficult time taking a 20-minute solo. If they completed this, they could set a goal of 40 minutes. Considering the context of the solo is critical to determining its length. We need to remember that just because a solo lasts for days, solo takers may not benefit if their attitudes are not receptive to being open to the experience.

Tom: Here's a related question: **How is the solo experience affected when participants stay in one place as opposed to moving about?** Mortlock (1987) talked about *static* versus *dynamic* solos.

Cliff: The answer to this question gets back to the main purpose of the solo. Some goals are better achieved by being sedentary and others by moving around. Perhaps many benefits of a solo can be achieved equally well either way. There are different safety considerations for each type. Most likely, for younger students, there would be greater risk in letting them move away from an assigned solo site. The logistics of managing solos on the move would be considerable. Perhaps the ideal setting for a solo depends on the person, the purpose, and the environmental conditions…

Tom: …and the duration. If the solo experience lasts just a few minutes, a class period, or even a few hours, it probably makes sense to have the soloist stay put. On the other hand, there is value in solo walking. Kurt Hahn used to require his students to take a daily solo walk to enhance reflection.

I remember one time being in a sweat lodge, and tuning out the stories that were being told. My thoughts went other places as I journeyed in my mind, and I was snapped back to the present when a friend pinched my shoulder. Memories of solo in the middle of a crowd make me think about another question. While doing research for this book, I came across a quotation from a descriptive overview to an Outward Bound trip to the Chihuahuan Desert. "Your course will include a 48-hour solo. A solo provides an important break from traveling and a unique opportunity to rest, reflect and practice self-sufficiency. With sufficient food and equipment, you will spend time alone at an assigned campsite. You will be within hearing distance of other group members, and your instructors will check with you at least once per day, more as necessary." That raised a question that has recurred repeatedly as I have edited papers for this collection: **Is it still a solo experience if one is only symbolically alone, with the guide or coach only a yell or whistle call away and if the instructor makes daily visits?**

Cliff: The fact is, it's very difficult to separate yourself from other humans. Few of us can travel to remote wilderness tracts for our solos. On my solos I've seen airplanes fly overhead and heard dogs and cars in the distance. And, conversely, I've felt very alone in a crowd. The real question may be: **How far from other humans should a person on solo be in order to feel isolated from the rest of the world?**

Tom: I think we may be talking about *perceived aloneness,* as we do about *perceived risk.* In risk situations, we attend to safety and factor out as much real risk as possible, but we still want the individual to feel some sense of danger. If we try to take out all real danger, then participants don't have to deal with the *on the edge* feelings that can bring lots of growth. Of course, it would be irresponsible to put our participants into extreme *real risk* situations. In the case of solos, we have to insure the safety of the participant but still create a situation where they feel isolated. We need to consider the age and the psychological readiness of the individuals going on solo. We have to ask: **What sort of solo experience will be both safe and yet involve perceived aloneness?**

Cliff: I'd certainly wonder about the value of sacrificing safety to achieve isolation. What good does it do to lose campers because no one can hear their distress signals? Like so much of what we do, there are lots of variables in how one responds to questions like this. It depends on the soloist's age and experience. It depends on the dangers in the area. It depends on the space available and the number of people in the group. In the end, it seems that we have to fully realize that a person can feel alone and isolated no matter how close others are.

Whenever I think about the question of safety, I find myself asking: **What are the minimal policies and techniques that should be employed to assure both physical and emotional safety for participants?**

Tom: For many people, just being out of sight and hearing range of others is indeed a very lonely feeling. Many believe that humankind is essentially a social being, and cutting off opportunity for peer and community interaction, even if only symbolically, produces feelings of aloneness — and sometimes loneliness. This reminds me of a quotation — from Gertrude Stein, I think — "When they are alone they want to be with others, and when they are with others they want to be alone. After all, human beings are like that."

Most programs offering solo experiences deal with the questions of safety by giving soloists whistles, using stone-pile *post office* sites where partners check in daily, or scheduling regular visits to the soloist's site. I suspect that the records would show that while hundreds of soloists are given whistles to send out distress calls, very few ever use them. I suspect that the stone piles for connecting buddies results in more positive exchanges of thoughts and feelings than actual pleas for help. These procedures for insuring safety have developed through time and seem to be quite appropriate.

This leads to my next questions: **What are the signs of a participant experiencing anxiety and fear before the solo? And how do we deal with individuals who experience emotional distress during solo?**

Cliff: Sometimes people are able to mask their emotional distress very well. The better we know a person, the better we are able to detect their stress level. What I've learned is that as leaders we must attempt to know the person we are preparing for solo as thoroughly as time allows. This raises two other questions. **How well should we know our clients before sending them on solo? What do we need to know in order to trust that they will benefit from the experience?** I wouldn't feel comfortable sending a person on solo unless I had been with them for a period of time. This warning presents problems when the solo is the primary purpose for the gathering of the group. The minimum time seems to be a matter of several days, but there are still risks. **Should we give those preparing for solo some kind of test or diagnostic intervention?**

The obvious signs of distress might be rapid talking, fidgeting, nervous laughter, and expressions of fear and distrust. If leaders observe these behaviors they should know that additional preparation might be necessary. I'm more worried about those who don't show or admit that they have fears. **Maybe a discussion about fears and anxieties with the solo takers before they go out is in order? How might a good leader facilitate this?** The more I think about this question, the more I believe we need to hire highly qualified leaders and appropriately train them in the basics of solo. Maybe this book will be a step in the right direction.

Tom: Pre-solo preparation is essential. I believe that helping the participants understand why they are taking a solo can contribute to a psychological readiness that minimizes emotional distress. What do you think?

Cliff: I believe leaders need to carefully prepare those who are about to embark on a solo. Ideally, this preparation should begin weeks before the actual event. This briefing should cover physical safety as well as emotional safety. Camps and adventure programs should have a comprehensive policy manual that defines the philosophy and practical aspects of the solo. Program leaders must be clear about what is accepted equipment and what is forbidden. Without a written philosophy of solos, these lists are impossible to methodically construct. Without a written philosophy of solos, knowing what framing or briefing is necessary is also difficult.

Tom: Two articles I recently read stirred my mind in regard to this question. Jon Hovelynck (*Australian Journal of Outdoor Education*, 2001, Volume 6, Issue 1) suggests that any pre-structuring or framing of experience prior to the event may limit the experiential nature of that event. He asks, "How much space is there for the learners' experience in so-called experiential education?" He says, " If the lessons to be learned from experience can be listed before the experience has taken place, and thus independently of the learners' experience, it seems misleading to call the learning experiential."

More recently, on his website, Roger Greenaway (www.reviewing.co.uk/rva.html) wonders if much of what we do is not "confirming by experience" rather than "learning by experience."

Even after writing papers for this collection about the value of pre-solo framing and pre-solo instruction on doing activities, I found myself raising this question: **Would there be more value in just taking the participants to the wilderness and letting the event unfold?** If we frame the solo in too much detail and provide the soloist with too much structure, then we may be greatly influencing the outcome. Still, I tend to think there is value in framing and briefing, especially if we have a clear philosophy of what we want to accomplish. **But how do we know if we are framing with too much detail or giving too much instruction?**

Cliff: Participants bring a great variety of prior experiences to their solos, so we can never be sure about what they need to help make the solo more meaningful. No one approaches a solo with a blank experience slate. A partial answer to this dilemma rests with knowing as much as possible about the participants in regard to their past experience with solo. We need to know answers to questions like: Why did they choose to take this solo? What do they want to gain from it? What are their fears and reservations about it? Would they like to change their lives as a result of this experience? If so, how would they like to behave differently afterward? I am not concerned with erring in the direction of giving too much preparation for a solo event. I think a person is likely to filter any framing or briefing and retain only what they need anyway.

Tom: You're suggesting that participants bring their experiential framework to us, and that we add some new suggestions and perspectives in our briefing and framing sessions. Whether we make those additions or not, the person just doesn't move to the experience with that *tabula rasa* — that blank tablet of the mind. Programs have goals and leaders have goals — and what we provide in the way of information and attitudes of expectancy becomes part of each participant's readiness and framework. It is still their experience, and they will take to it, and from it, what is important to them.

Cliff: I've been wondering about the best time for participants to experience solo, specifically: **What is the best sequence of events leading up to or following the preparation, actual solo, and follow-up reflection activities? Should the solo come near the beginning of the planned experience, in the middle, or closer to the end?** These questions about proper sequencing of program events puzzle me. My experience as a teacher has taught me there is no "best" way to order the components of a lesson, but that the order does influence outcome.

Tom: Many years back, I said, "You must sequence — but there is no sequence." The leader must understand the unfolding psychodynamics of the group and modify the sequence accordingly. Some groups would be ready for solo experiences early in a program, while others would not. I realize, of course, that the logistics involved require that the solo portion of a program be scheduled in advance. Still, the question of when to facilitate the solo is intriguing.

Cliff: Bill Quinn's case study (Chapter 14) clearly illustrates how solos can change participants' individual attitudes and, in turn, group dynamics, so it makes sense that the timing of the solo (near the beginning, in the middle, or toward the end) influences not just the solo experience itself but also the overall program experience.

Tom: Anyone who leads adventure groups, teaches classes, or works with groups in any capacity knows that every collection of people is unique. We speak of "good" and "bad" groups, with regard to mood, motivations, and the capacity of teamwork. When the adventure sequence includes the activity of solo, there are certainly effects on the post-solo attitude or *personality* of the group. Bill Quinn's group was only together for eight days, so they didn't have a lot of time to profit from the post-solo positive group attitude. Imagine if that had been a standard 21-day Outward Bound course. Bill would have been very glad that the solo portion of the program was after the sixth day, early in the sequence. Of course, if solo were to have negative impact on the group, then one would wish it didn't happened early. This is a tough question, just another one to which there is no right or wrong answer.

Cliff: You and I have discussed the role of prayer in the solo experience. Maybe a better way of addressing the issue is to ask: **What is the role of prayer in the person's life?** If prayer is an integral part of a person's life, they will take prayer on the solo with them. If it is not, they probably won't pray at all. If a person only prays in times of crisis, then prayer might come in if they face a physical or emotional challenge.

Tom: I wonder if any portion of a soloists self-talk could be considered prayer? I guess there may be a distinction between talking to self, talking to nature, or talking to the Divine or God, but I'm not sure if that distinction is obvious to everyone. There are nature theologists and pantheists who believe that one finds God or gods in nature. In a broad sense, the very essence of the solo experience might be considered to be prayer. I disagree with those who would narrow the definition of prayer to *talking only to God.* I would also question the practice of having the soloist take along printed prayers to read or chant when in solitude. Yet, if that is the stated purpose of the solo, then it might fit the need. Personally, I have had some very prayerful conversations with a special tree or a quiet waterway when on solo.

Cliff: In pre-solo discussions, maybe rather than guiding students to pray, leaders could help participants explore their relationship to prayer. Questions to consider might be framed as: **What is my philosophy of prayer? How did I learn to pray? When do I feel the urge to pray? Are there different types of prayers for different reasons?**

Tom: Which brings up a question about pre-solo prayer. As I understand it, the Lakota Sioux ask the Great Spirit for guidance, direction, and strength for the forthcoming fasting quest before actually going to the wilderness.

Cliff: Certainly, if the goal of the solo was to re-create an ancient indigenous ritual, prayer would be an important topic in the preparation. Traditional earth-based people weave prayer into their everyday lives. There is little separation of their spiritual and secular activities.

Tom: A few papers have been written about the relationship between people's *spiritual quest* and challenge/adventure programs, but more discussion is needed about this. I suspect that many outdoor adventure leaders are uncomfortable facilitating participants who interpret the significance of their learning in terms of spirituality. I like your idea about pre-solo discussions about prayer, but I wonder about the qualifications and comfort level of leaders to facilitate such discussions. Religion and politics are sometimes considered off-limit subjects in public education.

Let's turn to another question, one that you asked years ago. **Who decides what is an "inappropriate" use of cultural/religious ceremonies?** (Knapp, 1992). Like me, you were trying to clarify the issue of non-Natives adapting traditional rituals and ceremonies for contemporary outdoor and adventure education programs. I have argued that the wisdom of Native traditions is worthy of exploration, and that most Native elders are now willing to share ancient rituals and ceremonies (Smith & Quinn, 1998, 2004). However, there is still issue about who has adequate knowledge to try to teach sacred activities to others. With regard to solo the questions are: **How should we proceed in applying solo rituals and ceremonies grounded in Native American tradition? Should we offer solo experiences as vision quests?**

Cliff: Many Native American nations have conducted vision or fasting quests for hundreds of years. If a program staff is properly trained to share these traditional solo rituals with others, there should be few problems. The difficulty with this approach is finding appropriately trained leaders who have the depth of understanding required to honor Native tradition. I have had more than a dozen years of experience and teaching about Lakota and Ojibwe rituals, but I have no desire to lead any of these ceremonies. The more I learn, the more I realize what I don't know. On the other hand, I do feel comfortable in creating my own adaptation of a vision quest and leading others.

Tom: I like your reference to *adapting*. My first learning experiences with Lakota and Ho Chunk elders was in the 1960s, and I have facilitated modifications and re-creations of many Native rituals, ceremonies, and games. But, like you, I have neither interest nor comfort in teaching others about these activities as authentic. I would never call the wilderness solos I facilitate *vision quests.*

Cliff: For me, the key difference is in how I describe the origins of the ritual and conduct it. I wouldn't dream of leading a vision quest and calling it an authentic Native American ritual. I would explain that I adapted an ancient form of being alone outdoors but that it was certainly not authentic. You quoted someone in this book who avoided naming their created solo ritual a *vision quest* out of respect for Native people. I'm not sure I would go that far and avoid the term, but I know I wouldn't attempt to mimic my Native teachers and try to lead a solo the way they led me as a participant.

Tom: I have great respect for the work of Steven Foster and Meredith Little in facilitation and teaching about the vision quest (1983, 1992). Some of the contributors to this book are students of Foster's School of Lost Borders, and they are doing wonderful work. Although their version of the solo experience follows Native tradition fairly well, they do note that it is a 20th century adaptation of the ancient ceremony of *Hanbleceya.*

Here's another question. I know you have written about the importance of journals in outdoor education. My journal is always close at hand when I go on solo, and I often write in it creatively. **What is the place of journaling in solo?**

Cliff: One value of journal writing is that the participant can make a record of thoughts, feelings, and images at the time they are happening. Some thoughts, feelings, and images might become blurred or forgotten as time passes. If participants have a journal for recording important moments, they may treasure them for a long time. Journal entries can also provide discussion points in the reflection sessions that follow the solo experience.

Tom: If the soloist has good writing skills, then I think journals are great, but I wonder about their value when the participant has limited skill for wording ideas. **Should the student's solo journal be structured or open?** I've had great success using a structured journal with adolescents. That involves printing out sentence stems that require completion, giving some directions for what to write about and even supplying picture frames to draw within. I may simply write at the top of a page, "Write a letter home," or "Make a list of the best things about your world." When I have used a solo as part of a workshop on Native American traditions, I include a few words about the significance of the four directions and the four winds, and then have the students write about what they learned. My point is that we ought to help soloists transfer their thoughts and feelings into journals; I've found that blank pages without any structure can be overwhelming to many people.

Cliff: I agree that an inexperienced journaler would benefit from some structure, and children and youth often need some writing prompts before they are able to free-write. Most people would probably benefit from writing with structure and by writing freely. Why not encourage both?

Tom: Wow, is it possible that the time and energy it takes to journal thoughts and feelings actually reduces the impact of the sensory experience? I think that those who teach about *focusing* might advocate for letting the experience itself go deeper, and not take that moment to convert it to words. Journaling could be saved for later.

If we do want our soloists to journal, we may want to focus on this skill in the pre-solo preparation. We could have participants write down their thoughts and feelings about activities early in the program sequence, in lieu of or in addition to, the group processing session. In general, unless dealing with a sophisticated group, I think that handing out a blank journal just prior to the solo and telling people to write in it when on solo can have limited effectiveness. **I wonder how many young people spend frustrating and discouraging minutes staring at a blank page in their journal, not knowing how or where to start?**

Cliff: The field of phenomenology presents a rationale for sometimes not using a journal during an event. Phenomenologists believe that whenever we put words between our senses and the world outside our body, we change and distort the perception of the event. For example, some people are content to name a flower and then move on to the next one. Naming something is only one of the many perceptions that can be attributed to that object. If one remains fully open to the experience and doesn't let words interfere with connecting the senses to the world, the benefits can be great. This approach would take some instruction and practice, but that could be the role of the leader. I recommend a book by David Abram, *The Spell of the Sensuous* (1997), for more on this topic.

Tom: The question of taking journals on solo leads to another question I have long pondered. **What about taking other props and technical gadgets on solo?**

Cliff: Gadgets and technologies can detract from or enhance a nature experience — it depends on the main purpose of the solo. If learning about the constellations and planets is a goal, a star and planet guide would be helpful. If learning to identify local animals, birds, or fauna is a goal, some identification books might be of value. If inspirational thinking is a goal, there might be value in taking along a collection of readings. This is an important question to consider when creating policy and practice guidelines for conducting the solo. My personal preference is to leave behind as much technology as possible. In the "civilized" world of our Western society people are inundated with technology. Solo can be a time to practice simple living and better understand its value to our spirit and lifestyle.

Tom: I don't think anyone would argue for allowing soloists to take along radios, iPods, electronic games, or even a deck of cards. My question refers to things like knives for whittling and binoculars, or a pocket lens for nature study. I have seldom been on solo without my knife, but a folding pocket lens is also a must for me. Sometimes I spend long periods of time looking close up at a wildflower or a beetle. Doing that has always proved to be a spiritual experience for me. I suspect that some people would find whittling to be calming, mind-freeing, and a stimulus for reflection.

Historically, many outdoor programs facilitated solo experiences as an exercise in survival and set rigid restrictions on what the soloist could take. If the intention of solo is to develop nature awareness and reflective thought, some would allow greater creature comforts.

Cliff: If keeping warm at night is a goal, then blankets or a sleeping bag are in order. If keeping dry during a rain is a goal, then a tarp or tent would help. **How much comfort do we want the soloist to experience? What are the benefits of being uncomfortable?** These are questions that must be answered by program leaders.

Tom: I soloed one night on the coast of Maine and had to try to find body space along the rocky shoreline. I could not get comfortable, and I slept very little. Still, being awake to see the sunrise over the ocean was worth the discomfort. I think of those adages about having to see darkness in order to appreciate light, and having to experience coldness to know the warmth. I probably would not have sensed the wonder, the joy, and the energy of that morning sun with such intensity if I had not been through that lumpy-bumpy-rocky night.

I think the issue of safety comes into play here, too. It's probably not advisable to let younger children take a knife along, and you would want to be sure they had shelter appropriate to the weather. I can see where environmental safety might lead to a rule of "no campfires," but if that was not a problem, could soloists have a small fire?

How often do we see people enthralled and entranced by the flames of a campfire? **How does allowing a fire at the site affect the benefits of the solo experience?**

Cliff: Again, that depends on the location, current fire danger, and the purpose of the solo. If a fire is not a safety hazard to the person or the land, it can serve as a comforting companion. If the solo is a re-creation of the indigenous Vision Quest, I don't think a fire would be allowed. My bias is toward having a small fire, but this might mean trading some benefits for others.

Tom: Is fasting an important aspect of the solo experience?

Cliff: You might predict my answer to this from my previous responses. If one has the luxury of taking an additional day or two to rest after the solo is completed, I would recommend fasting for several reasons. First, fasting re-creates the conditions of many historic solos, such as those taken by Jesus, Buddha, and indigenous peoples. Second, fasting simplifies the experience, leaving more time for observing the outer world and thinking about the inner world. Third, by denying food and water during solo, one's appreciation of these necessities of life is enhanced. I can remember savoring the first sip of water and bite of food when I returned from my first solo. I have never looked upon thirst and hunger in the same way again.

Tom: On the other hand, I thought about the person who goes on a fishing solo to the wilderness. Part of the joy and enrichment of the whole experience is to take a trout and fry it over the fire. I also recall a group at an outdoor center that made muffins from freshly picked blueberries, and the leader assigned what he called a "muffin solo." Everybody had to leave the central campsite, go to a quiet spot and think about the wonderful gifts nature gives as they ate their muffin.

Even though a solo of a few hours might bring some feelings of hunger and thirst, I wonder if that can be considered fasting? Even on an overnighter, where the soloist might be in solitude for 24 hours, going without food might not be considered fasting. The bodily effects of going without food may not be felt until the second or third day. So the question relates to fasting on two-, three-, and four-day solos, and I think that the answer would depend on the organizational framework and purposes for the experience.

Cliff: So much of what we have talked about depends on the context for the experience, and the attitudes, goals, and expectations of the participants. Program leaders have to ask: **Why do we want to facilitate solos?** and **What is the most appropriate framework and procedures for those solos?**

Tom: And, what is the proper training for leaders who will facilitate those solos?

Cliff: The phrase "it depends" comes to mind again. Outlining the proper training program for leaders depends on program and participant goals, as well as the amount of time allotted for that purpose. For most frameworks it would take a whole book to do justice to the topic of leadership training. Each broad category of solo type would dictate a different program for preparation of leaders. However, there might be some common ideas and skills that apply across the wide variety of solo frameworks. Some general topics for consideration would be tips for knowing thyself, facing fears of loneliness and being alone, the values of solitude, and safety considerations for solo experiences. What do you think?

Tom: The question of appropriate training of leaders is the most important we have discussed. I think that leaders who consider using solo need to proceed through three steps. First they need to determine the framework and the nature of their solos. This would involve considerations of geography, duration, and the nature of the groups. Second, they need to spell out specific policies and procedures for their solos. Finally, they need to develop a solid training program for solo leadership. In general, experiential education and therapy programs are only as effective as the quality of the leaders. Without careful attention to the orientation and skill development of the leaders, any facilitation of solo experiences is less effective — perhaps not even effective at all.

When I think about general topics for consideration in any training program, two rise quickly to consciousness. The first you already mentioned — that of attending to the personal growth of our leaders, and giving them tips for the life quest of *know thyself*. The second has to do with questions of emotional safety — prediction, prevention, handling, and appropriate follow-up for psychological stress related to the solo experience. You're right, it would take a book to do justice to the question of leadership preparation.

Cliff: Though we've raised as many questions as this book answers, I hope this collection of papers results in many leaders discussing these and other questions related to the solo experience. And, if those discussions result in lots of "it depends," "I don't knows," and even more questions, that will be good enough for me.

References

Abram, D. (1997). *The spell of the sensuous.* New York: Vintage Press.

Foster, S. & Little, M. (1983). *The vision quest: Passing from childhood to adulthood.* Big Pines, CA: Rites of Passage Press.

Foster, S. & Little, M. (1992). *The book of the vision quest: Personal transformation in the wilderness.* Englewood Cliffs, NJ: Prentice Hall.

Hovelynck, J. (2001). Beyond didactic: A reconnaissance of experiential learning. *Australian Journal of Outdoor Education, 6*(1).

Knapp, C. (1992). Letter to the editor. *Journal of Experiential Education, 15*(3), 23–25.

Monaghan, P. & Viereck, E. G. (1999). *Meditation: The complete guide.* Navato, CA: New World Library.

Mortlock, C. (1984). *The adventure alternative.* Cumbria, UK: Cicerone Press.

Smith, T. & Quinn, W. (2004). *The challenge of Native American traditions.* Lake Geneva, WI: Raccoon Institute.

Vincent, S. M. (1995). Emotional safety in adventure therapy programs: Can it be defined? *Journal of Experiential Education, 18*(2), 70–75.

APPENDIX II

Quotations About and for Solo

The quotations contained in this appendix are some of the editors' favorites about solo, silence, and solitude. They have been photocopied or jotted down throughout the years. As a result, in many cases page references are not cited. It is our hope that you find these quotations useful and inspirational, nonetheless. References are cited at the end of this collection.

I became aware for the first time today of the immense silence in which I am lost. Not a silence so much as a great stillness — for there are a few sounds: the creak of some bird in a juniper tree, an eddy of wind which passes and fades like a sign, the ticking of the watch on my wrist — slight noises which break the sensation of absolute silence but at the same time exaggerate my sense of the surrounding, overwhelming peace. A suspension of time, a continuous present. If I look at the small device strapped to my wrist the numbers, even the sweeping second hand, seem meaningless, almost ridiculous. No travelers, no campers, no wanderers have come to this part of the desert today and for a few moments I feel and realize that I am very much alone.... I wait. Now the night flows back, the mighty stillness embraces and includes me; I can see the stars again, and the world of starlight. I am twenty miles or more from the nearest fellow human, but instead of loneliness I feel loveliness. Loveliness and a quiet exultation. —Edward Abbey, *Desert Solitude*

Nature Awareness....

> *Earth teach me stillness ... as the grasses are stilled with light.*
> *Earth teach me suffering ... as old stones suffer with memory.*
> *Earth teach me humility ... as blossoms are humble with beginning.*
> *Earth teach me courage ... as the tree which stands all alone.*
> *Earth teach me limitation ... as the ant which crawls on the ground.*
> *Earth teach me freedom ... as the eagle which soars in the sky.*
> *Earth teach me regeneration ... as the seed which rises in the spring.*
> *Earth teach me to forget myself ... as melted snow forgets its life.*
> *Earth teach me to remember kindness ... as dry fields weep with rain.*

—Ute Prayer quoted in Amidon and Roberts, *Earth Prayers from Around the World*, p. 176.

And when he had sent the multitude away, Jesus went up into a mountain apart to pray; and when the evening was come, he was there alone.   —Matthew 14:23, *The Bible*

There are no more deserts. There are no more islands. Yet one still feels in need of them. To understand this world, one must sometimes turn away from it: to serve men better, one must briefly hold them at a distance. But where can the necessary solitude be found, the long breathing space in which the mind gathers its strength and takes stock of its courage, —Albert Camus, *Lyrical and Critical Essays*

Silence is the great teacher, and to learn its lessons you must pay attention to it. There is no substitute for the creative inspiration, knowledge, and stability that comes from knowing how to contact your core of inner silence.   —Deepak Chopra, *Ageless Body, Timeless Mind*

When alone at night in the depths of these woods, the stillness is ... sublime. Every leaf seems to speak.
                    —John Muir, quoted in Cornell, *Journey to the Heart of Nature*

There is another kind of seeing that involves letting go. When I see this way I sway transfixed and emptied. The difference between the two ways of seeing is the difference between walking with and without a camera. When I walk with a camera I walk from shot to shot, reading the light on a calibrated meter. When I walk without a camera, my personal shutter opens, and the moment's light prints on my own silver gut. When I see this second way I am above all an unscrupulous observer.
                    —Annie Dillard, *Pilgrim at Tinker Creek*, p. 33

Once in a lifetime, if one is lucky, one so merges with sunlight and air and running water that whole eons ... might pass in a single afternoon without discomfort.   —Loren Eisely, *The Immense Journey*

To go into solitude, a man needs to retire as much from his chamber as from society. I am not solitary whilst I read and write, though nobody is with me. But if a man would be alone let him look at the stars. The rays that come from those heavenly worlds will separate between him and what he touches. One might think the atmosphere was made transparent with this design, to give man, in the heavenly bodies, the perpetual presence of the sublime. Seen in the streets of cities, how great they are! If the stars should appear one night in a thousand years, how would men believe and adore, and preserve for many generations the remembrance of the city of God which had been shown!

—Ralph Waldo Emerson, *Selected Essays*

There is a difference between loneliness and being alone; there is a choice of mind in being alone; but loneliness comes up through the heart into the throat.   —William Faulkner, *A Light in August*

The fruit of solitude is increased sensitivity and compassion for others. There comes a new freedom to be with people.   —Richard Foster, *Celebration of Discipline: The Path to Spiritual Growth*

The purpose of silence and solitude is to be able to see and hear.

—Richard Foster, *Celebration of Discipline: The Path to Spiritual Growth*

Here we discover the paradox of the contemplative life, that the desert of solitude can be the school where we learn to love others.

—Richard Foster, *Celebration of Discipline: The Path to Spiritual Growth*

The best remedy for those who are afraid, lonely, or unhappy is to go outside, somewhere where they can be quiet, alone with the heavens and God. Because only then does one feel that all is as it should be.

—Anne Frank, *Diary of Anne Frank*

I'm not here by myself, there just isn't anybody here with me.

—Nadine Funk, personal communication

Solitude is a silent storm that breaks down all our dead branches. Yet it sends out living roots deeper into the living heart of the living earth.   —Kahlil Gibran, *Sand and Foam*

All true wisdom is only to be learned far from the dwellings of men, out in the great solitudes.... To learn to see, to learn to hear, you must do this — go into the wilderness alone....

—Igjugarjuk, Caribou shaman, quoted in Joan Halifax, *Shamanic Voices: A Survey of Visionary Narratives*

We are thankful to the East because everyone feels good in the morning when they awake, and sees the bright light coming from the East; and when the Sun goes down in the West we feel good and glad we are well, and we are thankful to the West. And we are thankful to the North, because when the cold winds come we are glad to have lived to see the leaves fall again; and to the South, for when the south wind blows and everything is coming up in the spring, we are glad to live and see the grass growing and everything green again. We thank the Thunders, for they are the manitous that bring the rain, which the Creator has given them power to rule over. And we thank our mother, the Earth, whom we claim as mother because the Earth carries us and everything we need.

—Charley Elkhair, quoted in M.R. Harrington, *Religion and Ceremonies of the Lenape*

In solitude, we may find a new beginning, an opportunity to break old habits. In solitude, we may find increased sensitivity, compassion, and empathy. In solitude, we may find the truth of ourselves, restore our dulled senses, and clarify and reorder our priorities. Above all, in solitude, we may find God, and come to hear that voice. —Brigid Herman (Ed.), *Creative Prayer*

If there is a better cure for self-deception than solitude, it has yet to be discovered.

—Brigid Herman (Ed.), *Creative Prayer*

The friends of my solitude out-number by far those of my social life. This may be because Nature and Art are more easily approached than persons. These friends are not sticklers for conventions; they never demand a formal introduction; they never accuse me of neglect or deceit; they never condescend to apologies. —Shasta Leila Hoover, *Nature Magazine*, April 1930

Reflection should also include emotions. We cheat our students when reflection is confined to the levels of intellect and cognition…. I wonder if, in fact, we have reached a stage where the distinctions among the cognitive, affective, and spiritual aspects of mental work have outlived their usefulness.

—Bert Horwood, "Reflections on Reflection," *Journal of Experiential Education*, 13(2)

Religion is what one does with one's solitude.

—William James, *The Varieties of Religious Experience*

The perfect stillness of the night was thrilled by a more solemn silence. The darkness held a presence that was all the more felt because it was not seen. I could not any more have doubted that HE was there than that I was. Indeed, I felt myself to be, if possible, the less real of the two.

—William James, *The Varieties of Religious Experience*

Whenever we have a little free time, most of us seek some form of amusement. We pick up a serious book, a novel, or a magazine. If we are in America we turn on the radio or the television, or we indulge in incessant talk. There is a constant demand to be amused, to be entertained, to be taken away from ourselves.... Very few of us ever walk in the fields and the woods, not talking or singing songs, but just walking quietly and observing things about us and within ourselves.

—Jiddu Krishnamurti, *Think on These Things*

How many more generations will pass before it will have become nearly impossible to be alone even for an hour, to see anywhere nature as she is without man's improvements upon her?

—Joseph Wood Krutch, *Treat the Earth Gently*

From that time forth he believed that the wise man is one who never sets himself apart from other living things, whether they have speech or not, and in later years he strove long to learn what could be learned, in silence, from the eyes of animals, the flight of birds, the great slow gestures of trees.

—Ursula K. Le Guin, *A Wizard of Earthsea*

There are degrees and kinds of solitude. An island in a lake has one kind; but lakes have boats, and there is always the chance that one might land to pay you a visit. A peak in the clouds has another kind; but most peaks have trails, and trails have tourists. I know of no solitude so secure as one guarded by a spring flood; nor do the geese, who have seen more kinds and degrees of aloneness than I have. —Aldo Leopold, *A Sand County Almanac*, p. 29

We are all, in the last analysis, alone. And this basic state of solitude is not something we have any choice about. It is, as the poet Rilke says, "not something that one can take or leave." We are solitary. We may delude ourselves and act as though this were not so. That is all. But how much better it is to realize that we are so, yes, even to begin by assuming it. "Naturally," he goes on to say, "we will turn giddy." —Anne Morrow Lindbergh, *Gift from the Sea*

It is difficult today to leave one's friends and family and deliberately practice the art of solitude, for an hour or a day or a week. And yet once it is done, I find there is a quality to being alone that is incredibly precious. Life rushes back into the void, richer, more vivid, fuller than before.... For it is not physical solitude that actually separates one from other men, not physical but spiritual isolation. When one is a stranger to oneself, one is estranged from others too.

—Anne Morrow Lindbergh, *Gift from the Sea*

There is much that fasting can teach, but that teaching can never be explained to someone else. It is an experience in which all of the artificial barriers between self and universe crumble.

—Fred McTaggart, *Wolf That I Am*

The solitary life, being silent, clears away the smoke-screen of words that man has laid down between his mind and things. In solitude we remain face to face with the naked being of things. And yet we find that the nakedness of reality which we have feared, is neither a matter of terror nor for shame. It is clothed in the friendly communion of silence, and this silence is related to love. The world our words have attempted to classify, to control and even to despise (because they could not contain it) comes close to us, for silence teaches us to know reality by respecting it where words have defiled it.... Let me seek, then, the gift of silence, and poverty, and solitude, where everything I touch is turned into prayer: where the sky is my prayer, the birds are my prayer, the wind in the trees is my prayer, for God is all in all. —Thomas Merton, *Thoughts in Solitude*

It all adds up to one thing: peace, silence, solitude. The world and its noise are out of sight and far away. Forest and field, sun and wind and sky, earth and water, all speak the same silent language. —Thomas Merton, *Thoughts in Solitude*

Nature has presented us with a large faculty of entertaining ourselves alone; and often calls us to it, to teach us that we owe ourselves partly to society, but chiefly and mostly to ourselves. —Michel de Montaigne, "On Giving the Lie," in *The Complete Works of Montaigne*

One of our main problems is that in this chatty society, silence has become a very fearful thing. —Henri Nouwen, *The Way of the Heart: Desert Spirituality and Contemporary Ministry*

Solitude leads us to a new intimacy with each other and makes us see our common task precisely because in solitude we discover our true nature, our true self, our true identity. That knowledge of who we really are allows us to live and work in community. —Henri Nouwen, *Clowning in Rome*

I have had my share of solitude and know whereof I speak. It is beautiful to me, for it brings back perspective and a sense of timelessness. I come back to the friends I have left, stronger, better, and happier than when I went away. —Sigurd F. Olson, *Reflections from the North Country*

Over all was the silence of the wilderness, that sense of oneness which comes only when there are no distracting sights or sounds, when we listen with inward ears and see with inward eyes, when we feel and are aware with our entire beings rather than our senses. —Sigurd F. Olson, *The Singing Wilderness*

One does not have to be alone to enjoy silence. It has often been said that the ability to enjoy it with others is the mark of friendship and understanding. Only when people are strangers do they feel obliged to be entertaining. Where there is agreement and appreciation, silence is no bar to mutual enjoyment. —Sigurd F. Olson, *The Singing Wilderness*

Was solitude a matter of remoteness and primitive country or was it something within myself?
—Sigurd F. Olson, *The Singing Wilderness*

Detachment, as far as possible, from our normal routines, reliances, and roles — solitude, calls us to confront ourselves ... to learn who we really are and what we can rely on.
—Parker Palmer, *To Know as We Are Known*

In many societies, voluntary isolation from others is considered necessary for the completion of certain phases of personal growth. Adolescent males entering adulthood in certain tribal cultures are expected to wander alone in the forest, mountains, or desert for as long as several months at a time. During this period the solitary wanderer is instructed to communicate with the divine, compose a song, or experience a magic dream. Those who return without their dream may be sent back into the mountains and told to return when they are successful.
—Barbara Powell, *Alone Alive and Well: How to Fight Loneliness and Win*

Because solitude is a presence, not an absence, it is already here, already a potential. To find it, we must merely give it our full attention. We must watch where we place our interest and attention, not where we place our bodies. In order to know solitude, we do not first have to arrange our lives differently, control our emotions, or learn new techniques of thought control. Having said that, however, it should be obvious that some circumstances are more distracting than others. Surely all of us can make better choices about where we go and what we do, choices that lead us toward either greater chaos or greater simplicity.
—Hugh Prather, foreword to *The Wonders of Solitude*, edited by Dale Salwak

Solitude is wondrous because of what it contains, not what it lacks. Solitude is a place of stillness and joy that is found in the heart, and once found, becomes all-encompassing. It is a window from the soul that looks upon everything and sees unity. Because it resides in our heart, and not simply circumstances, solitude need never be delayed until a more convenient time..... Because solitude is a presence, not an absence, it is already here, already a potential. To find it, we must merely give it our full attention. We must watch where we place our interest and attention, not where we place our bodies.
—Hugh Prather, forward to *The Wonders of Solitude*, edited by Dale Salwak

Only those who learn to live with solitude can come to know themselves and life. I go out there and walk and look at the trees and sky. I listen. I sit on a rock or a stump and say to myself, "Who are you, Sandburg? Where have you been, and where are you going?"
—Carl Sandburg, *Home Front Memo*

The most valuable thing you can do for the psyche, occasionally, is to let it rest, wander, live in the changing light of a room, not try to be or do anything whatever.

—May Sarton, Journal of a Solitude

And therefore I come out to these solitudes, here the problem of existence is simplified. I get a mile or two from the town into the stillness and solitude of nature, with rocks, trees, weeds, snow about me. I enter some glade in the woods, perchance where a few weeds and dry leaves alone lift themselves above the surface of the snow, and it is as if I had come to an open window. I see out and around myself.... This stillness, solitude, wildness of nature is a kind of thoroughwort or boneset to my intellect. It is as if I always met in those places some grand, serene, immortal, infinitely encouraging, though invisible, companion, and walked with him.

—Henry David Thoreau, quoted in Shepard, The Heart of Thoreau's Journals, p. 170

The creative life of the artist, like the inner life of everyone, depends on silent intuition and reflection before anything can be put into words or images, sounds or lines. In this regard, we can see that silence is not the absence of something, it is the most powerful event, the precondition for reality.

—Donald Sooto, The Hidden Jesus: A New Life

When a young man has decided to make the final test, he immediately purifies himself with the sweat bath. A trusted friend selects for him a distant and secluded spot where he can fast without interruption. For after the fast has begun, nothing must happen to disturb his quiet communion with Nature.... He goes with a receptive mind and soul ready to see all and hear all. After days of fasting and praying, the young man feels himself getting closer in touch with mysterious powers.

—Luther Standing Bear, Lakota, My Indian Boyhood

It is incredible how much you can realize about your own existence by simply paying close attention to it and becoming more deeply aware of your own experiencing. Awareness is basic, and you can discover this through your own experiencing.... The revolution of awareness is happening because more of us are insisting on living our own lives. You can join us by living your own life, fully, with awareness. —John O. Stevens, Awareness: Exploring, Experimenting, Experiencing

Only in the oasis of silence can we drink deeply from our inner cup of wisdom.

—Sue Patton Thoele, The Woman's Book of Courage

I find it wholesome to be alone the greater part of the time. To be in company, even with the best, is soon wearisome and dissipating. I love to be alone. I never found the companion that was so companionable as solitude. —H. D. Thoreau, Walden, pp. 93-94

I suspect it was ... the old story of the implacable necessity of a man having honour within his own natural spirit. A man cannot live and temper his metal without such honour. There is deep in him a sense of heroic quest; and our modern way of life, with its emphasis on security, its distrust of the unknown, and its elevation of abstract collective values has repressed the heroic impulse to a degree that may produce the most dangerous consequences.   —Laurens van der Post, *Heart of the Hunter*

In many so-called primitive cultures it is a requirement of tribal initiation to spend a lengthy period alone in the forests or mountains, a period of coming to terms with the solitude and nonhumanity of nature so as to discover who, or what, one really is — a discovery hardly possible while the community is telling you what you are, or ought to be. He may discover for instance, that loneliness is the marked fear of an unknown which is in himself; and that the alien looking aspect of nature is a projection upon the forests of his fear of stepping outside habitual and conditioned patterns of feeling. There is much evidence to show that for anyone who passes through the barriers of loneliness, the sense of individual isolation burst, almost by stint of its own intensity, into the 'all feeling' of identify with the universe.   —Alan Watts, *Nature, Man and Woman*

References

Abbey, E. (1968). *Desert solitaire: A season in the wilderness.* New York: Ballantine Books.

Amidon, E., & Roberts, E. (1991). *Earth prayers from around the world: 365 prayers, poems, and invocations for honoring the earth.* New York: Harper San Francisco.

Camus, Albert. (1968). *Lyrical and critical essays.* New York: Alfred A. Knopf.

Chopra, D. (1993). *Ageless body, timeless mind: The quantum alternative to growing old.* New York: Three Rivers Press.

Cornell, J. (1994). *Journey to the heart of nature.* Nevada City, CA: Dawn Publications.

Dillard, A. (1975). *Pilgrim at Tinker Creek.* New York: Bantam Books.

Eiseley, L. (1957). *The immense journey.* New York: Vintage Books.

Emerson, R. W. (1982). *Selected essays.* New York: Viking Penguin.

Faulkner, W. (1990). *Light in August.* New York: Vintage International.

Foster, R. (1978). *Celebration of discipline: The path to spiritual growth.* New York: HarperCollins.

Frank, A. (1952). *The diary of a young girl.* Garden City, NY: Doubleday.

Gibran, K. (1926). *Sand and foam.* New York: Alfred A. Knopf.

Halifax, J. (1979). *Shamanic voices: A survey of visionary narratives.* New York: Penguin.

Harrington, M. R. (1921). *Religion and ceremonies of the Lenape.* New York: Museum of the American Indian.

Herman, B. (Ed.). (1998). *Creative prayer.* Brewster, MA: Paraclete Press.

Hoover, S.L. *Nature Magazine*, April 1930.

Horwood, B. (1990). Reflections on reflection. *Journal of Experiential Education, 13*(2).

James, W. (1994). *The varieties of religious experience.* New York: Random House.

Krishnamurti, J. (1964). *Thinking on these things.* Ujai, CA: Krishnamurti Foundation of America.

Krutch, J. (1957). *Treat the Earth gently.* Garden City, NY: Hanover House.

Le Guin, U. K. (1984). *The wizard of Earthsea.* New York: Spectra.

Leopold, A. (1949). *A Sand County almanac and sketches here and there.* New York: Oxford University Press.

Lindbergh, A. M. (1955). *Gift from the sea.* New York: Pantheon.

McTaggart, F. (1984). *Wolf that I am: In search of the Red Earth People.* Norman: University of Oklahoma Press.

Merton, T. (1958). *Thoughts in solitude.* New York: Farrar, Straus and Cudahy.

Montaigne, M. (1958). *The complete works of Montaigne.* Stanford, CA: Stanford University Press.

Noewen, H. J. M. (1981). *Clowning in Rome: Reflections on solitude, celibacy, prayer, and contemplation.* New York: Image Books.

Noewen, H. J. M. (1981). *The way of the heart: Desert spirituality and contemporary ministry.* New York: HarperCollins.

Olson, S. F. (1998). *Reflections from the North Country.* Minneapolis: University of Minnesota Press.

Olson, S. F. (1956). *The singing wilderness.* New York: Alfred A. Knopf.

Palmer, P. (1993). *To know as we are known: A spirituality of education.* New York: HarperCollins.

Powell, B. (1985). *Alone alive and well: How to fight loneliness and win.* New York: Rodale Press.

Salwak, D. (Ed.) *The wonders of solitude.* Novato, CA: New World Library.

Sandburg, C. (1942). *Home front memo.* New York: Harcourt Brace.

Sarton, J. (1973). *Journal of a solitude.* New York: Norton.

Shepard, O. (Ed.). (1961). *The heart of Thoreau's journals.* New York: Dover Publications.

Sooto, D. (1998). *The hidden Jesus: A new life.* New York: St. Martin's Press.

Standing Bear, L. (1931). *My Indian boyhood.* Lincoln: University of Nebraska Press. (159-60).

Stevens, J. O. (1971). *Awareness: Exploring, experimenting, experiencing.* Lafayette, CA: Real People Press.

Thoele, S. P. (1996). *Woman's book of courage: Meditations for empowerment & peace of mind.* Boston: Red Wheel/Weiser.

Thoreau, H. D. (1957). *Walden.* Boston: Houghton Mifflin.

Van der Post, Laurens. (1987). *Heart of the hunter.* New York: Vintage Books.

Watts, A. (1991). *Nature, man and woman.* New York: Vintage Books.

APPENDIX III

Activities for Solo

Tom Smith's paper "Exercises and Activities to Prepare for the Solo Experience," presented in Chapter 16, discusses how pre-solo activities can ready participants for solitude, and give them skills that will be useful when they are alone. His paper offers a brief overview to a number of activities that can be useful in preparing people for solo, and can introduce them to activities they may find useful when in solitude. Many of the other papers in this book have suggested activities that can focus people for silence and solitude. This appendix offers a collection of activities solo facilitators and soloists may find useful.

We also include an adaptation of the post-solo questionnaire that was used in the study reported by Bobilya, McAvoy, and Kalisch in Chapter 8. Solo leaders who wish to study and compare participant reactions to the solo experience may find it useful. Most of the activities overviewed are referenced, so the reader can follow the leads to find even more activities to use.

Activities

Connecting With Nature: Let your attention shift from one thing to another, noticing the tiniest detail. From time to time come back to sensing the whole scene, then let your focus hop to other things again. As you see the full moon, also hear the crickets and watch the trees shift in the breeze. While you engage everything around you, also be aware of your inner state. Every sight, sound, smell, and thought leaves tracks of sensation in your body. Notice these. They are part of the symphony too. Acknowledge each of these sensations, not giving more or less importance to one than the other. Enjoy.

(Kraft, Marty, Connecting with Nature, www.allspecies.org/ideas/conwnat)

See and Hear: Find a place in nature and spend time there. Take a notepad and begin to write down everything you observe. Try to be aware of everything you see (spiders, bees, clouds, leaves, birds, shadows, etc.) *and* everything you hear (birdcalls, bees buzzing, waves or rapids, wind rustling the leaves, etc.). When you *see* something, *listen* for associated sounds. When you *hear* something, focus on it to *see* what it is.

Breathing: Sit in a comfortable position.… Slowly allow the tension to flow out of your body. Breathe deeply and rhythmically. Your chest and abdomen should move together as you inhale and exhale. Direct your attention to a particular image: a stream, a quiet landscape. You can also concentrate on your own rhythmic breathing or a favorite word or phrase, which you can repeat aloud or silently to yourself.

(Passive meditation, Canadian Mental Health Association,
www.vc.bc.ca/rmdcmha/meditate)

Ritual of Thanks: Find a special place in nature and spend some time there. Before you leave, create a ritual of thanks. Set up a central point altar, and reflect on your experiences. Select some special things from the environment and ask them for permission to be placed at the central altar. Put them there one by one, and reflect on the gift they have given you. Later, return them to where they were and, respectfully, dismantle the altar.

Seated Centering: Sit comfortably in a chair with eyes closed. Empty your mind, intend to do nothing but be in the present, having your attention extroverted. Don't think *being there* or anything like that, just relax and do nothing. You can notice the space you are in and the sounds about you. If thoughts are going through your mind, just let them fade away and get back to just being there. You don't try to strain and force yourself to not think, you simply relax into a quiet space of just being there. Likewise with any physical reactions you might have. If you twitch or yawn, just notice that and get your attention back to just being there. You should be able to get to the point of doing this for a couple of hours, sitting relaxed without doing anything, but being alert. When you succeed in doing that, it is like time disappears and you can sit relaxed for any amount of time with your attention centered.

(Centering Exercise, www.worldtrans.org/TP)

Focusing: Take a moment to relax. All right, now pay attention inwardly, in your body, perhaps in your stomach or chest. See what comes *there* when you ask: How is my life going? What is the main thing for me right now? Sense the answers within your body. Let the answers come slowly from this sensing. When some concern comes, *do not go inside it*. Stand back; say *Yes, that's there. I can feel that, there*. Let there be a little space between you and that. Then ask what else you feel. Wait again, and sense. Usually there are several things.

(An Introduction to Focusing, www.focusing.org/sixsteps)

Transforming: Find an object in nature. Describe that object in objective terms — its characteristics, color, shape, smell, texture. Bring the object into awareness and try to get *inside* the object. Reflect on its characteristics, particularly what the words you use to describe it mean for you. Does the butterfly have a symbolic meaning for you about transformation? Do the surging waves have a message? Attributes of ourselves are highlighted in the objects we are attracted to. What do they tell us? What metaphors may pave the way for personal transformation?

(Adapted from Sylvie Shaw's *Connecting to Nature's Spirit*,
www.ecopsychology.org/gatherings8/html)

Surfaces: Take some time to touch and feel as many surfaces as possible (leaf, rock, tree, jeans, skin, water, moss, thistle, etc). Compare and contrast them. Think about what they remind you of, and let your thoughts flow with associations. Compare and contrast examples of natural and human-made parts of the environment, and reflect on what that means.

My Leaf: Have students select a leaf and examine it carefully. Note all aspects — the shape, the color, the veins, the signs of insects on it, etc. Then place all the leaves in a pile at the center of the group, and mix them up. Have students find their leaf. Make a group collage of all the leaves. Make up a story about your leaf.

(Adapted from "Sensory Awareness for Infants," www.seen.org.au/schools/fs)

Becoming Tom Brown: Immerse yourself in your environment. Jump into the swamp, play in the mud.... Close your eyes, minimize distraction and concentrate just on what you are hearing. Learn from a dog; when a dog hears its name, it looks in the direction of the sound and then perks up its ears.... Get down on all fours and crawl in the woods and notice all the smells around; push your nose right into the soil.... Close your eyes and touch an object. How does it feel in your hands? How does it feel against other parts of your body?

(Adapted from Tom Brown's *Field Guide to Nature Awareness.*)

Stick, Stone, Leaf: Find a small stick, a small stone (or nut, or berry), and a palm-size leaf. Sit with them and look carefully at their uniqueness. Feel them. Smell them. Taste them. Listen to them and hear their stories. Make up a solitaire game or puzzle that involves your three new friends. After the solo, pair off with someone and tell her/him about your stick, stone, and leaf. Then teach them the game you created. Listen to them tell you about their new friends, and have them teach you the game they created.

(Adapted from Smith & Quinn, *The Challenge of Native American Traditions*, 2004, p. 66.)

Dancing on the Skyline: Lie on the ground, preferably on high ground or a gentle slope, with feet pointed in the direction of the farthest visible skyline. Place your hands under your hips and raise your head so you can look over your feet at the horizon. Raise your feet about 6 inches and begin to dance along the skyline. Maybe you can rotate your body so that you keep turning until you have traced 360 degrees of skyline.

(Adapted from Smith & Quinn, *The Challenge of Native American Traditions*, 2004, p. 68.)

Just Walking: Go outside and find an open area in the park, a field, or even a parking lot. Using your imagination and no props, move as if you were:

   a. walking a tightrope 100 feet above the ground
   b. running over hot coals
   c. walking on stilts
   d. walking on railroad tracks
   e. walking through a briar patch
   f. walking among a flock of chickens
   g. crawling through deep mud
   h. walking through a cow pasture
   i. walking on water
   j. walking through a cornfield ready for harvest
   k. running in the ocean's surf
   l. walking in 4 feet of snow
   m. walking through a flower garden

(Adapted from Cliff Knapp, *Creating Humane Climates Outdoors: A People Skills Primer.* ERIC Clearinghouse on Rural Education and Small Schools, 1980, p. 51.)

Gifts From Nature: Spend several minutes by yourself in a natural area. Decide what kind of gift from nature you can give yourself and then experience receiving it. Do you consider the following to be gifts from nature? Shapes in the clouds? Flowers, soil, or weeds? Rocks to skip on the water? Trees to hug? Breezes that blow across your face? Wild berries? Enjoy your gifts, and give thanks to the Creator, Mother Nature, or whatever you want to thank.

(Adapted from Cliff Knapp, *Creating Humane Climates Outdoors: A People Skills Primer.* Eric Clearinghouse on Rural Education and Small Schools, 1980, p. 37.)

Colors: Observe the many colors of nature. Go to the paint store and get one of their color charts of paint samples. Take a slow walk and match the various colors to things you see. The paint samples may show many different shades of a color, but you can find all of them outdoors.

(Adapted from Cliff Knapp, *Activities to Nurture the Naturalist Intelligence,* unpublished paper.)

Wide-Angle Vision: Most of the time we see with *tunnel vision,* seeing only things on a small screen in front of us. Take time to view nature in wide-angle, wide-screen, Cinerama. Pretend the whole scene before you is a giant mural hanging on the wall. Look to the left, right, up, and down, and notice the interconnections. Turn your head to the left and to the right, and notice that the same picture continues. It is like a movie picture, for you will begin to see movement all about.

(Adapted from Tom Brown, *Field Guide to Nature and Survival for Children,* 1989.)

Fallen Tree: Look for a large fallen tree in a decomposing state. Observe it carefully. Remember the cycles of nature, where when a living entity dies, it then becomes the source of life for many other things. The tree was once a seed, then nourished by sun, water, and soil, it became a tree. It provided shade for others, produced oxygen and water, disposed of carbon dioxide, and helped make the whole planet a more livable place. Now it has stopped living and has become a source of life for others. It will start the cycle of life all over again. Talk to the fallen tree. Listen to the fallen tree. What does she tell you about your life?

(Adapted from Larry Crenshaw, *The Outward Bound Earthbook,* 1995.)

Gravitational Centering: This is an exercise sequence for relaxation, awareness, energy, balance, and focus. Once individuals learn to *center* themselves in balance with the Earth, they can find that relaxation and awareness rather quickly. It can be a valuable warm-up exercise for groups. It is even more valuable when the group is given instructions for reflection and introspection. After it is mastered, the procedure does not have to be followed in rigorous detail, but for the novice, it is important to take the time to learn the method.

The facilitator of the exercise should use a soft, slow, and relaxed tone of voice, and there should be pauses throughout the presentation to give students time to focus on the instructions. Space needs for the activity are minimal; people need only their own special space to stand. The task can be offered on a sunny hillside, in an open meadow, or in the forest beneath the trees. If the sequence is offered inside, there may be value in using a background tape of relaxation music or the sounds of nature.

The exercise begins with the instructions, "Close your eyes, breathe deeply, relax, and come to this place." The facilitator should allow several minutes for everyone to settle themselves into readiness, and then begin the narrative:

> Listen…
> There is a CENTER to the Universe…
> There is a CENTER to our Body…
> The Center of our Body is the Center of our Universe…
> The energies of the Universe, in their continuous flow through timespace
> pass through the Center…
> The gravitational, seasonal, and stellar energies of our world also transfer and
> recharge at our Center…
> Within each of us — to be known best when we find balance and harmony with
> the gravitational and Universal forces — lies our Centerpoint of peace, balance,
> and energy…
> Let us come to CENTER…

Stand up. Close your eyes. Relax your muscles and your thoughts. Take a few deep breaths. Listen to yourself breathe for a moment. Breathe in your stomach, breathe in your heart. Let your arms hang freely at your sides. Take a deep breath and hold it to the count of 10, and then let it out very slowly. Breathe again, and hold it, and then let it out slowly.

Spread your feet apart about 12 inches. Be aware of your ability to shift your weight from one foot to the other. Put all your weight on your right foot. Now shift all your weight to your left foot. Feel all your energy flow downward to that point of touching the Earth. Concentrate on a perfect balance, with half your weight on one foot and half your weight on the other. Move the weight back and forth until you find that point of balance at Center.

Now, be aware that you can also shift your weight forward and backward. Rock forward and feel the weight on the balls of your feet. Rock backward and feel the weight on your heels.

Again, concentrate on a perfect balance, with half your weight forward and half your weight backward. Relax. Find Center. Feel the peace and the balance. Feel the warmth and the energy at Center.

Focus on your knees. Note that you can stretch them to the back, tightening them in muscular lock. Hold that stiffness, feel the muscles pull. Now, relax the tension. Let your knees bend slightly, feel them moving forward. If you let them go you would fall down in a heap, but just be aware of that forward point. Backward again, tighten the knees, feel the tension. Forward, relax the tension, and find the Centerpoint. As you find that Center, be aware of your feet. Are you still at Centerpoint? Feel the Earth energy flowing upward, up through your legs, to Center, to Universe.

Move your concentration upward, to your hips, to the pelvic area. Feel the range of movement. Shift your weight to the right hip, then to the left hip. Forward. Backward. Feel the range of movement. Rotate your hips in a full circle, feeling the outer boundaries of the movement. Circle back the other way, and be aware of the weight off Center. Relax, balance, Center you hips. Then check back to your knees. Check back to your feet. Your body is coming to Center. Feel the warmth and the quiet at Center. A rod of energy is thrusting upward from the ground, right through your Center. Breathe deeply.

Focus on your arms. Concentrate on your hands. Center your hands. Clench your fist. Hold it. Feel the tension. Relax it, and feel the release. Wiggle your fingers, feel their movement, stretch them out. Feel the tension of that outward stretch. Clench your fist. Feel the tension of that inward stretch. Find Center. Find that point of unawareness. When you find that Center you will hardly know those hands are there. Be aware of your elbows. Notice that they usually hang in a very centered position. Lock them outward in tension. Feel the energy flow in your whole arm. Relax that tension. Bend your elbows slightly, feeling the muscles of your arm lift the weight of your hands. Then let the weight release. Find Center. Tight elbow is not right. A working elbow is not right. In the middle, relaxed, find that Center.

Move upward to your shoulders. Lift them. Let them drop. Lift them again, and hold that tension, and then let them drop. Roll your shoulders forward. Curl them around. Feel the tension. Hold it. Let it out. Roll your shoulders to the back. Feel the pushing across your shoulder blades. Feel the tension. Hold it. Let it out. Move your shoulders to find Center. Relax. Focus back on your elbows, Centered? Focus back on your hands. Centered? Shift attention to your hips, your knees, your feet. Find Center. Feel the energy building as you come to Center.

Now, think about your head and your neck. Drop your chin to your chest. Tip your head from side to side. Nod your head from front to back. Roll your head about. Feel the full range of movement. Find gravitational Center. Remember, it was not too far back that we walked on all fours, and we are still learning to carry our head straight up. Stretch your head to the back, to the sides, and to the front. Find that Centerpoint. Relax. Breathe deeply. As you find Center you will be unaware of your whole body. That rod of energy from the Earth is growing upward, through your feet, your legs, your hips, your full body, and your head. Balance. Center.

Breathe deeply. Listen to your breathing. Focus on the deepest Center. Midsection. Be aware of all that is inside. Feel the range of movement in those vital organs. Be aware of the rib cage. Breathe deeply. Send your eyes down inside to see the range of movement. Sense your ability to breathe up high, in the chest. Sense your ability to breathe down low, in the stomach. Find the Center. Just above the stomach, just below the chest. Breathe deeply, and come to that Center. Listen to the Earth. Hear the energy flowing upward through your Center.

Center. Everything is Centered. Check back to your feet … your knees … your hips … your arms … your shoulders … your head … your insides. Inside, at Center, deep in the Center is the Center. Breathe deeply. Feel the peace, the quiet, the balance, the harmony, the energy, the flow. It is as if you are rodded to the Earth. Draw up that energy from the Earth. Draw down that energy from the Universe. Energy from below. Energy from above. Energy concentrated at your Center. Breathe deeply. You are at Center. Breathe deeply. Let it out slowly. Listen.

> There is a CENTER to Our Universe…
>
> There is a CENTER to Our Body…
>
> The Center of Our Body is the Center of the Universe…
>
> The energies of the Universe, in their continuous flow through timespace
>
> pass through the CENTER…
>
> The gravitational, seasonal, and stellar energies of our world also transfer and
>
> recharge at our CENTER…

Nature Awareness Prayer Thoughts: Repeat the following prayer to yourself or out loud. After each line, pause to think about how that idea relates to you in that place.

> Earth teach me stillness … as the grasses are stilled with light.
>
> Earth teach me suffering … as old stones suffer with memory.
>
> Earth teach me humility … as blossoms are humble with beginning.
>
> Earth teach me courage … as the tree which stands all alone.
>
> Earth teach me limitation … as the ant which crawls on the ground.
>
> Earth teach me freedom … as the eagle which soars in the sky.
>
> Earth teach me regeneration … as the seed which rises in the spring.
>
> Earth teach me to forget myself … as melted snow forgets its life.
>
> Earth teach me to remember kindness … as dry fields weep with rain.
>
> (Ute prayer quoted in *Earth Prayers from Around the World*,
> Edited by Elizabeth Roberts and Elias Amidon.)

Solo Questionnaire

Instructions: Take a few minutes to think about your experience and answer the following questions. The process will help you clarify your recent learning. Your responses are completely confidential, but your leaders may choose to discuss some of your answers with you.

Please check all the blanks that apply.

1. How did you feel entering the solo experience?

___ Peaceful   ___ Anxious   ___ Excited   ___ Other

If other, describe: _____

Please explain why you felt like you did.

2. How would you describe your state of mind during most of your solo?

___ Peaceful   ___ Anxious   ___ Bored   ___ Other

If other, describe: _____

Please provide specific examples of your state of mind during most of your solo experience.

3. What was your favorite part of solo?

___ Solitude/Absence of Others   ___ Unstructured Time   ___ Wilderness Setting
___ Setting up a Shelter   ___ Journaling   ___ Fasting   ___ Weather
___ Lack of Activity/Rest   ___ Bored   ___ Other

If other, describe: _____

4. What was the most difficult part of solo?

___ Solitude/Absence of Others   ___ Unstructured Time   ___ Wilderness Setting

___ Setting up a Shelter   ___ Journaling   ___ Fasting   ___ Weather

___ Lack of Activity/Rest   ___ Other

If other, describe: _____

5. If you wanted to talk about your solo experience with a friend, how would you describe it?

6. During solo you spent your entire time in the natural environment. Did the environment play a role in your experience? If so, please explain how.

7. What are three lessons or outcomes you obtained from your solo experience, and how do you plan to apply these to your life?

a.

b.

c.

8. Is there anything else you would like to record as you reflect on your solo experience?

(Adapted from a questionnaire designed by Andrew J. Bobilya and Ken R. Kalisch to assist participants in reflecting on the solo experience.)

AFTERWORD

By Keith V. King

I have often wondered and still wonder what a solo really means. These papers have opened a few doors for me and expanded my understanding. I have thought, and I have learned.

I would like to begin with some statements so you, the reader, will know more about me and what I believe. Then you can accept, modify, or reject my ramblings more intelligently.

I believe that experience is anything about which I can think.

I believe that the only thing about which you can think is experience.

I believe the act of reading is best described as what I'm thinking about as I am looking at words.

I believe the act of thinking produces new dendrite connections or uses connections already made in the brain.

I believe that learning results only when we think.

I believe a solo can be a valuable experience.

I believe Dewey may have been right about the meaning of thinking all along. In *How We Think* (1910), Dewey stated that there are four levels (senses) of thinking.

The first level concerns anything that goes through our head, such as daydreaming or building castles in the air. Example? The loose flux of casual and disconnected material that floats through our minds. Most all of the time I'm thinking about something.

Dewey's second level of thinking refers to ideas that are accepted with no attempt to support or reject them. Example? Reading an item in a newspaper and not questioning its validity or its importance — just accepting it as information.

The third level of thinking is *reflective thinking*, which Dewey describes as an idea that is accepted, modified, or rejected by seeking more information. This could be as simple as discussing a new idea or fact with others, or as complex as doing research. The purpose of this investigation is to clarify and/or test the new informa-tion and its suitability for further use. This investigation is uncomfortable, as its pur-pose is to question the present position of the thinker. Reflective thinking not only involves a sequence of ideas, it determines or stimulates other ideas. It leaves a deposit that is used in the next thought level.

Dewey's fourth level of thinking, *critical thinking*, is the second stage of reflective thinking. It comes when alternative suggestions are turned over in one's mind — a hunt for additional evidence, ideas, feelings, and data that will bear out or shoot down an idea. Critical thinking is not a case of spontaneous combustion. Critical thinking is trou-blesome because it involves overcoming the inertia that encourages uncritical thinking. Critical thinking involves a willingness to endure a condition of mental unrest and dis-turbance. Critical thinking requires maintaining a state of doubt while carrying on sys-tematic inquiry.

The papers is this book have stimulated Dewey's four levels of thinking in me, especially the third and fourth levels. Here are a few observations that were stimulated by my thinking as I looked at the words in this collection.

This very morning there was a fleeting moment in time when I saw an orange full moon slipping behind the hills to the northwest. I have seen the moon do this so infrequently in my life that it was significant, and I chose to stretch it out for a few more moments and savor it. It was an opportunity for reflection, and it was my choice to use it. Because there were no other distractions, and I was alone, I was able to make it a solo.

There have been many such moments — of different intensities and lengths, some spontaneous and others intentional — all significant. I have experienced the offi-cial Outward Bound (OB) solo, consisting of four long days and three very cold nights in the northern New Hampshire wilderness. I'm proud of how I survived those days and nights, but I didn't reflect much during that solo — I was too busy just trying to survive it. Only after reflection, when the buzz of doing it had worn off, did the experience have its full impact. I still reflect on it, and through these reflections I am still learning.

The same holds true for my first encounter with the classic solo experience — flying a small plane alone. Wow! And later, there was the solo flight with no directional radio over the mountains, rivers, roads, and railroads of northern New England using only charts and my brain. What a ride! Again, the full power of these events continues to unfold.

Then there was the solo on which I embarked the day after my 57th birthday. It remains the most significant solo bike ride of my life. I started at the eastern rim of the Grand Canyon and rode to Atlanta, where my sister lived. I rode because I wanted the forced soloness. I needed to be in a strange place, away from everything I knew, uncomfortable and hungry. I needed a shift in perspective. And if there's one thing riding across a desert affords, it's the opportunity to see things in a new light. Riding a bike on an interstate with nobody else around and out in the pucker brush, you either go crazy or you start thinking. So I started thinking. As I was crossing the Arizona desert, I focused on turning points in my life. I thought about the moment in time when my father became my dad. Not until I turned 10 did he become my friend, my buddy. And not until I turned 57 did I realize the shift in our relationship had even occurred or the significance of that shift. Taking that time alone and choosing to ride alone in an often unforgiving and barren landscape allowed me to see pivotal life events more clearly, and to reflect on them and, in turn, to learn from them.

So I've soloed. And I don't recall how many OB and Operation LIVE (an adventure program at Keene State College) solos I have set up and overseen, but there have been hundreds. And still, despite decades of personal and professional experience, these papers have opened my eyes to things I should have done, could have done, might have done, and should not have done.

Similarly, writing and rewriting this Afterword has raised a few questions.... Why does a solo have to be in a strange place? Example? As my waking brain discovers a new day, before I can ponder the happenings of yesterday and the plans for today, can't I make that a solo? Isn't a solo whatever the soloist makes of it? That's one of the conclusions I've drawn after having the experience of reading (see my definition of reading) these papers, reflecting on the thinkings within them, and trying to get these thoughts down more clearly (see my definition of experience).

Isn't the act of learning the responsibility of the learner? And isn't it the job of the teacher to expose the learner to experiences about which the doer can think and, as a result, learn?

Why don't we use solos more often in our teaching? After all, it really doesn't take a trip to the wilderness to experience solo. A true solo doesn't come often in our lives.

There are unique things that happen during a solo. Some of those things are risky, some are not, but isn't all learning somewhat risky? These papers do an excellent job of outlining some of the ways to control the risks. These papers describe some of the things that can happen on solo. These papers show how solo can be used by individuals, teachers, and other leaders.

I have read. I have enjoyed. I have thought. I have read again, and I have learned. I now have to use these ideas — and continue to learn and try to teach — using experience as the teaching modality.

Reference

Dewey, J. (1910). *How we think*. Boston: Heath.

About the Authors

The Editors

Clifford Knapp has been an experiential educator for most of his 40-year career, working in K-12 schools and at the university level. He has held positions as a science teacher, outdoor education director, and professor of outdoor/environmental education at Southern and Northern Illinois Universities. He has also served in summer camp leadership roles for several years, and co-directed his own camp dedicated to human relations and adventure skills. His interests include nature study and interpretation, values education, reflection/processing skills, indigenous cultures, curriculum development, place-based education, and environmental ethics. Currently, he is an educational consultant, author, parent, grandparent, reader, writer, and thinker. Contact him at cknapp@niu.edu or at Box 313, Oregon, IL 61061.

Thomas Smith has been a clinical and school psychologist, a wilderness guide and therapist, and an experiential and humanistic educator for more than 50 years. His professional career has been guided by two lessons learned long ago: There is a wilderness beyond, and there is a wilderness within. He is founding director of the Raccoon Institute, which provides consultation and leadership training in challenge education and outdoor therapy. He introduced the theory and practice of *Raccoon Circles* a decade ago, and is a frequent presenter at regional, national, and international conferences for professionals who want to learn about the power and potentials of the circle. He received the Association for Experiential Education's Kurt Hahn Award in 1996. He has been married more than 50 years, and is the proud father of six children, grandfather of nine and great-grandfather of two. He resides in Lake Geneva, Wisconsin. Contact him at tsraccoon@earthlink.net.

The Contributors

Elias Amidon is co-director, with his wife Rabia, of the Boulder Institute for Nature and the Human Spirit (www.boulderinstitute.org), which runs national and international training programs in support of human rights, citizen peacemaking, environmental ethics, and indigenous cultures. During the '90s he taught in the master's program of Environmental Leadership at Naropa University in Colorado. He is a trained wilderness quest guide and has led quests for the past 14 years. He is the Pir (leader) of the International Sufi Way (www.sufiway.org). Over the years, Amidon has studied and practiced Sufism in America, Europe, India, North Africa, and the Middle East. He currently resides in Boulder, Colorado. Contact him at elias@boulderinstitute.org.

Mary-Laurence Bevington began teaching in the outdoors as an intern with Wolfcreek Wilderness School in 1988. Since then she has primarily instructed and directed courses for the Colorado Outward Bound School (now known as Outward Bound West), in the mountains, deserts, and on the rocks. In the mid-1990s, Mary guided for First Ascent Joshua Tree and served Tuolumne Search and Rescue. She also taught leadership at Regis University. Currently, Mary is a freelance writer and the founder of Chasm View Productions, a Colorado theater company. She is grateful to the natural world for providing so many doors of perception. Mary lives in Boulder, Colorado. Contact her at marybevington@mac.com.

Andrew J. Bobilya began researching the experience of solitude while a graduate student at Minnesota State University at Mankato and the University of Minnesota. He is currently an assistant professor in the Outdoor Education Department at Montreat College in North Carolina. Andrew's research interests include outcomes of first-year college-student transition programs, and the role of solitude and other course components in wilderness programming. He has served as an instructor, trainer, and program director for various outdoor and adventure programs. Most of his work investigating wilderness solitude has been supported through collaboration with Wheaton College's High Road wilderness program. Contact him at abobilya@hotmail.com.

Michael Bodkin has been executive director of Rites of Passage since 1987. His first vision quest was with Stephen Foster and Meridith Little in 1980. Trained by Foster and Little, he was certified as a vision quest guide in 1982, and shortly thereafter began leading programs for the organization. Michael has been a Californialicensed marriage and family therapist since 1978, and has more than 25 years' experience working with youth, couples, and families in counseling and wilderness programs. Michael is a member of an intentional community in Northern California. Contact him at mikeb@ritesofpassagevisionquest.org.

Brad Daniel is Professor of Environmental Studies, Biology, and Outdoor Education at Montreat College. He holds an M.A. in Biology from Appalachian State University, an M.S. in Outdoor Teacher Education from Northern Illinois University, and a Ph.D. in Environmental Studies from Antioch New England Graduate School, where he also serves as adjunct faculty. Brad was the principal author of the B.S. in Outdoor Education at Montreat College, where he has led multiple extended wilderness expeditions since 1986. His research interests include significant life experiences in outdoor settings, environmental theology, and field-based environmental education. At Montreat, he has been honored twice with the Distinguished Professor Award and four times as Teacher of the Year. Contact him at bdaniel@montreat.edu.

Faith Evans is an experientially based process consultant/trainer. She has been a college professor, kindergarten teacher, and summer camp program director. She is founder and director of Playfully, Inc., based in Colorado. She specializes in learning with small and large groups in schools, corporations, and summer camps, and is co-author of the popular book *99 Best Experiential Corporate Games We Know*, and *The More the Merrier, Games for Large Groups* and *From Adversity to Zeal: An A to Z Guide* (in press). Faith received the Association for Experiential Education's Kurt Hahn Award in 1998, and was active in the founding of Play for Peace, an organization that brings children of conflicting cultures together to sow seeds of cooperation. Contact her at FaithEvans@aol.com.

Deborah Eads Greene currently teaches middle school science in Anchorage, Alaska, and has taught for both the wilderness and education programs of the University of Alaska. She began her teaching career at Towson University in Baltimore, Maryland, working for Project Marj, an adapted Outward Bound program for incoming freshmen. She has worked as an Outward Bound instructor and course director, and as an educator for Boulder Valley Public Schools in Colorado, where she developed PASSAGES, an optional program for middle school students struggling to find purpose and meaning in their education. Several personal trips have opened the international doors of climbing, and she was the first American woman to attempt Manaslu without use of oxygen or high-altitude Sherpas. In 1991, she was awarded the International Practitioner of the Year award by the Association for Experiential

Education. She has incorporated the solo experience throughout her wilderness experiences and her teaching career. Contact her at greene_deborah@asdk12.org.

William F. Hammond earned his Ph.D. at Simon Fraser University in British Columbia. He is a founding professor of Ecological and Interdisciplinary Studies in the College of Arts and Sciences at Florida Gulf Coast University, and is completing his 45th year as a professor, science teacher, and director of Instructional Services and Environmental Education with the Lee County Schools in Florida. He has worked as a consultant to government agencies, organizations, businesses, and Fortune 100 companies. He is a published author and has served on many international, national, regional, state, and local boards of directors and not-for-profit organizations (including Project Wild and Project Learning Tree). Contact him at whammond@fgcu.edu.

Chris Heeter is the founding director of The Wild Institute, which offers wilderness trips for women and customizes unforgettable wilderness experiences for women, both for business and pleasure. Chris speaks professionally across the country, bringing the wisdom of wild places to corporations, associations, and environmental groups. She has guided women's trips for more than 20 years and is the author of *Daily Degradations for Women Who Should Know Better*. She also writes a weekly poem about our connections with nature and sends it out via e-mail to all who subscribe (at no cost). Contact her at Chris@thewildinstitute.com.

Bob Henderson has been teaching outdoor education for more than 25 years. He got his start leading canoe trips for a summer camp, which led him to McMaster University, where he now teaches. His classes involve summer and winter travel, theory, and workshops in experiential education and environmental education, and pay attention to how we dwell with nature/place, culture, and lifestyles. Other interests include heritage-based travel and story-telling, learning the game of basketball to support a daughter and son's intense interest, and to explore how we — in different cultures — genuinely meet the earth. Contact him at bhender@mcmaster.ca.

Kenneth R. Kalisch has many years of experience in the field of outdoor adventure education, as a teacher, camp director, researcher, and author. He is the author of the classic *The Role of the Instructor in the Outward Bound Educational Process*, and is currently an assistant professor at HoneyRock, Wheaton College's Northwoods Campus, in Eagle River, Wisconsin. Kalisch has facilitated students of all ages in wilderness programs designed for leadership development and camp-related ministries. Contact him at kkalisch@honeyrockcamp.org.

Keith V. King is one of the respected elders of the profession of experiential education. During the second half of his 30-year tenure at Keene State in New Hampshire, Keith taught in a physical education professional preparation program and ran Operation L.I.V.E. (Learning in Vigorous Environments), a modified Outward Bound Program designed to fit into the college calendar and schedule. Since his retirement in 1987, he has turned his attention and energies toward his family, AEE, local summer camps, and using his homemade 31-foot wooden schooner as a teaching base. He lives with his wife of 55 years on the shores of Lake Winnipesauke in New Hampshire and is currently helping his son and grandsons build their large log home. Contact him at kvk@wordpath.net.

Leo H. McAvoy is a professor at the University of Minnesota. He has many years' experience in teaching and conducting research on the outcomes of adventure education programs. He has published numerous articles and research reports related to outdoor education and recreation, and is co-editor of *Stewards of Access, Custodians of Choice: A Philosophical Foundation for the Park and Recreation Profession*. He has long been a consultant and program facilitator for Wilderness Inquiry, a Minneapolis-based program that integrates persons with and without disabilities for outdoor adventure and recreation, and is co-editor of *Integrated Outdoor Education and Adventure Programs*. Contact him at mcavo001@umn.edu.

John Maxted is a faculty member of the School of Physical Education at the University of Otago, New Zealand, where he has coordinated outdoor education fieldwork since 1996 and come to recognize adventure as a profound medium for the merging of self, nature, and culture. John's Ph.D. examined the meaning and significance of solo experiences for adolescent males immersed in a broader outdoor education residential experience. As the father of three boys and a former high school teacher, John is especially interested in the role of local natural places in the journey toward manhood. He spends much of his free time gardening, planting trees, crafting wood, and exploring special places in southern New Zealand. Contact him at jmaxted@pooka.otago.ac.nz.

Burke Miller is an executive coach, leadership consultant, relationship coach, and wilderness vision quest guide. He is the founding director of the Spirit River Institute in Colorado. He has a master's degree in environmental philosophy from Antioch University, and trained with Stephen Foster and Meridith Little at the School of Lost Borders and with the Coaches Training Institute. He writes and teaches about the interconnections of consciousness, nature, and human development. He has 20 years' experience conducting leadership seminars, leading wilderness retreats, and coaching senior executives and other corporate teams. Burke resides in Boulder, Colorado. Contact him at burke@spiritriverinstitute.com.

Tim O'Connell is on the faculty of the School of Outdoor Recreation, Parks and Tourism at Lakehead University in Thunder Bay, Ontario, Canada. He has worked with elementary school, high school, and university students across North America. He works as a guide for Wilderness Inquiry of Minneapolis, Minnesota, and serves as a senior instructor at SUNY Cortland's Department of Recreation and Leisure Studies outdoor practicum in the Adirondacks. Tim's research and writing interests include journaling, outdoor leadership, sustainability education, group dynamics, psychosocial dimensions of outdoor recreation, integrated wilderness travel, and sea kayaking. He spends much time climbing, paddling, and skiing with his wife, Mary Breunig, and their dog, Ridge. Contact him at toconnell@lakeheadu.ca.

Rev. Tom Owen-Towle has been a parish minister since 1967, serving congregations in Wisconsin, Iowa, Michigan, and California. For 24 years, he and his lifemate, Carolyn, were co-ministers of the First Unitarian Universalist Church of San Diego, where both are presently ministers emeriti. Tom is the author of 17 books that emphasize personal, relational, and spiritual growth. His volume entitled *Sauntering: A Soul Journey in the Woods With Thoreau as My Guide*, from which the essay in this book is taken, was the result of a month-long sabbatical solo in a wooded retreat. Contact him at uutom@cox.net.

Tom G. Potter is on the faculty of the School of Outdoor Recreation, Parks and Tourism at Lakehead University on the North Shore of Lake Superior in Thunder Bay, Ontario, Canada, where he teaches courses in group dynamics, outdoor adventure education and leadership, and inclusive and special recreation. He enjoys introducing people to the wonders of the boreal forest and the beauty of the waters of Northwestern Ontario. A teacher of 20 years, Tom has taught at a variety of levels (primary, secondary, college, and university), both inside and outside the classroom, and has served as a college director of student services. He enjoys sliding on all forms of water and ice, be it while paddling, sailing, skating, or skiing. Tom and his wife, Teresa Cocha, actively share their passion for leisure pursuits in wild places with their two children, Stephanie and Andrew. Contact him at tpotter@lakeheadu.ca.

William J. Quinn is a professor at Northeastern Illinois University in Chicago, where he teaches undergraduate courses in challenge and adventure education in the

Physical Education Department. He is founder and president of Cliffs & Cables, a company that builds ropes courses and climbing walls, and offers training workshops for teachers and counselors in the theory and practice of challenge education. Contact him at w-quinn@neiu.edu.

Linda Sartor received a Ph.D. in Integral Studies, after receiving an M.S. in environmental education, and is now a faculty member at two graduate schools. She trained with the School of Lost Borders and Rites of Passage, and has been leading wilderness trips for 20 years. Sartor works with the Rites of Passage program, teaches research methods, and is a field team member of the Nonviolent Peaceforce. She is a member of an intentional community in Northern California. Contact her at lsartor@inreach.com.

David T. Sobel is director of Teacher Certification Programs in the Education Department and director of the Center for Place-Based Education at Antioch New England Graduate School. He is a member of the editorial board of the *Encounter: Education for Meaning and Social Justice* journal and a correspondent for *Orion Magazine*. His published books include *Children's Special Places, Beyond Ecophobia, Mapmaking with Children,* and *Place-Based Education*. Sobel is currently co-director of Project CO-SEED (Community-Based School Environmental Education), which creates partnerships between communities, school districts, and environmental organizations in a collaborative effort to improve schools and support community development. Contact him at dsobel@antiochne.edu.